HISTORY OF THE
1st BATTALION SHERWOOD FORESTERS
IN THE BOER WAR

LIEUT.-GENERAL SIR H. L. SMITH-DORRIEN, K.C.B., D.S.O.

[*Frontispiece.*

HISTORY

of the

1st Batt. Sherwood Foresters

(NOTTS. AND DERBY REGT.)

IN THE BOER WAR, 1899=1902

BY

CAPTAIN CHARLES J. L. GILSON

WITH AN INTRODUCTION BY

LIEUT.=GEN. SIR H. L. SMITH-DORRIEN, K.C.B., D.S.O.

(Colonel of the Sherwood Foresters)

WITH 10 PLANS, &c., AND 4 PORTRAITS

LONDON

SWAN SONNENSCHEIN & CO., LTD.

25 HIGH ST., BLOOMSBURY, W.C.

1908

Printed and bound by Antony Rowe Ltd, Eastbourne

INTRODUCTION

In 1899 the 1st Battalion Sherwood Foresters was quartered at Malta, and on the 2nd October, H.E. the Governor-General, Sir Francis Grenfell (now Lord Grenfell), lunched with the Battalion, and in telling the officers that all preparations for a war with the Boers was in full course of completion, and that war appeared inevitable, gladdened our hearts by predicting that the Battalion would be almost sure to go.

On the 8th October it seemed that the Governor's prophecy was going to be fulfilled, for a private cable arrived from Captain Maurice of the Regiment in England, containing the one word, "Nottingham," the interpretation of which was that the Battalion was to mobilise and proceed to take part in the great Boer War which, by that time, had become a reality. But gladness was turned into sorrow by the arrival of another cable on the 12th October, contradicting the previous one. We hadn't long to wait, however, for our mental barometers to rise again, for on the evening of the 31st an official cable ordered the Battalion to the Cape. Curiously enough, on the 25th October, the 2nd Battalion, under Lieut.-Colonel Bulpett, had arrived from Aden, and were doing a period of quarantine at Fort Manoel, and so when this exciting news arrived the two Battalions were practically alongside each other, an event which seldom happens in the history of a regiment. I will pass over the hearty congratulations from our comrades in the 2nd Battalion, and the earnestly expressed wishes that both Battalions might soon meet in South Africa, and will proceed to the 21st November, when the Battalion embarked in the good transport ship "Dunera." Seldom has a Battalion been given a heartier send off. H.E. the Governor, published a general order, of which we were very proud, and Sir Francis Grenfell himself, with the Naval Commander-in-Chief, Admiral Sir John Fisher, in the Admiral's barge, accompanied the ship to the mouth of the harbour. All the ships of the Mediterranean Fleet, which were in Malta harbour at the time, were manned, and the "Dunera" passed down the line and out of the harbour with ringing cheers, which were heartily responded to. I do not here propose to enter into the causes of the War, which are fully described in the *Times* and official histories, but I will give the briefest outline of the first stage of the campaign, which had resulted in reinforcements (the 1st Battalion Sherwood Foresters amongst the number) being sent out with all despatch.

It was after the failure of the Bloemfontein Conference in June, 1899, that the British Government realised that war was possible. For such a war the Imperial Troops at that moment in South Africa, viz., 9,000 to 10,000, were manifestly inadequate. In June, 1899, the then Commander-in-Chief, Lord Wolseley, advised mobilisation, but the Government were opposed to a policy of menace.

From June to September, however, defensive preparations on a small scale were carried out.

Early in September the Natal Ministry asked for reinforcements to prevent an invasion of that Colony, and on 8th September the Cabinet decided to raise the force in South Africa up to strength adequate for defence of the whole territory of the Colonies. An additional 10,000 men were thought sufficient for this purpose, and were to be drawn from India and the Mediterranean, and General Sir George White was sent out to command in Natal.

In the meantime it was decided to occupy Natal as far

north as Newcastle. By the end of September Major-
General Sir W. P. Symons moved the Ladysmith troops
to Glencoe, in the direction of Newcastle.

In Cape Colony the defence of the line of the Orange
River had been delayed. On the 19th September Colonel
Kekewich was put in command of a garrison at
Kimberley.

Detachments were also placed by the end of the month
to guard the bridges over the Orange River, and the railway
from De Aar to Mafeking. In addition, every endeavour
was made with the troops available to guard the Rhodesian
frontier against invasion.

On the 7th October mobilisation was ordered at home,
the result of which was that, by 4th December, 47,000
reinforcements had been landed in South Africa.

The command of the whole of the forces in South
Africa was assigned to General Sir Redvers Buller, who
sailed from England on 14th October.

The plan of campaign decided on was an advance
through Cape Colony. To carry out the latter the army
corps to be sent out was to be landed in three parts,
viz., at Cape Town, Port Elizabeth and East London,
and to concentrate, *via* De Aar, Naauwpoort and Stormberg
upon Norval's Pont and Bethulie.

The Boer plan of campaign was roughly as follows:—A
large force was to invade Northern Natal from west,
north and east, crush the little garrisons of Dundee
and Ladysmith, and then rapidly overrun Natal down
to Durban; other forces were to seize the British towns
scattered along the Bechuanaland Railway, Mafeking,
Vryburg and Kimberley, and then to advance south.

By 11th October 38,000 Boers were in the field, and
were disposed as follows:—The main body of the
Transvaalers—in all, some 8,000 to 9,000 men—were at

Sandspruit, twelve miles from Laing's Nek. In front of
the main body two smaller forces, numbering 1,800 to 2,000
strong, were at Wakkerstroom Nek; 12,000 were on the
Klip River, west of Majuba; 1,500 to 2,000 were camped
at the foot of the Doornberg, twenty miles from Dundee.
The Free State commandos, numbering 6,000 to 6,500,
were concentrated at Van Reenan's Pass. In all, there
were 20,000 Boers on the Natal frontier. The Orange
River was watched by some 2,500 to 3,000 Free
Staters. The Basúto border, and the frontier from Orange
River to Jacobsdal, was being patrolled by 2,500 men.
North of these 3,000 to 4,000 Boers were at Boshof ready
to pounce upon Kimberley. North of the Vaal 800 were
watching the border from Fourteen Streams to Vryburg.
Beyond these some 7,000 were at Ottoshoop near
Mafeking. Detachments threatened Lobatsi, Crocodile
Pools and Deerdepoort. The rest of the Northern
frontier was guarded by 1,600 men on the Limpopo.
A few men were posted at Kumati Poort, and 800 to
1,000 burghers watched the Swaziland frontier. Lastly,
a small force remained in or near Johannesburg.

Sir George White's task when he landed at Durban on
7th October was a most difficult one. He finally decided
to concentrate at Ladysmith, and a force was retained at
Dundee, General Symons being given the command in that
region. General Forestier Walker in the old colony, with
vastly inferior numbers, found it almost impossible to hold
the whole frontier, or even the line of the Orange River
in the western field of operations. The defence of the
Rhodesia and Bechuanaland frontiers were entrusted to
Colonel Baden Powell, who placed one regiment under
Colonel Plumer at Tuli, while he himself with another
withdrew into Mafeking, and placed it in a state of defence.
The long line of frontier from Orange River Bridge to

Mafeking was assigned to Colonel Kekewich, who determined to hold Kimberley in force.

The campaign actually commenced on 11th October.
The invasion of Natal was carried out between 12th-19th
October; the Transvaal forces closing in on Dundee by
the latter date.   In the meantime the Free Staters were
engaged in keeping Ladysmith occupied.

It was becoming evident that the Boers were contem-
plating the complete envelopment of the British forces
north of the Tugela.   Sir George White, whilst fully
realising the somewhat isolated situation of General
Symons command about Dundee, decided not to withdraw it.

On the 19th October Elandslaagte was occupied by the
Boers, who thus established themselves on the Ladysmith-
Dundee lines of communication.

On the 19th October the Boers east of the Buffalo determined to make a night march on Dundee.   On the 20th
October the battle of Talana was fought and won by the
British, General Symons being mortally wounded.   After
the battle the Boers retreated across the Buffalo.

The eastern wing of the Boer invasion was thus disposed of for the moment.   General Sir George White, on
hearing of the Dundee success, determined to clear the line,
and on 21st October sent a force, under Major-General
French, to operate against the Boers at Elandslaagte.
On reaching there General French found himself very
inferior in numbers, and asked for reinforcements from
Ladysmith, which were sent.   The battle of Elandslaagte
ensued, and resulted in a complete victory for the British
after a very stubborn fight.

On the 22nd October, however, it was found necessary
to hurriedly evacuate Elandslaagte owing to the danger
threatening Ladysmith itself.   Next day Elandslaagte was
reoccupied by the Boers.

Meanwhile Colonel Yule (who now commanded the Dundee Column) decided to retire from that place on Ladysmith on 22nd October. Sir George White, on the 24th, moved out to cover this retirement.

The action of Rietfontein which resulted enabled communication with the Dundee Column to be established. On the 26th the Dundee Column reached Ladysmith. On the 23rd the Boers had occupied Dundee, but not for long. They moved down the Glencoe Pass on the 25th, and advanced on Ladysmith, which they approached on the 27th. Thus the forces of the two republics had joined hands, and were posted in strong positions so near Ladysmith that the movements of our troops could be easily watched. On the 30th Sir George White determined on a general action outside Ladysmith. The battle of Ladysmith ensued, and ended in failure; our force had to retreat into Ladysmith again with disaster—especially at Nicholson's Nek.

Sir George White then decided to defend Ladysmith itself.

During the above operations in Natal those on the western field were less dramatic but more successful. The Boers, wasting no time, crossed the frontier on 12th October. Between the 13th and 31st operations round Mafeking took place, and the Boers realised that they had a hard task before them to capture this place.

North of Mafeking, along the western frontier and along the Limpopo, fighting took place during October.

Vryburg, south of Mafeking, was occupied by the Boers on 18th October. Operations round Kimberley were successfully carried out by Colonel Kekewich up till 4th November, on which date the siege of that place may be said to have begun.

By the end of October, also, President Steyn had set in

motion the Free State commandos across the Orange
River, *i.e.*, the southern frontier.

On 31st October Sir Redvers Buller landed at Cape Town.

Between 1st and 3rd November the Free Staters crossed
the Orange River, and Sir Redvers Buller withdrew from
Naauwpoort and Stormberg. On 3rd November the Garrison of Colenso was reported to have fallen back on Estcourt.

Sir Redvers Buller then decided to deviate from the
original plan of campaign and divert a part of the army
corps to Natal. In pursuance of this decision the dispositions arranged were as follows :—Hildyard's and Barton's
Brigades were diverted to Ladysmith; Lord Methuen was
to advance rapidly on Kimberley to relieve it ; Clery,
Gatacre and French were to watch the whole of the front
from Orange River Station to Aliwal North.

By the 15th November it was found necessary to further
break up the army corps by sending more reinforcements
to Natal. General Clery was therefore sent to take command,
and arrived at Durban on the 19th November.

Fourteen thousand men had now collected south of the
Tugela, but the situation was becoming worse. On 22nd
November Hildyard at Estcourt was completely cut off by a
Boer force, numbering 7,000. Barton was being bombarded
at Mooi River, and Nottingham Road was being threatened.
This necessitated a still further portion of the army corps
being absorbed in the vortex of the Natal complication.

On 22nd November Sir Redvers Buller left Cape Town,
bound for Durban and Natal. Leaving Natal for the
moment, the following are briefly the events which took
place elsewhere :—

On 9th and 10th November the Belmont Reconnaissance,
under Colonel Gough, was unfortunate in its results. On the
12th Lord Methuen arrived on the Orange River and took
over command.

The Free Staters made a slow advance into Cape Colony, and Olivier entered Aliwal on 13th November.

On the 14th the Boers entered Colesburg, and the British reoccupied Naauwpoort on the 19th.

Meanwhile the advanced body of the Bethulie burghers had entered Burghersdorp on the 15th.

Olivier, on the 18th November, occupied Jamestown, Lady Grey and Barkly, but it was not till 26th November that Stormberg Junction was occupied by the Boers.

Gatacre reached Queenstown on the 18th November, and had the Naval Brigade not been withdrawn to join Lord Methuen on the Orange River on 16th November, it is possible that the reoccupation of Stormberg might have been safely effected. North of the Orange River, except for Kimberley, Kuruman and Mafeking, the whole of British Bechuanaland and Griqualand West was annexed to the two republics.

On the 21st November Cronje and 4,000 men were withdrawn from Mafeking and entrained at Klerksdorp, being at once sent, *via* Johannesburg and Bloemfontein, to meet Lord Methuen's advance.

To return to Natal — by the 4th of November the investment of Ladysmith had been completed, and the British at Colenso had fallen back on Estcourt. Up to the 13th the Boers had contented themselves with the task of investing Ladysmith and spreading themselves over Northern Natal, and it was not till that date that they decided on an expedition south of the Tugela. A picked force of 3,000 to 3,500 men having been collected at Colenso for this purpose.

On the 14th the Boer patrols reached Estcourt, which resulted in great alarm both at that place and at Maritzburg.

On the 15th an armoured train, sent out from Estcourt, was surprised and captured by the Boers at Frere. Elated at this success, the Boers, during the 15th to 20th November, moved round Estcourt in two bodies, and finally effected an undisturbed junction on the 21st, establishing themselves on the heights of Brynbella Hill, south and south-east to Joubert's position, between Estcourt and the Mooi River.

Barton meanwhile remained inactive at Mooi River, thinking that he was opposed by very superior numbers.

This brief history of the early days of the War sets forth the military situation up to the date the Battalion embarked.

It will be seen from the above that the state of affairs, at the time we left Malta, were such as to lead us to believe we might, with luck, be in time for very considerable fighting, but over and over again fears were expressed that we might be too late. None, I think, anticipated that before the Battalion would again settle down under peace conditions two and a half long years of war were before them. On board the "Dunera" we found many officers of the Battalion, and a splendid body of reserve men, who had embarked in England to bring the Battalion up to fighting strength. The names of the officers, and the strength of the Battalion and the reserves will be found in the history itself. We were now all complete, except for a detachment of 100 men with Lieutenants Radford, Anley and Percival at Cyprus, and these were picked up at Limasol on the 24th November. At Aden Major-General O'Moor Creagh, V.C. (originally an officer in the 2nd Battalion, the 95th), gave us a hearty welcome, and at Zanzibar, where the ship stayed one and a half days, the Battalion landed and greatly impressed the inhabitants by taking a short route march in the island, about 1,100 strong, with the band playing. Here the greatest hospitality was extended to the Battalion by H.H. the Sultan, his Prime Minister, General Mathews, and the British Consul, Mr. B. S. Cave, C.B. It is interesting to note that Colonel

Broadwood (now Major-General), who had already made for himself a great name as a dashing Cavalry leader, was, with a few other officers and details, *en route* for the War in our ship.

At 5 a.m. on Thursday, the 14th December, on a cold, fresh morning, the "Dunera" dropped anchor in Durban Harbour, and I am sure I am right when I say that there wasn't a heart in the Battalion which didn't beat faster. "Are we too late? What is the latest news? Shall we be lucky enough to join a fighting force at once, or shall we be relegated to the line of communication?" were the sort of questions on everybody's lips. After an hour of impatient waiting, a tug came off ordering us to East London at once, and from what we could glean from a local newspaper—for we were allowed no chance of conversation—the situation was as follows:—

Sir Redvers Buller's Force was moving to within three miles of Colenso, and a great battle was hourly expected. Mafeking and Kimberley were still being besieged. Lord Methuen was apparently still fighting on the Modder River, and General Gatacre had had a serious reverse at Stormberg.

News was depressing enough, but there was an undoubted look of relief on the faces of most, for although the British arms had met with serious reverses, they were bound to triumph ultimately, and we, the 1st Battalion Sherwood Foresters, were not too late to dip our spears and share in the glories of that triumph.

It had originally been intended by Sir Redvers Buller that the Battalion should be sent to reinforce his own force at Colenso, and it was merely the news of Gatacre's reverse, on the 9th December, which had induced him to order us to East London.

At 8 a.m., after disembarking a few details for Durban, the "Dunera" was again heading for the open sea for a run of 252 miles to East London, where we landed the next day.

It was there that we learned the exact state of affairs and the disposition of our forces.

In order to enable the reader to follow the narrative of the campaign from the time we sailed from Malta to the 15th of December, the date of our landing at East London, I must give a brief resumé of what had happened in South Africa during that period. I will first take the reader back to affairs as we left them in Natal on the 21st November. Next day Mooi River was shelled by the Boers, but Hildyard, at Willow Grange, on the same date decided to attack the Boers on Brynbella. The action was indecisive, and the British withdrew to Estcourt again.

The Boers now decided to return to Colenso, which they did, unmolested, between 24th and 27th November. The British moved up to Frere without attempting to pursue the Boers in their retreat.

From 26th November to 15th December a general concentration took place at Frere preparatory to an advance for the relief of Ladysmith.

The military situation at the end of November may be summed up by saying that Natal, south of the Tugela, was cleared of the Boers. The first stage of the War, viz., the Boer invasion of British territory was over. In Natal, as also in the Western Theatre of War, the Republican forces were also on the defensive, determined to retain their hold on the territories they had annexed, and to starve out the British garrisons they had invested.

On the 21st November Lord Methuen started from Orange River to march to Kimberley. He got into touch with the Boer outposts almost at once, and the battle of Belmont, on the 23rd November, resulted in the Boers falling back from their first selected position on the Kimberley Road. The next position taken up by the Boers was at Rooilaagte or Enslin—here again the British were successful on the 25th November, the Naval Brigade, however, suffering very heavy losses.

The Boers now assembled at Jacobsdal to deliberate on their next move. They finally decided to hold the line of the Modder River.

Lord Methuen having at first decided to move forward by Jacobsdal, eventually determined to establish himself on the Modder River. Early on the 28th November the advance began on Modder River Bridge. The battle fought that day consisted in a number of detached engagements. As darkness came on the battle died away, and during the night the Boers evacuated their position, riding off to Jacobsdal, while the British collected at Rosmead Dam. On the 29th November the British crossed the river unopposed. The news of this battle at home resulted in the announcement that a sixth division would be mobilised and sent off without delay.

Turning to the north-eastern part of Cape Colony, on the 27th November Sir W. Gatacre had moved from Queenstown to Putter's Kraal. He determined to reoccupy Stormberg by a *coup de main*. He started the enterprise on the 9th December, but it failed, and a disastrous retreat on Molteno was the result. A further retreat to Sterkstroom took place next day, where headquarters were established.

After the battle of the Modder River the Boers took up a position at Spytfontein, their numbers being reinforced to 8,000 men.

On the 4th December, however, the Boers, leaving their position, advanced to Magersfontein, and entrenched the foot of the ridge. Lord Methuen had been reinforced on the Modder River, and on the 10th December the attack on Magersfontein Hill began. During the night of 10th-11th December, the disastrous Highland Brigade night-attack took place, and the battle ended during the afternoon of the 11th in failure. On the 12th December Lord Methuen retired to the Modder River Camp.

Meanwhile Sir Redvers Buller arrived in Maritzburg on 25th November, and the Ladysmith Relief Force had assembled at Frere. Sir Redvers Buller at first decided to attack the Boers at Colenso by way of the Upper Tugela, but on 12th December it was decided to make a direct frontal attack on Colenso. On 13th-14th December the Boer position was shelled. The attack on Colenso took place on 15th December, and ended in a further disaster. An armistice was agreed on for 16th-17th December. Such was the news which greeted us as we reached East London : " Our forces driven back all along the line." The past week had indeed been a black one for our arms, but I am afraid there was a distinct feeling of satisfaction amongst " the old stubborns " that they were not too late, and that they would still see plenty of glorious fighting.

The actual part the 1st Battalion Sherwood Foresters played in the War, the full details of all the fighting it took part in, and the hardships it underwent, are fully set forth in the following history.

Admiral P. H. Colomb, in his sketch of the Sherwood Foresters, published in August, 1894, briefly describes the many over-sea expeditions and wars the Battalion took part in from the date of its birth as a Marine Battalion in 1739, and he sums up its characteristics in the following words :—

" A review of the history of this Regiment exhibits two leading features: its steadiness and reliability under every change of circumstance, and its experience of sea-life. It never wanted dash, it never failed to show endurance, but its reliability at all times, whether of sudden shock or of prolonged trial, whether in peace or war, has been the characteristic which strikes the reader of its story most forcibly as he follows the phases of its career."

We have only to take Admiral Colomb's summary of the characteristics for which the Battalion has always been famous, and to apply it to those who fought under the old colours in 1899 to 1902, to obtain an accurate description of the bearing of the Battalion throughout that War, and it will be as great a source of pride to all who have ever had or ever will have any connection with the Sherwood Foresters, the Notts and Derbyshire Regiment, as it is to me, the Colonel, who took them out to the War, to read that the 1st Battalion, individually and collectively, has added nothing but lustre to the Regiment's glorious past.

H. L. SMITH-DORRIEN,

Lieut.-General,

Colonel of the Sherwood Foresters,

The Notts and Derbyshire Regiment.

QUETTA, *May,* 1907.

PREFACE

This Record has been compiled from the South African War Record by request of Lieutenant-Colonel C. N. Watts, commanding the Battalion. The former Record, which was printed in Hong-Kong in 1904, was conceived, and for the most part executed by Lieutenant-Colonel H. C. Wylly, C.B., then in command, and was intended for a foundation upon which a more permanent and accurate Record might arise.

With regard to the chapters (vii. to x.) written by Lieutenant-Colonel Wylly in the original edition, comparatively little has been added or suggested by officers, and they remain in much the same form as that in which they first appeared. But in the remaining chapters, especially those dealing with Ian Hamilton's march, such is far from being the case; and the whole has been carefully rewritten, with a strict regard for truth, upon all the evidence supplied, and, in such cases where conflicting statements have been received, the opinion of the majority has only been accepted as correct.

Indeed, the sole aim throughout has been to attain the true story of the services of the Battalion during the War while the events are still comparatively fresh in the memory of those whose names are mentioned in the following pages, in order that a link may be forged of some value in the future to the Regimental Historian.

As such, in Colonel Wylly's words in the Preface of the original Record, upon which this is founded, "it is offered to all ranks of those who served with the Battalion in South Africa as a memorial to those who died in its service, and as a Record for all who happily survive."

CHARLES J. L. GILSON, Captain.

London, 14th November, 1906.

To Colonel H. C. Wylly, C.B., late commanding 1st Battalion Sherwood Foresters, is due the credit of the inception of the idea of a History of its performances during the War in South Africa. During his tenure of command he compiled the "South African Records" of the Battalion, from which Captain C. Gilson has written this consecutive History.

To both these officers I tender the thanks of the Battalion for their labour of love in adding yet another Chapter to a Record dating back to 1741.

C. N. WATTS,
Brevet-Colonel,
Commander 1st Battalion Sherwood Foresters,
(Nottinghamshire and Derbyshire Regiment),
Late 45th (Nottinghamshire) Sherwood Foresters.

BANGALORE, *June,* 1907.

CONTENTS

LIST OF ILLUSTRATIONS

1st Battalion Sherwood Foresters in the Boer War

CHAPTER I

THE EARLY DAYS OF THE WAR

ON the 10th of October, 1899, President Kruger of the South African Republic presented an ultimatum to the British Agent in Pretoria, demanding a reply within forty-eight hours. His requests were extreme, and compliance was beyond the question. In the words of the Colonial Secretary, the sands had long since been running down. Public opinion ran high at the time, and, as the ultimatum left the British Government no alternative but hostilities, by 5 p.m., Transvaal time, a state of war came into existence.

Sir George White, with troops from India, was already in Natal; the defence of Cape Colony was left to Providence, and a few isolated detachments, until the Army Corps, the command of which had been given to Sir Redvers Buller, arrived upon the scene. But in the meantime, Sir George White's position was precarious; for, as had been anticipated, the Orange Free State immediately declared war against England; and, on the 12th, the Boers, mainly upon the urgent advice of President Steyn, invaded British territory. England, however, remained confident and serene. The Crimea was a thing of a past generation, and men profit

A

little by the experience of their fathers, and though the '81 war was still fresh in the memory of the British public, no one foresaw the magnitude of the task upon which the Government had embarked.

It is but necessary here to sketch briefly the events from the commencement of hostilities to 1st November, on which date the regiment—then quartered in St. Elmo Barracks, Malta—received orders to mobilise. General White had established his headquarters at Ladysmith; and, solely for political reasons, on the advice of Sir Hely-Hutchinson, he had advanced Sir Penn Symons' Brigade as far north as Dundee. This brigade became immediately isolated; and on the 19th Lucas Meyer, with a large force of Free Staters, occupied Talana. Symons did not hesitate to attack. A frontal advance, the capture of a wall, and thence the driving of the enemy from the crest of their position, all in due accordance with the finest traditions of the British army, brought forth a roar of applause from the Empire, which a moment after stood aghast at Symons' death, and Yule's hurried retreat on Ladysmith. Late in the evening of the following day, Ian Hamilton, stirring his infantry with visions of London posters, cleared the enemy from Elands-laagte, putting General Kock into the scales with Symons. General French had covered the retreat of the Dundee force with some success, and 300 wounded remained in his hands. Some months were destined to elapse before England heard of another victory as worthy of the name. But these two actions had cost a hundred killed, two hundred and thirty wounded, and four hundred and twenty prisoners and missing; and nothing had been gained: indeed Sir George White's position, isolated in Ladysmith as he was, was even alarming. Rietfontein on the 24th retrieved nothing; and on the 30th White, turning gambler per force, attempted, once and for all, to drive back the enemy, fast closing in upon his force. Colonel Grimwood, however, fails him. There is six hours' heavy fighting; we hear of the first appearance of Christian de Wet at the northern end of Tchrengula; the whole of Colonel Carleton's force surrenders; the remainder of White's army falls back in disorder, and the Siege of Ladysmith begins. Nicholson's Nek was indeed a disaster. Buller's army corps was still at sea, and three more regiments—the Sussex, the Essex and the Sherwood Foresters —were mobilised the following day, as corps troops to replace casualties.

On the 7th, 8th, and 9th parties of reservists marched through the streets of Derby, *en route* for temporary quarters in Victoria Barracks, Southampton, amid scenes of the wildest enthusiasm. The road was densely packed with a cheering multitude; bunting was displayed from every window; people had even mounted to the roofs. At the station itself the men had literally to fight their way through the crowd, who had broken through the police and were beyond restraint. Their enthusiasm knew no bounds. Many had climbed to the topmost lattice-work of the arched roof, and there cheered lustily, until the train steamed out of the station.

On the night of the 9th a detachment of 8 officers and 356 men, under Major E. A. Gosset, were assembled in the barracks at Portsmouth; and, on the 11th, the party embarked on the British India Company's s.s. "Dunera," detailed to convey the regiment to the Cape.

On 21st November the "Dunera" arrived at Malta, where the Battalion embarked without delay. The reservists were posted to their original companies; several old soldiers, veterans of the Tirah Campaign, were transferred from the 2nd Battalion, also stationed in Malta, and two officers —Lieutenants Keller and Watson—exchanged with two newly-joined officers—2nd Lieutenants Gibson and Luther.

A list of officers who sailed on board the "Dunera" will be found in Appendix "D"; it is only necessary to note the names of Major and Brevet Lieut.-Colonel Cunningham, who joined the Battalion soon after its arrival at Sterkstroom, and Major Duncan, R.A.M.C., who filled the post of Medical Officer to the regiment for a period of eighteen months.

At Gibraltar, the "Dunera" had passed down the lines of the Channel Fleet, who had accorded a hearty send-off to their more fortunate comrades of the sister service; but this was as nothing to the scene, when, at 4 p.m. on the 21st, the "Dunera" steamed slowly out of the Malta Grand Harbour. The ramparts, from Ricasoli to Tigne, were packed with cheering thousands; flags and handkerchiefs fluttered in the air; bands struck up in every direction; the boats of the Mediterranean Fleet, with oars uplifted, formed an avenue down which the transport steamed; and the Governor, Sir Francis Grenfell, and Sir John Fisher, commanding the Fleet, in their own launches, followed far out to sea. There was "God Speed" in every token; and there was not an officer or man who did not second the telegram Colonel Smith-Dorrien sent back from Port Said :—

> "The Sherwood Foresters deeply appreciate the splendid send-off given them by the Royal Navy as they left Malta."

After embarking " E " Company, under Captain Radford, which had been for some time on detachment duty in Cyprus, at Limasol, the "Dunera," picking up details at Suez and Aden, proceeded down the East coast of Africa to Zanzibar.

During the voyage every precaution was taken to keep the Battalion in the best of training. Companies paraded daily for physical drill; a target towed astern afforded opportunities for musketry practice for the reservists and machine-gun detachment. Also, the men's straps were washed in permanganate of potash to stain them a dark colour, and orders were issued that buttons and belt-plates were not to be cleaned. Officers discarded their Sam Browne belts for men's equipment. In short, Colonel Smith-Dorrien prepared his regiment in every possible way for immediate work in the field on arrival at the Cape.

At Zanzibar permission was obtained to land the Battalion, which, headed by the band and drums, marched through the town to the Recreation Ground, much to the wonder and delight of the cosmopolitan population of the place. This fact is particularly worthy of note, as the Battalion was the first British regiment that ever set foot upon the island.

At last, on the night of 13th December, the "Dunera" lay at anchor in Durban Roads, and the long voyage had ended. No communication with the shore could be gained that night; but with the morning's light came the news of Gatacre's defeat at Stormberg and the order from Sir Redvers Buller to proceed to East London and thence to reinforce the defeated General.

On the night of the 15th the Battalion was billeted in the Agricultural Hall, East London. The townsfolk could talk of nothing else but the terrible news of Stormberg; and newspaper boys displayed posters proclaiming :—" Fierce battle now raging in Natal" : this, of course, was Colenso, while a day or so afterwards came the tidings of Magersfontein; for the regiment had landed in the country during what was afterwards known as "Black Week," when the whole Empire shuddered under three successive disasters, and then gathered itself in unison and responded to the call.

In three train-loads the Battalion, consisting of 28 officers, 1 warrant officer, and 980 rank and file, leaving 2nd Lieutenant de Pledge and 102 N.C.O.'s and men at East London as a Base Company, proceeded northwards by the Eastern Government Railway to Sterkstroom and joined the so-called Third

Division, which consisted of the 2nd Northumberland
Fusiliers, the 2nd Royal Irish Rifles, the 1st Royal Scots,
the 77th and 74th Batteries of Field Artillery, under Colonel
Jeffreys, and a large force of Mounted Infantry, comprising
the Cape Police, the Cape Mounted Rifles, the Kaffrarian
Horse, the Frontier Mounted Rifles, the Berkshire Regiment,
M.I., and De Montmorency's Scouts.   Shortly after the
regiment's arrival, the Northumberland Fusiliers—who,
with the Irish Rifles, had suffered so severely in the
Stormberg disaster, and were in consequence very weak in
strength—departed for East London for duty.

Such then was the force which, already prostrated by
reverse, was destined to several weeks of practical inactivity
at Sterkstroom.   For General Gatacre's orders were on no
account to again attempt to dislodge the enemy from their
extremely powerful position, thirty miles to the north: his
instructions were essentially those for passive defence.

The country around the small township of Sterkstroom,
which lies at an altitude of some five hundred feet above sea-
level, and at a distance of two hundred miles from the sea,
may be described as the final plateau, lying below the Storm-
bergen and Bamboes Mountains, before the level of the veldt
proper is attained.   Beyond these mountains there are hills
in plenty, but such as it is possible to obviate, and which do
not stand out across the country, in ranges a hundred miles
in length, as great barriers to the north.   The great unbroken
plain, in the centre of which Sterkstroom lies, stretching from
Bushman's Hoek to Putter's Kraal, is bounded on the west by
the hills of the Tarkstad Valley, and on the east by the great
Donkerhoekberg and Pen Hoek.   Through the mountains to
the north—with which we are chiefly concerned—lie only
two passes—Pen Hoek and Bushman's Hoek—leading to the
higher plateau, which terminates at Stormberg Junction.
General Gatacre, based on Sterkstroom, contented himself

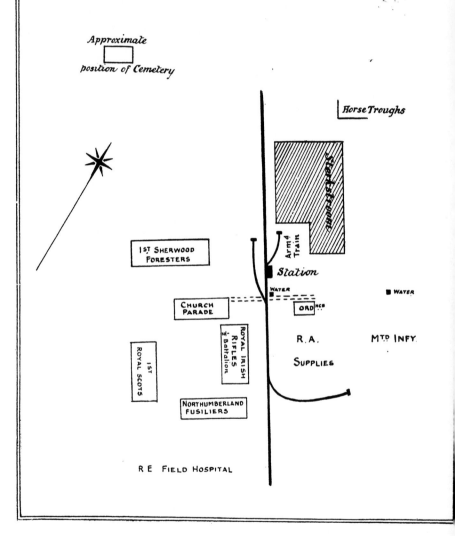

PLAN OF STERKSTROOM CAMP.

Approximate
position of Cemetery

Horse Troughs

Sterkstroom

1ST SHERWOOD
FORESTERS

Arm.d
Train

Station

WATER

WATER

CHURCH
PARADE

ORD NCE

ROYAL IRISH
RIFLES
½ Battalion

R.A.

M.T.D INFY.

1ST
ROYAL SCOTS

SUPPLIES

NORTHUMBERLAND
FUSILIERS

R E FIELD HOSPITAL

[To face p. 7.

with holding the southern range at these two points of access; Commandant Olivier, evidently with similar orders from his General-in-Chief, rested passively at Stormberg. Both places were railway junctions; the former with the small coaling line to Indwe, affording easy communication to Pen Hoek—(the main line itself passed through Bushman's Hoek)—the latter of the main line with the Steynsburg line, which connected with the central Cape Railway to Norval's Pont. Strategically, therefore, Stormberg was by far the more important place; but General Gatacre's orders were emphatic: he was to content himself in enforcing loyalty from Sterkstroom to the south.

The enemy ushered in the New Year by advancing beyond Molteno to a hill called the Looperberg, whence they shelled the Bushman's Hoek detachment, and, having by this means treated many officers and men of the Regiment—at the time upon one of its daily route marches—for the first time to the sound of a shot fired in anger—though it was but luke-warm anger at the best—they departed whence they came; and two more weeks passed without event.

By this time Lord Roberts, with Lord Kitchener as his Chief of Staff, had arrived at Cape Town. In the meantime General French alone had met with some success, and was now throwing out a cordon around De Wet at Colesberg. These operations, by drawing large bodies of the enemy over Norval's Pont, fitted in admirably with Lord Roberts' plan; though curiously enough General French, together with all the other divisional Generals, was in entire ignorance of what course the Commander-in-Chief had decided to pursue. Neither he nor General Kelly-Kenny were made aware of the plan which led to the relief of Kimberley and the advance on Bloemfontein until the day before French's troops left the Naaupoort line and commenced the operation itself.

Gatacre's orders under the new Commander remained

practically the same: he was deprived of most of his Colonial mounted troops, which were sent to Dordrecht as an independent command, under Brigadier - General Brabant, to threaten the enemy in the direction of Aliwal North; and, beyond an occasional reconnaissance, to satisfy himself that Stormberg was still held in force, he was to avoid becoming in any way seriously engaged. But though the division as a whole remained inactive, there were several collisions between the patrols of the hostile forces before the year had ended. One body of men in particular were frequently engaged. They were composed of picked men from the neighbourhood, and were commanded by Captain de Montmorency, V.C., of the 21st Lancers, whose reckless gallantry was of such a degree that could alone be due to an absolute ignorance of the meaning of fear. It is in the character of all men to admire a truly brave man, and the whole division gave to this one his share; yet, in the nature of things, it was hardly probable that he could have lived throughout the war.

On the 19th of January the Battalion left Sterkstroom for Bushman's Hoek, where a strong advanced post was formed, under the command of Colonel Smith-Dorrien. "A," "C" and "E" Companies, under Major Shaw, held the Hoek itself, the remainder of the regiment camping on the northern slopes of the hill at Phillip's Farm. The position also included the Looperberg—the hill before mentioned whence the enemy were able to shell the Hoek—which was held by 500 Kaffrarian Rifles. It was at Phillip's Farm that No. 1 Company Mounted Infantry was formed. The command was given to Major Godley, with Lieutenant Casswell—who was succeeded in the Adjutancy by Lieutenant Keller, 2nd Lieutenant Rhodes becoming Transport Officer — and Lieutenant Watson as subalterns.

On 1st February Major Shaw's detachment relieved the

Kaffrarian Rifles, who joined Brabant's Colonial Division, on the Looperberg; and the following day Colonel Smith-Dorrien bade good-bye to the regiment. All knew that it was for the command of a brigade, that that brigade would lead to a division, and that his old regiment would never see him more as a regimental officer all were equally certain; but where that brigade was, and what that brigade was to do, were facts at that time only known to Lord Roberts, Lord Kitchener, and perhaps five staff officers.

This left Colonel Cunningham in command of the advanced force; and Major Gosset took over command of the Battalion, which the following day moved its camp five miles forward to Cyphergat, a small colliery at the base of the Looperberg.

Colonel Cunningham's force comprised all three arms, and now lay within striking distance of the enemy's head-quarters. Its position at Cyphergat was amply secure. Major Shaw's detachment, with two 12 pr.-naval guns, commanded the country for miles around, and kept up communication with Sterkstroom and Pen Hoek from the summit of the Looperberg; whilst " F " and " G " Companies held a rocky ridge to the north of the Cyphergat Camp itself.

In the foreground of the plain to the front lay the town of Molteno, and ten miles to the north the Stormberg Hills, composed of the Rooikop and the Kissieberg. The former rose conspicuously from the undulating plain, a great barren, treeless hill, to the east of the Nek over which the railroad passed. Further to the east lay a range of lofty and inaccessible mountains, rendering any attempt at a turning movement on that flank futile from the beginning. The Kissieberg, a low, three-pronged ridge, running in a north-westerly direction, protected the other flank. It was at the foot of these hills that the disaster of 10th December had taken place. But any further attempt was now beyond the question. Gatacre's force, even had he wished to again hazard an attack, was not of sufficient strength; and though in the early days of February there were one or two minor skirmishes of little importance, and Pen Hoek was twice attacked in a half-hearted fashion, the month was well advanced before any news of Lord Roberts' operations reached the outside world. After Buller's defeat at Spion Kop, the outlook had appeared more gloomy, and it seemed as if the signal for an advance would never come.

Moreover, these long weeks of waiting in a standing camp were beginning to produce their inevitable result, and dysentery and enteric were rapidly filling the hospitals. On 11th February Captain England was removed from the Looperberg to the Station Hospital at Sterkstroom, suffering from enteric fever. For thirteen days he fought hard for his life, but on the 24th, to the great grief of the regiment, his death was announced. He was buried in the little cemetery at Sterkstroom. He was the only officer of the Battalion who embarked on board the "Dunera" who was destined never to see his native shores again.

By this time the Free State had come to be regarded as a kind of "promised land," towards which the patience of the children of Israel was as nothing. Consequently, the news that not only was Lord Roberts across the Orange River and Kimberley was relieved, but that he had even surrounded and captured the whole of Cronje's army, came upon the Third Division, as it came upon the world, as a thunderbolt of surprise. The absolute secrecy with which the whole operation had been planned and carried out was a master-piece in itself, and completely nonplussed the enemy. At first, owing to French's activity at Colesberg, they had made sure that Norval's Pont was the objective of the British General, and had strongly reinforced that line, which was then only held by a small force under General Clements. Then, after the feint at Koodoosberg, they fully believed that

the English were going to hurl themselves once again against
the Magersfontein entrenchments; and the army corps crossed
the river to the east wholly without their knowledge. It was
not the line of advance that had been recommended by the
War Office, for it had the disadvantage of being without any
adequate line of communication; but for that very reason
perhaps the manœuvre was all the more unexpected. The
relief of Kimberley was but a side stroke from the general
movement; for a greater object was now rendered possible,
in the fact that Cronje's army had not yet moved, and the
British army corps lay across his line of retreat. What
actually happened is history; and from the moment that the
white flag of surrender ran up from the laager at Paardeberg
the whole tide of the war, from Kimberley to Ladysmith
—for even although the Natal laagers were in no way
diminished, the fact remains the same—was completely
and reversely changed. On the evening of the day that
the news came to the little camp at Cyphergat, the
Commander-in-Chief's health was drunk in the corrugated
iron hut, which answered for an officers' mess, with the
greatest enthusiasm; for all knew now that the long period
of inactivity had ended, and the darker clouds, which had
hung over the earlier days of the war, had at last lifted and
dispersed.

CHAPTER II

STORMBERG AND BETHULIE BRIDGE

THE presence of Lord Roberts in the Free State naturally rendered the Boer positions, south of the Orange River, no longer tenable. An early evacuation of Stormberg was anticipated ; and therefore, to ascertain whether the Rooikop was still occupied by the enemy in any appreciable strength, General Gatacre made a reconnaissance in force on 23rd February.

His force consisted of four companies of Mounted Infantry, the Royal Scots, the Berkshire Regiment, the Royal Irish Rifles, the Cape Police, De Montmorency's Scouts, the 74th and 77th Batteries R.F.A., and 500 men of the Battalion— " E " and " A " Companies remaining in camp.

General Gatacre's idea was twofold : firstly, to ascertain the approximate strength of the Boer force, and secondly, to take up a defensive position before the Rooikop with his infantry and guns, and, by thrusting forward his mounted troops, to endeavour to entice the enemy out. The ground offered certain facilities for such a plan ; for, by sending his infantry by rail to Molteno, it was possible for them, by advancing well to the west of the railroad, to approach to within a few miles of the Stormberg hills under cover of a series of low-lying kopjes which lay scattered in that direction. Before the Rooikop itself, overlooking Pinnear's Farm, a rocky ridge extended from east to west, parallel to the Boer position, which, with a good field of fire across the valley, was admirably suited to the General's purpose. Upon this ridge, therefore, he placed his guns, the 74th Battery on the right and the 77th on the left, the bulk of the infantry being posted behind the 74th Battery.

The mounted troops were then advanced in the following order :—De Montmorency's Scouts on the right, the Irish Rifles M.I., Berkshire M.I., Derby M.I., Royal Scots M.I., and the Cape Police on the left. The engagement was soon opened. The advanced Scouts were greeted with a heavy rifle fire from the lower slopes of the Rooikop. Thereupon, estimating the enemy at two or three hundred, they fell back upon their companies, who began a steady retirement, cautiously followed up by the enemy. Thus, on the British left, all went well; for the Mounted Infantry had not only drawn the enemy's fire and obliged them to bring a gun into action, but the Boers had actually advanced from their position ; and this had so far been accomplished without any loss of life, though several horses were hit. But on the right there was trouble. The ground at this end of the valley was more broken, and several small boulder-covered kopjes lay within easy rifle range of one another. De Montmorency had pushed across the valley with characteristic eagerness ; and, anxious to gain an advantageous position, he had advanced his men well to the front of the general alignment at the very time the remainder of the mounted troops had begun to retire. The Boers instantly seized this opportunity, and galloped for the hillock from the north, while De Montmorency, with Colonel Hoskier (a volunteer officer) and sixteen of his men, approached the same kopje from the south. General Gatacre immediately realised the danger to which the gallant officer was exposed, and both batteries poured their shell across the valley in the hope of checking the on-coming Boers; while the regiment was immediately ordered across to that flank. But all was in vain, the Boers reached the hill first ; and then, in spite of the greatly

increased fire along the whole length of the valley, calmly
awaited their man. De Montmorency, well in front of his
Scouts, had reached the crest of the hill, when he fell dead
with a bullet through his heart. Several of his men,
including Colonel Hoskier, went down with him, and the
remainder, seeking what cover they could, lay helpless on
the hill. There was no thought then of the original plan:
the sole idea was to extricate the Scouts, no easy matter;
for the Boers, creeping round both sides of the kopje,
covered their only line of retreat. The whole of the fight
now centred itself around the fallen body of this celebrated
officer. The Mounted Infantry and Artillery, believing only
that De Montmorency was in danger, and little suspecting
the truth, entered heart and soul into the fray; and finally
the more advanced Boers were forced to fall back, no
doubt with some loss. This gave the Scouts a chance of
escape which they were not slow to take. But the appearance of the first man was the signal for a roar of musketry
from the "Mausers": through the dust of their bullets he
galloped back across the valley, and, one by one, his
comrades followed, until all who were unharmed were safe
again. But it was as if each man of the thousand there
had heard the news of a personal loss, when the word
went round that De Montmorency had not come back.
Almost immediately the general retirement commenced;
and, sadly, in the pouring rain the force wended its way
back to Molteno, reaching camp long after dark.

There is an act of devotion which may as well have
its place here as anywhere else; for Trooper Byrne was
well known to many men of the regiment, having sailed
to Egypt at the beginning of the year in the s.s. "Verona,"
which carried a draft to the Battalion in Malta. He had
been De Montmorency's servant for some time, and had
gained the Victoria Cross on the same day as his gallant

master. When he heard that De Montmorency was among
the missing, the brave fellow was unable to bear the
suspense, and, mounting his master's Arab, he rode straight
for the enemy's laager. Whilst there was no news there
was still hope; but the following morning, a solitary
waggon, bearing something white, followed by a solitary
man on a white horse, slowly approaching across the plain
towards Molteno, told its own sad tale. He was buried
at Molteno on the 25th February.

Lord Roberts' army was now rapidly closing on Bloemfontein; and, as the Norval's Pont and Bethulie lines join
at Springfontein, several miles south of the capital, the
lines of communication of both the Colesberg and Stormberg
laagers were thereby seriously threatened. A reconnaissance,
on the 2nd, showed the enemy's force greatly decreased in
numbers; and, without doubt, as proved by subsequent
events, it was only a weak rearguard which then held the
place. On the 3rd the advanced camp moved two miles
forward to a position overlooking the town of Molteno,
where they were joined by the remainder of the division.
Here another company of mounted infantry was raised, the
command of which was given to Captain Leveson-Gower,
with Lieutenants Burnett - Hitchcock and Wybergh as
subalterns. As Lieutenant Hitchcock shortly afterwards
was posted to the Headquarter Staff, Lieutenant Percival,
before going to the Army Service Corps, served with the
company for a short time: Lieutenant Wybergh, however,
remained with them throughout the entire war. No. 1 and
No. 2 M.I. Companies were respectively the original "B"
and "G" Companies of the Battalion, as the commanders
naturally desired to have as many men as possible from
their old companies; though, of course, many men from
other companies, with M.I. certificates or a previous knowledge of horses, were drafted into each. The regimental

Mounted Infantry were destined to take part in an entirely different set of operations than those in which the Battalion served; and for that reason, in order to pursue, as far as possible, a consecutive narrative, the doings of each are confined to separate chapters.

On the 5th of March General Gatacre personally conducted another mounted reconnaissance. On reaching the foot of the Rooikop, without drawing fire, the troops dismounted, fixed bayonets, and advanced up the hill. The position had been evacuated; and, so leaving the Royal Scots M.I. in occupation, the General returned to camp, and the following day the Battalion and the guns marched into Stormberg.

Much, no doubt, as he would have liked to, Gatacre was unable to push on, as the Boers had done considerable damage to the railway in their retreat northwards; culverts had been destroyed, and, in some places, hundreds of yards of the metals had been blown up and the sleepers burnt. In five days, however, during which the remainder of the division arrived at Stormberg by driblets, the engineers had the line again ready for traffic. On the 8th the mounted troops and guns set out in pursuit of the enemy.

The distant sound of firing soon announced that they were in touch; and word came back that four hundred of the enemy were still south of the Orange River. It was obvious, therefore, that the Bethulie bridges were still intact; and it thereby became General Gatacre's primary duty to save those bridges if he could.

The direct lines of communication to Bloemfontein, from Cape Town, Port Elizabeth and East London, lay across the Orange River at Norval's Pont and Bethulie. At the latter place the river is some two hundred yards across, deep, and the current, in the rainy season, exceedingly rapid. To build a temporary pontoon bridge, such as was afterwards erected at Norval's Pont, necessarily involving a deviation of the permanent way, would naturally be a matter of some time. Now Lord Roberts had come from Koodoosberg with only twenty-eight days' rations; and one of the first incidents of his now famous operations had been the loss of his reserve supply column. But the Commander-in-Chief, entirely undaunted by this mishap, had continued his march through a country almos' devoid of supplies, with only just sufficient food to carry his army corps to the capital itself. The victory of Paardeberg had considerably delayed his advance; and he reached his destination on his last day's rations. As the supplies in Bloemfontein would be rapidly consumed by his great force of four divisions, it would have been indeed a serious matter for him had all the Orange River bridges been destroyed. Therefore Gatacre's force, after months of inactivity, at last had a definite and fixed object before them.

The mounted troops pushed vigorously forward; and on the morning of the 11th, the Cape Police, under Major Nolan Neyland, and De Montmorency's Scouts, now under Captain M'Neil, came upon the Bethulie bridges. There they found that five of the eight piers of the railway bridge had been already demolished; but the road bridge, although already mined with dynamite, was still secure. The initial credit for the success of the action is due to Major Neyland; without a moment's hesitation—and a delay of a few minutes even might have proved fatal—the Cape Police threw themselves into a small farm, which commanded the bridge at the Cape Colony end, and immediately opened fire on the enemy, who were, even then, actually engaged in laying down a fuse with which to fire the mines. But the ready action of the Colonials forced them to desist; and forthwith the struggle commenced from either side of the river. In the meantime word had

B

been sent back for the remainder of the Mounted Infantry
and guns, both of which quickly arrived upon the scene.
The guns came into action on the heights on the southern
side of the valley at Klipbankfontein, and a Boer gun,
from the hills above Bethulie town, vigorously shelled
the farm at the bridge. The Mounted Infantry, dismounted
and extending, advanced to within a range of 800 yards,
No. 1 Company of the Sherwood Foresters being on the
extreme right—the road bridge being situated at the left
centre of the British line. For all that day and all that
night the mounted troops retained their position ; while
urgent word was sent back for the Battalion to come to their
assistance. The regiment entrained at Stormberg in haste,
and reached Olive Siding, which, owing to a demolished
culvert, was the temporary terminus of the East London
line, just before midnight on the 12th. Without delay
the whole battalion, horses, mules, and carts, were immediately detrained, difficulties being heartily overcome,
and the four buck-waggons lifted bodily from the trucks.
At dawn all was completed; and, as the booming of the
guns and the sharp rattle of musketry recommenced for
the day, the regiment deployed across the hill.   " D "
Company was detailed as escort to the guns, and " C "
Company, under Major Shaw, with Lieutenants Percival
and Popham, were ordered to occupy the farm. In order
to do so, they were obliged to pass under a very heavy
fire ; but, by advancing in twos and threes, Major Shaw
managed to gain his destination without a casualty.
Thereby the Cape Police and De Montmorency's Scouts,
who had passed the last twenty-four hours so profitably,
were enabled to retire ; but in all other respects the
situation remained unaltered ; and if the Boers were
unable to discharge their mines, the British were equally
unable to remove them.

In the afternoon General Gatacre ordered Major Gosset
to make a demonstration with his Battalion towards the
river, under cover of which the batteries were to move to
a more advanced position. On approaching the river the
regiment came under a very severe fire; but, fortunately,
only two men were hit; and, when the guns satisfactorily
changed their position, the Battalion retired in good order.
Towards evening "D" Company, under Captain Rigby and
Lieutenant Wilkin, which had acted as artillery escort
throughout the day, was ordered to reinforce "C" Company
at the bridge farm with the machine gun, under Lieutenant
Sadler. Under cover of darkness this party reached the
bridge without mishap; whilst half of "A" Company took
their place as escort to the guns.

At nightfall the firing, which had been practically
continuous throughout the day, had gradually died out.
A picquet posted behind a barricade, erected about a
hundred yards from the southern end of the bridge,
rendered it impossible for any of the enemy to cross to
the Cape Colony bank; but Major Shaw was naturally
anxious with regard to the other side of the river; for in
the darkness—although they had not dared to do so on the
previous night, it might have been possible, for ought he
knew—as it indeed subsequently proved to be—for a few of
the enemy to creep to the edge of the stream and there
connect their fuses with the mines at the northern piers.
He therefore ordered Lieutenant Popham to post a smaller
picquet on the enemy's side of the river. This was done,
apparently unperceived by the enemy, and Popham returned
to the farm. There, with Major Shaw's permission, he called
for volunteers to reconnoitre the enemy's trenches and the
ground in the vicinity, and Privates Topham, Holmes,
Sullivan, and Woods, all of "C" Company, immediately
stepped out of the ranks. This officer with his four men

then silently crossed again, and cautiously crept under the
bridge on the northern bank. At the base of the first pier
they found two large boxes, a large quantity of wire, a
Mauser rifle, a still smoking pipe and a dog, which
immediately started barking. The dog was instantly
silenced with the butt-end of a rifle. Lieutenant Popham
ordered the men to pick up the boxes, while he himself
took the coil of wire; and, thus laden, the party began
their retreat back across the bridge. But the alarm had
already been given; the interval which ensued was just
sufficient to enable the Boers to seize their rifles and for
Lieutenant Popham and his men to get back to the Cape
Colony side of the river, when a rapid rifle fire broke out
upon the bridge. But owing to the darkness, and no doubt
to the suddenness of surprise, the Boer fire was wild and
erratic: the bullets, for the most part, flew high, though the
iron gates at the northern end of the bridge were afterwards
found to be splashed white with lead, and a small pig, which
ran out from the farm, got shot. As soon as Popham and his
men had rejoined the company, Major Shaw replied to the
enemy's fire and brought the machine gun into action. But,
as the night was quite black, there is no reason to believe
that any of the enemy were hit, or that the total casualties
of the incident amounted to any more than 1 dog and 1 pig.
Nevertheless, this in no way detracts from what credit is due
to all concerned ; for the boxes, of course, contained dynamite.
More mines had been laid at the central piers ; but these were
beyond the reach of the enemy, by reason of the picquets at
either end of the bridge. For nearly thirty hours a fierce
struggle had continued for a few yards of ground on the
Free State bank; but now Lieutenant Popham and his
volunteers, by their gallant action, had attained the whole
object of the British force. The importance of the Bethulie
Road Bridge to the Commander-in-Chief—especially now

since both the railway bridges at that place and at Norval's
Pont had been destroyed—has already been mentioned ; and
it was for some time expected that Lieutenant Popham would
be awarded the Victoria Cross. He received, however, the
Distinguished Conduct Medal for his conduct in Lord
Kitchener's despatch of 23rd June, 1902 ; but the men who
had volunteered to accompany him remained unrewarded ;
although Private Holmes, for gallant behaviour at Vlakfon
tein, was afterwards promoted King's Corporal.

On the following morning, after a salvo of fifteen shells
fired into the farm at dawn, the enemy, it now being beyond
their power to work any harm, retired in the direction of
Smithfield and Rouxville. The same day the rest of
Gatacre's force arrived upon the scene, and Colonel Allen,
the C.S.O., was placed in command of the Infantry Brigade,
his place on the staff being taken by Colonel Cunningham.
On 15th March the mounted troops, under Colonel Sitwell,
who commanded the newly-formed 10th M.I., crossed into
the Free State on the heels of the retreating commandos ;
the Battalion, continuing still in advance of Gatacre's
headquarters, marched across the bridge at 5.15 p.m. on
the same day, and bivouacked some three miles to the
north of the town of Bethulie, at a spot where an empty
goods train lay upon the line.

As was to be expected, the Boers had run most of their
rolling stock to the north of Bloemfontein ; but Captain
Pope-Hennessy, of the Cape Police, and Captain Gordon
Turner, of De Montmorency's Scouts—who gained the
Victoria Cross for his conduct on the day that De
Montmorency lost his life — had found a solitary engine
at Bethulie on the previous evening. By means of a
revolver, levelled at the engine - driver's head, they ran
into Springfontein Junction that night; and by the
same process forced a few burghers, whom they found

asleep in the station waiting-rooms, to hand over their Mausers. They then ordered the reluctant driver to connect with a train which rested in the station siding, and thence steamed back to Bethulie. It was a strange thing, seldom as Gatacre's troops came into contact with the enemy, that almost every occasion brought forth opportunities for individual action which were never lost, of which this was by no means the least dashing.[1]

In this train the Battalion left Bethulie at 4 p.m. on the 16th, the line having been reported clear of the enemy as far as Springfontein, which station was reached soon after dark, as the Guards' Brigade, under General Pole-Carew, who had been sent down to clear the way for General Clements, went north again to Bloemfontein.

Clements, whose guns at Norval's Pont had been audible at Bethulie, advanced into the Free State in the direction of Philippolis; and Brabant's Colonial Division had crossed at Aliwal North, into the vicinity of the Caledon River. The Southern Free State was in fact now in the hands of the British; and, in the Natal theatre of war, Ladysmith, after the fierce ten days' battle of Pieter's Hill, had been relieved, and only the northern corner of that colony remained still invaded.

Thus the whole aspect of the war was changed. And now, for two weeks at Springfontein, and a month at various posts along the line, another period of inactivity ensued. But it was not of the same dreary nature as

---

[1] There was an instance at Dordrecht, on the last day of the year, when a few men of the Cape Mounted Rifles gallantly stuck to the body of their dying officer; there were the several exploits of De Montmorency, more especially the occasion when, with only ten men, he charged a rebel laager at Indwe, and put the lot to flight; there was Gordon Turner's bravery on the 23rd February; and at Bethulie the actions of Major Neyland and Lieutenant Popham; and, finally, this almost impertinent occupation of an important railway junction by two men.

the long days of Sterkstroom and Cyphergat had been ;
for everyone knew that the main army at Bloemfontein
merely waited for supplies, and that, since every day
spent in the capital only added more to the already long
lists of victims to the ravages of dysentery and enteric,
the Commander - in - Chief would not delay his further
advance a day longer than was necessary. To this end
Bethulie became a scene of the greatest animation and
energy. A large working party was already busily
engaged in repairing the destroyed railway bridge : a
deviation of the permanent way had carried the line
across the road bridge, but it was then discovered that
the bridge was not sufficently strong to bear the weight
of a full-sized engine and heavy goods train ; miles of
additional siding were therefore laid down on either bank,
and, on the Cape Colony side, thousands of loaded trucks
from the coast lay awaiting their turn ; while, night and
day, a light engine carried them over, three at a time.
Further south, at all the principal depôts on each of the
three main lines, Kaffirs never ceased to load truck after
truck as they came from the north. Every hour the full
trains rattled northwards through Springfontein or back
again empty ; from Cape Town to the Modder there was
but one watchword :—"Supplies for Bloemfontein."

While the British were so employed, the Boers did not
remain idle. Realising that it would be some time before
Lord Roberts could continue his advance, a large force, under
Christian de Wet, returned to the South-eastern Free State,
and invested Brabant's Division at Wepener. The Colonials,
more especially the Cape Mounted Rifles, offered a most
determined resistance, and held the enemy gallantly at bay,
until they were eventually relieved. But the British forces
were not everywhere as fortunate ; for both at Sanna's Post
and Reddersburg they suffered serious reverses. At the

former place De Wet surprised General Broadwood's 2nd
Cavalry Brigade, despatched by Lord Roberts to protect the
Bloemfontein Waterworks, inflicting on them severe losses;
and, at the latter, the same indefatigable General surrounded
and captured a detachment of the Royal Irish Rifles and
Northumberland Fusiliers, sent out by General Gatacre to
garrison the town.

The Commander-in-Chief was determined that, if possible,
De Wet's commandos, then considerably south of the capital,
should not escape him.   Therefore he despatched General
French's Cavalry Division, Ian Hamilton's Mounted Infantry,
and infantry brigades under Generals Paget, Colville, and
Smith-Dorrien, in the direction of Ladybrand.   The Colonial
Division and a mixed force, under General Brabazon, were
already to the south of the same district; and thus, though
the headquarters of the main army, with Tucker's and Pole-
Carew's Divisions, remained in Bloemfontein, the only active
scene of operations, in the last week of April, lay to the east
of the capital.

CHAPTER III

THE ORANGE FREE STATE

In spite of the impatience at home during Lord Roberts' six weeks' halt at Bloemfontein, his sudden movement northward must have come as a surprise to many. For, at that time, the majority of the mounted troops were engaged in the east with Ian Hamilton, at Houtnek and in the country around Thaba Mountain.

During this fighting at Wepener, Reddersburg, and Dewetsdorp, the Battalion held posts along the railroad from Van Zyl's Spruit to Bethanie. Along this line the greatest vigilance was necessary; for supply trains ran hourly to Bloemfontein, and Christian de Wet was known to be in the district—his guns had been heard in Edenburg, where the regimental headquarters had been established, Shut in, as he was, by the Basutoland border to the east, and an overwhelming British force to the north, the thinly-garrisoned line of railway to the west offered but little of a barrier to his escape. After Sanna's Post more troops were hurried east from Bloemfontein; and it seemed as if the Boer force had little chance of striking north again.

The fighting which took place around Thaba Mountain, from 22nd April to 1st May, was severe, General Smith-Dorrien's Brigade especially being heavily engaged and at one time almost surrounded. Under cover of a feint attack from either flank, Louis Botha, who had taken supreme command, managed to bring his convoy through the British troops and thence cover its retreat northwards. The manœuvre was finely executed, and called forth unanimous praise from the correspondents who witnessed it; but Botha had need for all his ingenuity, for French and Hamilton clung to him like leeches, changing their direction north.

It may have been coincidence, or it may have been the express intention of the Commander-in-Chief, but at that moment the whole British force, as a great khaki wave whose destination was Pretoria, rolled out of Bloemfontein upon the heels of the enemy. The concentration had been brought about with such secrecy and rapidity that even the troops themselves had little suspected what they were about.

On the 20th the Riet River and Bethanie Companies had commenced their march to Bloemfontein: the Van Zyl's Spruit and Jagersfontein - Road detachments, relieved by Militia Companies, had reached Edenburg on the 21st: the Volunteer Company, under Captain Turner-Lee, had already joined, and on the 23rd a hundred Section D Reservists had arrived from East London, under Lieutenant Taylor. On the 25th a half battalion of the Suffolk Regiment had run through to Bloemfontein by train, the other half battalion having preceded them: the same day the Edenburg Garrison had gone north; and on the 26th, as the last shower of the rainy season fell, the headquarter half battalion had arrived at Kaffir River Station, where it was immediately entrained. At 3 a.m. the train had passed through Bloemfontein, and by daybreak had arrived at Glen, on the Modder River, some seven miles north of the capital. Here the half battalions, again united, had joined the newly-formed 21st Brigade, the command of which had been given to Major-General Bruce M. Hamilton. Movements such as these had been in steady progress for some days, and by the last day of the month all preparations were completed.

The composition of the 21*st Brigade* was as follows :—

Major-General—Colonel (local Major-General) Bruce M. Hamilton.

Staff—A.D.C.—Lieutenant P. W. N. Fraser (Cameron Highlanders).

Brigade-Major—Major F. C. Shaw (Sherwood Foresters).

Signalling Officer—Lieutenant J. W. Cohen (C.I.V.).

Foraging Officer—Second - Lieutenant R. S. Popham (Sherwood Foresters).

Assistant Provost-Marshal—Lieutenant R. Bellamy (R. Sussex Regiment).

Brigade Transport Officer—Major G. H. Cardew, A.S.C.

1st Battalion R. Sussex Regiment (Lieut.-Colonel B. D. H. Donne).

1st Battalion The Sherwood Foresters (Major E. A. G. Gosset).

1st Battalion The Queen's Own Cameron Highlanders (Lieut.-Colonel T. A. Watson Kennedy).

The City of London Imperial Volunteers (Colonel Mackinnon and Lieut.-Colonel the Earl of Albemarle).

Section 9th Company Royal Engineers (Lieutenant L. Evans, R.E.).

Escort to General—Troop. Lock's Horse.

21st Supply Column (Lieutenant C. T. Lloyd, A.S.C.).

20th Field Hospital (Major J. Ritchie, R.A.M.C.).

20th Bearer Company (Major C. Reilley, R.A.M.C.)

76th Battery Royal Field Artillery (Major H. M. Campbell, R.A.).

The Officers of the Battalion at that time were as follows:—

Commanding—Major E. A. G. Gosset.

Second in Command — Major and Bt.-Lieut.-Colonel E. G. Cunningham, D.S.O.

Adjutant—Lieutenant R. H. Keller.

Quartermaster—Lieutenant F. Tyler.

Transport Officer—Second-Lieutenant H. V. Rhodes.

Medical Officer—Major Duncan, R.A.M.C.

"A" Company—Captain T. H. M. Green, Second-Lieutenant G. L. H. Manby.

"C" Company—Lieutenant L. St. H. Morley.

"D" Company—Captain P. G. Rigby, Second-Lieutenant W. H. Wilkin.

"E" Company—Captain F. J. Radford, Lieutenant P. F. R. Anley.

"F" Company—Captain F. H. Weldon, Second-Lieutenant C. J. L. Gilson.

"H" Company—Lieutenant A. S. Murray, Second-Lieutenant W. R. Frend.

"I" Company (Reservists)—Lieutenant R. F. Taylor, Second-Lieutenant M. B. Webb.

Volunteer Company—Captain Turner-Lee, Lieutenants Ellis and Wright.

On Sunday morning, 29th April, the whole Brigade paraded for Divine Service. In the afternoon, crossing the river by a temporary bridge, and leaving the demolished railway bridge to the right, Bruce Hamilton's force marched in a north-easterly direction, away from the valley of the Modder, to Klein Ospruit, on the high, down-like country of the watershed, where the first of many successive bivouacs was formed.

From Klein Ospruit, to the east and to the west, the camp-fires of many a British brigade lay scattered over the veldt. Swiftly indeed had a force of some thirty thousand men been conveyed to the same tactical area; and the whole army awaited the morrow's advance.

The Boer position in the vicinity of Klein Ospruit lay along a ridge running due north and south, from Vlakfontein to Kranzkraal. Its right flank rested in the direction of Brandfort. It appears this force of the enemy was independent of the commandos under Botha, above referred to, although they were practically upon the same alignment, and a small commando lay between.

At daybreak the 21st Brigade was under arms, and moved forward in the following order:—The Camerons on the right supported by the Sussex Regiment; the Sherwood Foresters on the left, supported by the C.I.V.; simultaneously General Tucker advanced from Spytfontein, on Bruce Hamilton's left, with Vlakfontein as his objective, and soon became engaged with pom-pom and long range rifle fire. The Brigade moved forward with alacrity; but it was not here that they were to receive their baptism of fire. The Camerons swung round, and joining hands with the 14th Brigade, under General Maxwell, which came from the direction of Genaden Dal in the south, encircled the Kranzkraal hill. Had any of the enemy remained upon the position, they would most assuredly have been captured. But seeing that two brigades menaced their front, another their left, while General Broadwood's 2nd Cavalry Brigade was well to the east, driving back the small commando which served in some measure to keep up communication with Botha's force, their position was rendered untenable; and long before nightfall their commandos were cantering northwards; and General Hutton had driven the enemy from the vicinity of Karree Siding.

The hills north of the valley of the Modder had offered no mean facilities for a more determined resistance; but it seems that the secrecy with which the great combined movement was carried out had been of some avail, and the enemy were wholly taken by surprise.

But the 30th had not passed thus peacefully for Ian Hamilton. He had advanced to Thaba 'Nchu at his own request ; and there a force of some 4,000 Boers offered him a determined resistance. Neither he nor General Smith-Dorrien failed to recognise in Thaba Mountain the key to the enemy's position; and all that day the lofty plateau was the scene of the fiercest struggle. At nightfall, owing largely to the gallantry of Captain Towse, Gordon Highlanders, who gained the Victoria Cross at the grave cost of his eyesight, a strong foothold had been obtained upon the hill. May-Day witnessed the continuance of the battle, the ultimate issue of which could scarcely have been any longer in doubt. Hamilton, however, helioed to General Bruce Hamilton for assistance; and the 21st Brigade immediately set out to his aid from Kranzkraal, taking with them two additional batteries—the 81st and 82nd—and two 5-inch guns, under Colonel Waldron, R.A., from the 14th Brigade. At Kaalfontein Broadwood's Cavalry were found encamped ; and the whole force advanced towards Houtnek. Early in the day General Smith-Dorrien's Infantry had cleared the plateau: and late in the afternoon, Bruce Hamilton's imposing force came upon the enemy from their right rear, and Botha had no alternative but to retire in haste. The cavalry followed close upon their heels; and some work with the sabre was even accomplished before the night came on and the curtain fell on ten consecutive days fierce fighting.

A force, the effective fighting strength of which amounted to 11,000 men and 38 guns, lay that night at Jacobsrust, under the command of General Ian Hamilton.

Its composition was as follows :—

2nd Cavalry Brigade—Brig.-Gen. Broadwood.
Household Cavalry (Lieut.-Colonel Calley).
10th Hussars (Lieut.-Colonel Fisher).
12th Lancers (Lieut.-Colonel Earl of Airlie).
" Q " Battery R.H.A. (Major Phipps-Hornby, V.C.).

2nd Mounted Infantry Brigade—Brig.-Gen. R. Ridley.

    2nd Corps (Lieut.-Colonel de Lisle, D.L.I.).

    5th Corps (Lieut.-Colonel Dawson, I.S.C.).

    6th Corps (Lieut.-Colonel Legge, 20th Hussars).

    7th Corps (Lieut.-Colonel Bainbridge, Buffs).

    " P " Battery R.H.A. (Major Mercer).

19th Brigade—Major-General Smith-Dorrien.

    2nd Duke of Cornwall's L.I. (Lieut.-Colonel Ashby).

    2nd Shropshire L.I. (Lieut.-Colonel Spens).

    1st Gordon Highlanders (Lieut.-Colonel McBean).

    Royal Canadian Regiment (Lieut.-Colonel Otter).

    74th Battery R.F.A (Major Macleod).

21st Brigade—Major-General Bruce Hamilton.

    (Composition already detailed).

Divisional Artillery—Lieut.-Colonel Waldron.

    81st Battery R.F.A. (Major Simpson).

    82nd Battery R.F.A. (Major Connolly).

    Two 5-inch B.L. Guns.

General Ian Hamilton's orders were to advance on Winburg, the most important town in the district, which it was calculated he would be able to reach by the 7th. The Highland Brigade, under Generals Colville and MacDonald, had received instructions to follow Hamilton's force at a distance of ten miles in support. After Winburg had been occupied, however, the Highlanders remained in the town as a garrison for the time being, and afterwards continued their advance as far as Heilbron, more or less as an independent column.

The whole army now lay at the disposal of Lord Roberts for the general advance, with regard to which Ian Hamilton's column formed the "Army of the Right Flank." The Eleventh Division, consisting of General Stephenson's and General Inigo Jones' (Guards) Brigades, under General

Pole-Carew, were to accompany the Commander-in-Chief, advancing along the railway line. The Seventh Division, under General Tucker—Brigades under Generals Wavell and Maxwell—were to move to the right of, and in touch with, Lord Roberts' force. The front of both divisions was to be covered by General Hutton's 1st Brigade of Mounted Infantry. Gordon's Cavalry Brigade was already to the left of the main body ; and the halt at Jacobsrust during the 2nd was in all probability to give time for General French, with the two remaining cavalry brigades, namely, those of Generals Dickson and Porter, to join him. General Kelly-Kenny was to remain in command at Bloemfontein. General Rundle, commanding the Eighth Division, received instructions to "exercise a vigilant control east of the railway, and prevent the enemy reinvesting Wepener or moving towards Smithfield by the Dewetsdorp-Wepener gap."

On the 3rd Ian Hamilton continued his advance on Winburg ; and the Commander-in-Chief's divisions moved forward, passing through Brandfort towards Smaldeel.

Soon after Ian Hamilton had left his bivouac at Isabella-fontein, on the morning of the 4th, heavy rifle fire broke out along the entire front of his column. The Houtnek Boers had taken up a position at Welkom Farm, south of the Klein Vet River, covering the town of Winburg. This position proved to be an extensive line of low kopjes, in the form of a huge crescent or horse-shoe, the left of which rested abruptly on a formidable-looking feature, known as "Impediment Hill." The Dutch had decided upon a plan to arrest Ian Hamilton's progress, which, although simple, was not altogether devoid of ingenuity. It involved the time-honoured idea of the concentration of two forces upon the actual battlefield itself—an operation difficult indeed to accomplish, but which if fully realised invariably meets with success. The ground was admirably suited for such tactics. Without doubt it was the intention of the enemy to enclose the British force within the aforesaid " horse-shoe " of hills, coming upon it simultaneously from the east and west, and seizing the ridges on either side. But to successfully carry out such a manœuvre, requiring as it does the most accurate calculations as to time and space, combined with perfect organisation and discipline, was more than Louis Botha had reason to expect of his commandos. The idea may have been excellent, the position may have been admirably selected, but he had not, in his ill-disciplined, ragged troops and inexperienced staff, the wherewithal to accomplish it.

By the time Hamilton's Infantry had entered the semicircle of kopjes, " Impediment Hill " was already strongly held, and a large force of Boers were riding in rapidly upon the other flank, from the direction of Brandfort; although their advanced scouts were already in possession of the western ridges, the main body was at least an hour too late. Yet an hour was a small margin: the situation admitted of no delay. General Broadwood acted promptly, and moved his brigade to the west towards the on-coming force of the enemy.

By 9 a.m. the action became general, and a heavy fire opened on Ridley's Mounted Infantry from " Impediment Hill." The two Infantry Brigades, under General Smith-Dorrien, came under shell fire from the front and right, as they moved forward within the " horse-shoe " of the hills, the City Imperial Volunteers leading the advance. The 5th M.I., who became engaged to the front, were repulsed, and received the order to retire ; and at the same time the Household Cavalry and Kitchener's Horse were unable to dislodge the advance body of the enemy from the western ridges. It must have been at this time that General

c

Smith-Dorrien was first made acquainted with the gravity
of the situation and the magnitude of the Boer force, which
was rapidly approaching his left flank, for he immediately
ordered the three rear battalions of the 21st Brigade—
namely, the Sussex, the Sherwood Foresters, and the
Camerons—to wheel to the left and deploy, advancing at
right angles to their original direction in support of the
cavalry.

The bulk of Broadwood's Brigade had made a detour
round the western kopjes of the "horse - shoe," and
Kitchener's Horse, a squadron of the 12th Lancers, and
another of the Household Cavalry alone remained to dislodge the enemy's advanced troops. But the Boers clung
tenaciously to the ridge, pouring a heavy fire into the
dismounted cavalry, who found themselves unable to make
any headway, and received orders to make way for the
infantry battalions moving to their support. As Kitchener's
Horse retired through the advancing infantry, the shell fire
from "Impediment Hill" increased in severity. Broadwood
was advancing with great caution, and the western Boer
force had now greatly diminished the distance between
themselves and their goal. On that day it was the next
few minutes alone that could have brought forth any cause
for anxiety. Neither Captain Rose, of the Royal Horse
Guards, nor the Earl of Airlie, who commanded the detached
portion of the cavalry, could tell how near the approaching
Boers were to the reverse side of the hill on which they lay.
But these were not officers to hesitate. Realising the importance of occupying the kopjes without delay, and seeing the
supporting infantry close at hand, they gave the order to
mount, and charged the hill. The rattle of musketry which
greeted them lasted but a moment; and then the enemy
fell back in panic. The Sherwood Foresters, hastening in
their wake, quickly seized the ground so gallantly gained,

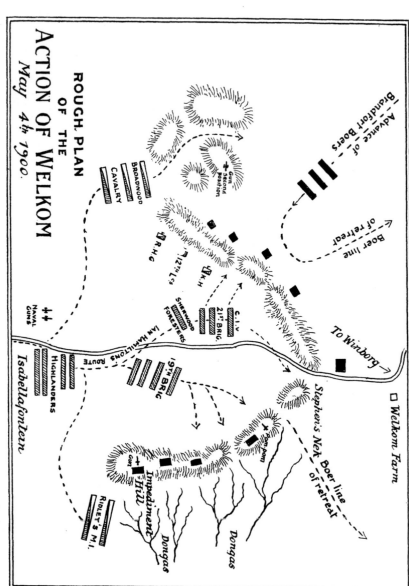

ROUGH PLAN
OF THE
ACTION OF WELKOM
May 4th 1900.

CAVALRY

BROADWOOD

+ Gun. Second position

R.H.G.

12th Ls

K.H

NAVAL GUNS

SHERWOOD FORESTERS

21st BRIG.

C.I.V.

Advance of Brandfort Boers

Boer line of retreat

To Winborg →

□ Welkom Farm

HIGHLANDERS

IAN HAMILTONS ROUTE

19th BRIG.

Isabellafontein

Stephen's Nek Boer line of retreat

+ 1 pom pom

+ Gun

Impediment Hill

RIDLEY'S M.I.

Dongas

Dongas

[To face p. 35.

and any union of the two Boer forces south of the Klein
Vet River was rendered impossible. It is believed the
initiative for this dashing movement came from Captain
Rose. Be that as it may, that gallant officer led the
charge and fell mortally wounded upon the crest of the
hill, adding but one more to the long list of keen soldiers
and brave men whose graves are now scattered across the
veldt.

From the position thus gained it was found that two hills
still lay to the front; the one, at about 3,000 yards range,
on which the Boers had posted guns, and the other, which
concealed their riflemen, at about half that distance. On
the plain beyond, the convoy of the enemy, now brought to
a timely halt, was visible.

Though for half an hour a heavy fire was directed upon
the ridge, neither any attempt to regain the lost position,
nor a counter movement of any sort was attempted by the
enemy. Their original plan had been frustrated, and it
appears that no other was forthcoming. As is, and must
always be the case with undisciplined armies, any diversion
from the original intention of the commander invariably
results in confusion. Seeing the enemy in possession of
the heights they themselves had intended to hold, the
western Boer force, on the 79th Battery coming into action,
retreated whence they came, leaving their comrades on
" Impediment Hill " to extricate themselves as best they
could.

Ridley's Mounted Infantry were well away to the east,
and the C.I.V. had gained the gap known as Stephen's Nek,
at the extremity of the " horse-shoe," the whole 19th Brigade
in support. The Highlanders had also appeared upon the
scene, and their naval guns, directed against " Impediment
Hill," thundered down the valley.

With no longer any hope of uniting their forces, with

the enemy in possession of their entire position, with the exception of "Impediment Hill," the Boers had no alternative but to retreat; and soon after 11 a.m. the incident was closed. The engagement had lasted but three hours. The casualties were inconsiderable, and principally confined to the mounted troops. A Boer pom-pom, which had the breech blown out by a bullet passing down the barrel and exploding the shell inside, fell into the hands of the British.

The action of Welkom, although it unfortunately disclosed to the enemy the strength and composition of the "Army of the Right Flank," could scarcely have been attended with greater success. The road to Winburg had been opened, and a force of 4,000 Boers had been dispersed in all directions; and this with trifling loss of life. But in the death of Captain Rose, Ian Hamilton's force sustained the loss of a gallant and devoted soldier.

A good defensive position now lay along the northern bank of the Klein Vet River in the thickly-wooded ridges, which, one behind another, roll back to the town of Winburg itself. But the enemy had had enough, and all considered they had some reason to be satisfied. This same force of Boers had come from the Basuto borderland, whither they had been led by Christian de Wet. From the siege of Wepener to the action of Houtnek, encouraged by such successes as Reddersburg and Sanna's Post, they had been busily engaged. But their most determined resistance—at Houtnek—had dismally failed, and for a fortnight they had been obliged to fall back day by day before Hamilton's masses. Had that General blundered, or had his troops been less ably handled, they might have still fostered some hope; but such was not the case. At Houtnek they had been severely taught to realise that to cling to a position with such tenacity only meant the sabres of the cavalry in the end. Before the huge force deployed at Welkom they appear to have utterly lost heart; and calling in their commandos from the south, and leaving Winburg and the surrounding country to its fate, they resolved to mass their forces at the Zand River, and there once again to hazard an engagement.

The following day the silver municipal keys of the town of Winburg were placed in the hands of the British General, and the Union Jack floated above the town. Philip Botha, arriving from the north with a force of Germans and Hollanders, had endeavoured to stir the inhabitants to a futile resistance, and even threatened to shoot Captain Balfour—the General's A.D.C.—under a flag of truce. But the townsfolk had heard descriptions of the deployment at Welkom, and had some notion of the great force which was upon them, or Botha's words might not have fallen upon such deaf ears.

At 4 p.m. the Infantry, with the pipes of the Camerons and the band of the Sherwood Foresters—the only one in the division—passed through the town amid the cheers of the British portion of the community, and camped upon the slopes to the north. That night a congratulatory message from Lord Roberts arrived for Ian Hamilton's force. The Commander-in-Chief's headquarters were then at Smaldeei his advance had been but feebly opposed.

The column did not move until late in the evening of the 6th, leaving the Highland Brigade in possession of Winburg. The march, which lay along the Ventersburg Road to Dankbaarfontein, was fortunately a short one. For the night was dark, and the route lay for the most part away from the road, and many meerkat and ant-bear holes lay scattered about the veldt.

Throughout the march from Welkom to Winburg the Boer convoys had been held in sight, even by the infantry.

General Colville now generously supplied Ian Hamilton with additional mule waggons, and the advance assumed the nature of a pursuit. The General desired to gain the Zand River drifts, and thus cut off these stragglers.

Unfortunately Ian Hamilton's column, imposing as its numbers may have been, was but a pawn upon the chess-board of the war. The Zand River Valley offered the most suitable line of defence, south of Kroonstadt—the then capital of the Orange Free State—which the enemy were hardly likely to concede without a struggle. Lord Roberts counted upon resistance there ; and rather than involve one column in an engagement, which would certainly entail considerable bloodshed, for the sake of a straggling convoy, he resolved to force the passage of the Zand River with the united strength of his entire forces, and ordered Hamilton to halt at Dankbaarfontein on the 7th and 8th. By the 9th his preparations were completed ; and Hamilton's column moved forward to Bloemplaatz, two miles south of the drift on the Winburg - Ventersburg Road. Tucker's division had come up to within three miles of Hamilton's left ; and the balloon of the Commander-in-Chief's main force shot up over the railway line.

As the great columns converged upon the re-entrant bend of the river, each covering, with its advanced guards and flanking patrols, a considerable frontage, vast herds of game were driven before them. Blesbok and springbok were startled from their mid - day slumbers, but in whichever direction they turned to fly came fresh troops ; until, at last, driven by Tucker's Mounted Infantry on to Hamilton's force at Bloemplaatz, and being crowded as a flock of sheep, they became panic-stricken and galloped madly into the brigade lines. In a trice bayonets were fixed ; many were bayoneted ; but the majority cleared the bivouac and broke out upon the plain beyond. Then, before the staff could stop it, the sporting instinct had the better of the Mounted Infantry; wild firing was opened from every direction upon the herd, and an unlucky Australian was shot in the stomach. But that night the "Army of the Right Flank" dined on venison.

A great army bivouacked upon an open plain, with the dark masses of its parted convoys, its myriads of stationary and moving lights, and the smoke rising from its fires, giving one the impression of a vast and busy city, full of animation and teeming with life. Thirty thousand troops lay that night on the southern bank of the Zand River, and their bivouac fires, which extended for more than twenty miles, must have been in full view of the enemy from their position to the north. Small wonder if they showed but little heart for fighting on the morrow.

Shortly before sunset that evening an order came that the Battalion was to march on to the river, and occupy the drift without delay. General Smith - Dorrien, with reminiscences of Paardeberg, realised the facilities for a passive defence afforded by a South African river - bed, and wished to guard against a similar experience. To pack up, fall in and cover the two miles necessary, was short work in those days, and the Battalion soon in its place.

The drift had been previously reconnoitred by mounted troops, and found unoccupied. The right half Battalion, under Colonel Cunningham, wading up to their waists in water—the drift was but ankle-deep had they been able to find it in the dark—crossed to the northern bank, and there entrenched themselves; while the left half followed suit upon the southern side. Later in the evening, General Tucker, unaware that Hamilton had already done so, sent the Cheshire Regiment to occupy the drift; and the two Battalions nearly opened fire upon each other in the dark.

That this precaution was wise there can be little doubt, since early the following morning the Boers sent down a party to occupy the place. They approached close to the position, but finding themselves forestalled were obliged to retire. Captain Radford's company mistook this force in the dull half-light of daybreak for British cavalry, or they would have opened fire.

When the sun climbed up the eastern slopes of the hills along the Kool Spruit Valley, on the morning of 10th May, 1900, the great British force upon the plain was already under arms. Among the hills to the north, and along the river itself, except for the men at the drift, who, stiff, hungry and wet, dragged themselves out of the trenches where they had vainly endeavoured to sleep, there was no sign of life. The yellow water flowed sluggishly westward between its silent, wooded banks, and except for the continual splashing of an occasional miniature waterfall, the whole valley was quiet and still, when the heavy report of a 5-inch gun burst upon the air. The challenge came from the southern bank, and the shell, flying across the valley, burst in the northern hills, where its columns of thick green smoke were lit by the morning sun. Time and again went the challenge, and still no reply came from the other side; until, as if weary of the work, the great guns ceased to speak, and the silence in the valley seemed more intense than before. Then, and not till then, a report came from the northern bank, and at the same time the head of a great column of infantry moved down into the drift; and the battle had begun.

The enemy's position extended for near upon twenty miles, from a point some two or three miles west of the railway line to the junction of the Zand River with Kool Spruit, near to which Hamilton's Column was encamped. Lord Roberts, as before mentioned, intended to utilise the whole of his great force in the passage of the river. In consequence,

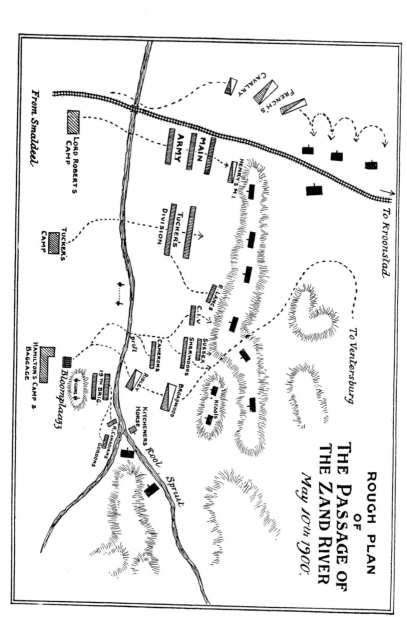

ROUGH PLAN
OF
THE PASSAGE OF
THE ZAND RIVER
May 10th 1900.

To Kroonstad

To Ventersburg

CAVALRY

FRENCH'S

MAIN ARMY

HENRY'S M.I.

From Smaldeel

LORD ROBERTS CAMP

TUCKERS CAMP

TUCKER'S DIVISION

E.LANCS

C.I.V.

SHERWOODS

SUSSEX

CAMERONS

RIDLEY

BROADWOOD

Kraals

HAMILTON'S CAMP & BAGGAGE

Bloomplaats

GUNS

19 TH BRIC

R. CANADIANS

GORDONS

KITCHENERS HORSE

Drift

Rooi Spruit

there was no greater or more extensive operation in the whole war. It was stated that a force of 12,000 Boers, with 25 guns, opposed the crossing; but an Army Corps, with two mounted divisions and a vast preponderance in artillery, lay at the disposal of the Commander-in-Chief.

The three infantry divisions were to deliver frontal attacks, Tucker in the centre, Hamilton on the right, and Pole-Carew on the left upon the railway line. French, with the Cavalry division, was to work round the enemy's right flank, closing in again on Ventersburg Road Siding, which lay some six miles north of the railway bridge. Broadwood was to assist Hamilton by similarly turning the left flank; while Ridley was to await the moment when the infantry of Hamilton's Column had pierced the position, when he was to dash through and attempt to join hands with either French or Broadwood. General Ian Hamilton decided to hold the 19th Brigade in reserve until the transport was safely across the drift, leaving the infantry work to the front to General Bruce Hamilton.

No sooner was the 21st Brigade safely across the river, than the engagement became general along the whole line, and close upon a hundred guns came into action upon the British side. French, who had crossed two of his brigades the night before, became heavily engaged. Again and again throughout the day he endeavoured to follow out his instructions and strike towards the railway; but each time only to meet with more determined opposition and to become more closely embroiled. Suffice it to say that he never reached Ventersburg Road Siding until the following day; and thus the entire plan proved abortive, as far as a large "bag" of prisoners was concerned.

But to return to Ian Hamilton's portion of the field: General Smith-Dorrien, in charge of both infantry brigades, resolved to give the artillery ample time to prepare the way for the attack. " E " Company, under Captain Radford, had previously been ordered forward to a low ridge, about 1,500 yards from the position, to draw the enemy's fire. This they succeeded in doing; and a pom-pom came into action to their immediate front.

At 10 a.m. General Bruce Hamilton deployed the Sussex Regiment for attack, moving the City Imperial Volunteers to their left and the Sherwood Foresters in support; the Cameron Highlanders he retained in reserve. General Tucker, who was but feebly opposed, rendered material assistance by diverting one of his regiments—the East Lancashire—to his right.

Soon after 11 o'clock the infantry of both divisions rose and advanced upon the enemy, while the artillery redoubled their efforts. The air was alive with shells, and the crest of the enemy's position was fringed with a cloud of smoke. During the advance the regiment became sadly mixed up with the Sussex, but, curiously enough, though the latter had three men killed, and one officer and seven men wounded, suffered no casualties. The position was captured without difficulty, the guns had for the most part done the work. For it is beyond doubt that many burghers, seeing the tremendous shell fire concentrated on the hill, refused to man the crest, and most of those that had the courage paid the penalty with their lives. One Boer gun, cleverly concealed within a mud kraal, had for some time baffled the telescopes of the artillery officers ; until, finally discovered, a lyddite shell smashed the gun, killed the crew, and levelled the kraal to the ground at one blow. Of the dead that lay upon the hill few were killed by the bullet.

While this main attack was in progress a large force of Boers advanced from the neighbourhood of the Kool Spruit Valley upon the flank of Hamilton's Force, and established themselves in the river-bed. Kitchener's Horse, under Major

Fowle, failed to dislodge them ; and General Smith-Dorrien sent the Gordons and Royal Canadian Regiment to their assistance. Nevertheless the enemy still clung to their position at the junction of the two streams ; and Hamilton, seeing that their presence not only threatened the rear of Bruce Hamilton's Brigade, but seriously menaced the transport column, applied to his C.R.A. for a battery. Now "P" Battery had gone forward with Broadwood, who was well across the river, although he had given up all idea of the wide turning movement, which he considered was more than he could do. But "Q" Battery, which had been unable to keep up, was close at hand ; and it was obvious, therefore, that "Q" was the battery needed. There seem to be various opinions as to how the mistake occurred : but the fact remains that the orderly went to "P" Battery ; and General Broadwood, being thus deprived of his guns, and hearing heavy firing directly to his rear, hesitated to advance further. Thus, although the general enveloping movement had already failed, owing to French's difficulties, all chance of any local capture of any importance had vanished before the mistake could be rectified. General Broadwood then moved direct on Ventersburg, and thus the proposed operations and those actually carried out became two very different matters.

But the Boer force, although obliged to retire, was by no means demoralised, and a strong rearguard, opposing Broadwood's advance, brought him to a standstill before Boschkop to the south-west of Ventersburg. He moved further to his right, awaiting the arrival of the C.I.V., who eventually occupied the hill.

The most notable feature of the engagement was the extreme accuracy of the artillery fire. During the fight General Smith-Dorrien sent back the following message to Colonel Waldron : "I congratulate you on your artillery fire, the accuracy of which is marvellous

Every shot is telling." Although the last shot was not fired until late in the afternoon, the casualties in the whole army were but few, French, Hamilton, and Hutton dividing the losses amongst them. That evening Hamilton occupied Ventersburg, and his division bivouacked upon the banks of Erasmus Spruit outside the town.

During the following morning the troops were allowed a rest, a short move on to Twismeit being made in the evening. The Ventersburg cross-roads, on a high ridge of veldt commanding many miles of country, was reached before sunset. Thence, far to the west arose mile upon mile of dust-clouds, rolling slowly northward. General French was not visible: the cavalry General had pushed on to Kroonstad, over the hills to the north; but along the vast horizon, lit by the setting sun, the whole of Lord Roberts' army stretched as far as the eye could reach. And this was but the spine, as it were, of a giant body, whose grip was even then closing upon Newcastle in the east, and Mafeking away upon the outskirts of the Kalahari desert.

On the 12th General French came upon Kroonstad, the temporary capital of the Orange Free State, and, unaided, drove the Dutch from the kopjes south of the town. President Steyn fled hastily to Lindley, taking with him such members of his Government as chose to follow, and placing himself and his portable Downing Street paraphernalia in the hands of Piet de Wet for protection. That evening Lord Roberts' headquarters were established in the town; while the three infantry divisional bivouacs lay around, Tucker and Pole-Carew to the north, and Hamilton to the south-east.

During the next two days Ian Hamilton's force was permitted to rest after their labours. The first being Sunday, there was a divisional church parade, and the

following day the column was inspected by the Commander-in-Chief, accompanied by Lord Kitchener.

The main body remained at Kroonstad for a week, and
finally moved slowly on towards the Vaal ; but more active
work was allotted to the "Army of the Right Flank."
Steyn was at Lindley, and a force under Piet de Wet
was known to be in that district ; but it is doubtful
whether this consideration alone would have induced the
Commander-in-Chief to detach a force for the occupation
of the town. Between him and the Vaal lay the Rhenoster
position. Here the hills, which are high, downlike, and
treeless, stand up across the veldt as a great wall, from
Rhenoster Kop eastward. Lord Roberts had reason to
fear this place, and resolved to repeat the tactics which
had been so successful throughout the last fortnight, upon
a larger scale, turning the position by a wide detour of
Ian Hamilton's Force. The following words came from the
lips of a Boer prisoner, taken later in the war :—" At the
Rhenoster we meant to fight you, it was a better place
than the Vaal, and there we intended to hold our ground.
First we saw a great column of dust moving round our right
(i.e., French) ; then we heard of another far to the east
moving round our left towards Villiersdorp (i.e., Hamilton) ;
at last when your main army came, covering the whole
of our front, well—we went away, for what was the use
of staying ? The dust of your columns was on every
side, and we were being slowly but surely surrounded."
This speech in itself illustrates the fact that there was
a greater reason in sending Hamilton to Lindley than
the mere temporary occupation of the place itself. The
Commander-in-Chief's object was to gain Pretoria, and that
as rapidly and with as little loss of life as possible. He
doubtless expected at least one pitched battle, and preferred that it should take place outside the walls of the

Transvaal capital itself, after which his weary troops might rest and his supplies be replenished.

So it was that at 8 a.m. on the morning of the 15th of May, Ian Hamilton's Column commenced its march to Lindley by passing through General Wavell's camp at Kaalfontein Nord. Three days later the infantry marched into Lindley, which General Broadwood had occupied on the 17th; for Hamilton had received intelligence that a large Boer force, driven north by General Rundle, were retiring on the town, which they intended to reach on the 18th. He therefore ordered Broadwood to push on in all haste and surprise the place, which indeed he did, the enemy's convoy, including President Steyn's exchequer, all but falling into his hands.

With the exception of the pursuit of Christian de Wet in July and August, the Lindley march was perhaps the most trying and wearisome the regiment performed. The country of the Valsch River Valley was intersected in every direction by innumerable dongas and water courses, in consequence of which the transport was invariably left far behind. Few who were there will forget the drift of the Eland's Spruit, east of Kaalfontein bridge, when the last of the brigade baggage did not reach camp until 2.45 a.m. on the following morning (18th May). On this account, the General, to safeguard his straggling transport, left the 19th Brigade behind, twelve miles west of Lindley, with instructions to rejoin the column on the Heilbron road. In addition to the difficulties of the country, the weather was now bitterly cold at night; and, fatigued after the day's march, the men were obliged to wait patiently for their food and blankets till the transport arrived. The officers of the regiment had every reason to be grateful to their commanding officer, Major Gosset. He carried a roll of blankets on his spare horse, and these he most ungrudgingly bestowed on his officers at nightfall.

But these hardships were fast thinning the ranks of Ian Hamilton's battalions. Lieutenant Ellis (Volunteer Company) and many men were overcome by exhaustion; Lieutenant Frend went back to Bloemfontein from Kroonstad with dysentery; Captain Weldon had been left at Winburg for the purpose of bringing up a fresh supply of boots and clothing; Second-Lieutenant Manby fell sick with enteric after the long march to Houtnek, whence he was taken to Bloemfontein hospital. There he developed double pneumonia, followed by dysentery, and was subsequently invalided home. In consequence of these casualties Captain Green and Lieutenant Murray were left without other officers in "A" and "H" Companies respectively, and Second-Lieutenant Gilson had since Winburg been in command of "F." The casualties among the rank and file were even more serious. Every day a company officer paraded a fast-diminishing company. Those who fell out of the ever-moving column had little chance of ever rejoining it, and these days did but forestall that one of three months later, when the ragged remains of a regiment, the companies of which barely averaged thirty men, dragged itself into Krugersdorp.

When the regiment halted outside the little township of Lindley, to allow the band to pass to the front, there were few who were not thoroughly exhausted; and without doubt, had not the town been in view for some distance, many would have fallen out.

Lindley is situated in a hollow in the hills, through which the Valsch River flows. The ridge to the south lies close upon the town. To the north a particularly prominent hill, known as "Lindley Hill," and destined to fame in connection with the disastrous yeomanry incident a few weeks later, rises above its fellows. But the surrounding hills were not such as the Dutch most love. They were bare and, except

for an occasional ant-heap, they afforded little cover, and
therein lay the danger of the country for an inferior force;
for the hills were many and within decisive artillery range
of each other.

It was reported to General Ian Hamilton, on his entering
the town, that commandos lay camped around to the south
and to the east. Piet de Wet, who was in command, and
whose conditional surrender Lord Roberts refused to accept
on the 18th, was by no means idle. All the following day,
while the column rested on the outskirts of the town, he
continued to harass the picquets by long range rifle fire.
"F" Company watched the country to the south; "D" to
the east; and "I" to the north-east. Large parties of
Boers were observed coming in from the south—doubtless
the commandos that General Hunter had driven north
from Senekal—and a playful interchange of shots was
sustained until nightfall, without however any damage
being done.

The Mounted Infantry relieved the picquets soon after
daybreak on the 20th, and the regiment, acting with the
rear-guard of the column, under Colonel Cunningham, re-
crossed the Valsch River to the high ground north of the
town. The enemy, who had already attempted to cut off
"I" Company picquet, showed up all around; and musketry
fire soon became audible in every direction. Suddenly the
southern picquet of mounted infantry, with Piet de Wet's
men close upon its heels, was seen approaching at the gallop.
Even before they cleared the town to the north the Boers
had entered from the south. Then rifles were hastily
snatched from hidden places, and the townsfolk, who had,
to do them justice, welcomed the British troops but sourly
at the best, joined the commando and opened fire upon the
retiring mounted infantry. Large parties of Boers were also
observed moving rapidly to the north-east, and then the

General feared for his right flank. The sound of guns, far
on the Heilbron Road, conveyed the news that the advanced
guard was also seriously engaged, and the presence of General
Smith-Dorrien's Brigade to the west probably accounted for
the fact that the left flank alone was unmolested. It was
evident that the force was beset from three quarters; things
began to look serious; and the General, leaving the rear-
guard in the hands of Colonel Cunningham, rode hastily to
the centre of his column. The advanced guard had been
roughly checked, with the loss of two officers and a dozen
troopers, at the Rhenoster River, eight miles north of Lindley.
General Broadwood had been obliged to wait for infantry to
clear the way; and the City Volunteers and Sussex were at
one time somewhat sharply engaged. As for the rear-guard,
upon the 82nd Battery coming into action upon "Lindley
Hill," the column, which had opened out considerably during
these actions, was for the time being extricated and enabled
to close up.

For two hours the march continued in peace. A halt was
called five miles clear of Lindley, and the news came that all
had gone well in front and that the drift across the Rhenoster
had been secured. The same staff officer brought the intelligence that Colonel Mahon had relieved Mafeking on the 15th,
which was received with cheers.

The regiment, closed well up upon the convoy, had been
again upon the march for half an hour, when the sound of
distant rifle-shots was heard far away on the right flank, and
almost immediately heavy musketry fire broke out in rear.
Colonel Cunningham had barely time to get his infantry and
guns into position when Bainbridge's Corps—forming the
mounted infantry of the rear-guard—were beaten back, and
at the same time Colonel de Lisle's men came in from the
right flank at the gallop with several riderless horses in their
midst.

D

Piet de Wet had already done much to avenge Lord Roberts' refusal of his offer of surrender.   The fighting to the flank and rear had been exceedingly sharp, and was not characterised wholly without dash on the part of the burghers.   They had inflicted some sixty odd casualties, mainly on the right flank guard in a running fight of some twenty minutes, and followed close upon the heels of the retiring mounted infantry.   But they were in no mind to face infantry and guns in position.   They came in from the right and rear in considerable numbers, and were received by the shells of the 82nd Battery.   In reply they opened fire upon the infantry position, on to which the mounted troops had retired, but seemed almost immediately to change their minds ; for, ceasing fire, they cantered down the valley, parallel to the position of the rear-guard, hoisted the white flag above the only farmhouse in the neighbourhood, and finally wheeled sharply about for Lindley, vanishing as suddenly as they came, and leaving the column to continue its march along the Heilbron Road in peace.

Those who were with the regiment that night are scarcely ever likely to forget it ; for the Battalion of the rear-guard did not reach the divisional bivouac until 8 a.m. on the morning of the following day.   The night was bitterly cold ; for although no frost was visible upon the ground at daybreak, a piercing wind blew across the open country from the west.   Owing to some mistake no guide had been sent back, and after being fourteen hours upon the march, and wandering aimlessly about the veldt till 10 p.m., hungry and tired, the Battalion lay down upon the banks of the Rhenoster, chilled to the backbone, and without fuel or blankets.   The men were more fortunate than their officers ; for they, at least, carried a blanket and the residue of the day's rations.   However, later in the night General Smith-Dorrien, with his usual thoughtfulness for the old regiment

in which he had served so many years, sent over the
Shropshire Light Infantry reserve of bully beef—for by
then communication had been established with divisional
headquarters.

The regiment rejoined the column as it marched out of
camp the following morning, and continued its way along the
Heilbron Road. With an intermediate camp at Wytpoort, Ian
Hamilton reached this town on the 22nd. Shortly before his
occupation, Christian De Wet, with a small convoy, reached
Heilbron from the direction of Kroonstad. But no sooner
had he outspanned than Broadwood's Cavalry came upon him
unexpectedly from the hills to the south. A running fight
over some four miles of country ensued, and finally resulted
in the capture of De Wet's convoy and 17 prisoners.

Ian Hamilton did not remain in Heilbron, but changing
his direction from due north to north-west, marched to
Spitzkop on the following day. Of the enemy, which had
so persistently hung upon the outskirts of his force during
the last week, the majority had returned to Lindley, the
remainder, mostly Transvaalers, going north to Villiersdorp,
where they naturally expected that he would cross the river.
It appears a strong Boer force awaited Ian Hamilton's arrival
at the drift at that place. The fact that they waited in vain
speaks much for the inefficiency of their own scouting ; for
they remained totally unaware that, firstly, Hamilton
changed the direction of his advance at Heilbron and rejoined the main British army at Vredepoort Road Station
on 24th May, and secondly, that on the following day the
"Army of the Right Flank" crossed the front of Lord
Roberts' divisions and made for the Vaal at Boschbank,
where there was not a soul to oppose him. By this movement Ian Hamilton's force became the "Army of the *Left*
Flank" ; and the force of Boers which attacked Hamilton's
rear-guard on the 24th May must have mistaken it for a

limb of the main army ; for certain it is that the Villiersdorp commandos received no intimation that Hamilton had crossed to the other flank.

On the evening of the Great Queen's last birthday, for the third time the three divisions were again concentrated ; and this time the dark hills of the " promised land," across the Vaal, rose on the northern horizon. Consequently the army was in a cheerful mood, and that night from among the bivouac fires of 20,000 weary soldiers again and again came the strains of " God save the Queen "—the great sovereign whom they were so soon to lose—sometimes loud and near at hand, sometimes faint in the distance of remoter camps ; but the song was everywhere the same, followed by cheer upon cheer. And then the news was passed down the lines that French was across the river, and that Hunter had some days before entered the Transvaal from Fourteen Streams, Baden Powell and Plumer from Mafeking, and Buller through the Drakensberg Passes ; and they themselves knew that Lord Roberts' army lay but a few miles from Vereeniging ; and the Transvaal, after six long months of war, was at last to be indeed invaded.

Not that in these days light-heartedness was any exception to the general rule. Perhaps it may have been that the days themselves were not passed altogether pleasantly, that the never-ceasing tramp of the column, striking the self-same note of monotony, was little conducive to pleasantry of any sort, that in the evenings laughter arose on every side. Perhaps it may have been that every step carried the army nearer to Pretoria and the supposed termination of the war, and every day brought forth a fresh success, for the following year, when officers and men were less hardly worked and better fed—in the days of the luxury of a Field Force Canteen—such was not the case. Be that as it may, the bivouac fires of Hamilton's Column were nightly surrounded by ragged, bearded soldiers, in the highest of animal spirits, all perfectly oblivious of the fact that many a poor fellow who in the morning had sloped his rifle or mounted his horse with a joke upon his lips, now lies buried where he fell, dropping quietly out of the great column which goes laughing northwards, leaving behind it little groups of hardly recognisable graves. Some are marked by a heap of stones, some are not ; a few may have a hurried inscription scrawled in indelible pencil upon the back of a biscuit-box wherein some faithful comrade had sacrificed his fuel ; some have not even a single stone to mark the spot. But all are alike in one thing ; for in each, stiff and cold, wrapped in the blanket he carried on his back, lies the same immutable silenced spirit.

CHAPTER IV

JOHANNESBURG AND PRETORIA

ON the 25th a march of fifteen miles carried Hamilton's Column to the basin of the Vaal; and at sunset on the following day the infantry waded across the drift at Wonderwater, covered by General Broadwood's cavalry, who had crossed that morning and secured the northern bank. French was some twenty miles to the north-west; so the three forces moved into the Transvaal in echelon—French' the most advanced, on the left; Hamilton in the centre; and the main army to the right. Lord Roberts intended to advance *via* Germiston, seizing the junctions of the Natal and Krugersdorp railroads with the main line; and with this object in view French was ordered to move upon Johannesburg *via* Driefontein, and Ian Hamilton by way of Florida. The Commander-in-Chief gave his lieutenants but three days for the operation; and Hamilton in consequence marched nearly twenty miles on the 27th, camping at Rietkuil; while French pushed rapidly on towards the Klipriversberg. The result of these movements was to draw the greater bulk of the Boer forces to the westward; while Lord Roberts seized the railway junctions before the enemy had time to demolish the line, capturing large quantities of much-needed supplies and rolling stock.

On the 28th General French engaged the enemy in the Klipriversberg, and Hamilton's Force marched up to Cypherfontein, within a few miles of support of the cavalry division. Once clear of the valley of the Vaal the aspect of the country had materially altered—picturesquely for the better, tactically for the worse. From the high hill at Cypherfontein a vast panorama lay extended to the view. To the north-west the Klipriversberg, rugged and red, stretching far to the east in range upon range of lofty mountains. To the north-west the hills diminished in altitude, and the neks and passes became both wider and more frequent; and here and there, visible only through the passes and over the smaller hills, lay the level ridges of the Witwatersrand itself and the smokeless chimneys of the Rand.

General French, at the close of the day's engagement, reported the Klipriversberg clear of the enemy, who had fallen back upon a less extensive position, intending there to defend their " Golden City " to the last.

On the morning of 29th May, Hamilton's Column moved off in a north-westerly direction, and almost immediately the mounted infantry, becoming engaged with parties of the enemy that had returned during the night, were held in check.

General French, under cover of their defence, moved off to the west, intending to advance upon his destination (Driefontein) *via* Florida, and at the same time outflank the enemy's position. This movement met with the required result; the Boers retired, and Hamilton moved his infantry over the hills by Van Wyk's Rust without the necessity of a deployment.

Here the Boer position came into view. A great valley, lying between the Witwatersrand and the Klipriversberg, extended from Florida in the west in the direction of Germiston. Upon a group of low kopjes to the front, situated in the centre of the larger valley, the mounted infantry, who had swiftly followed up the retreating enemy, were already under a heavy fire ; while French, who had now wheeled north again, encountered a determined resistance at Doornkop, and was obliged to dismount his cavalry. At the base of the steep, smooth slopes of the Witwatersrand lay a rocky ridge, running from Florida six miles to the eastward and terminating, or nearly so, at its eastern extremity in a formidable hill, known that day as "One Tree Hill," but in reality already christened "Crow's Nest." To the west lay a "Burnt Hill," entirely isolated from the longer ridge, but tactically covered and affording reciprocal defence. South of this kopje lay the Doornkop ridges, the losing scene of Dr. Jameson's pilgrimage. The large valley was thus subdivided into two minor depressions, the enemy's main position coinciding, for the most part, with the line of subdivision.

Such was the Boer position as viewed by General Ian Hamilton from the pass high up in the berg. He took little time to decide upon his plan; the division never halted, but once clear of the mountains, wheeled to the west and marched towards Doornkop, parallel to the enemy's line. He placed his infantry under General Smith-Dorrien, Colonel Spens of the Shropshire Light Infantry, the well-known Hampshire cricketer, taking over command of the 19th Brigade, which formed for attack opposite "Crow's Nest." The 21st Brigade continued their march west, relieving the 14th Hussars in occupation of the Doornkop ridges. Both brigades now came under heavy shell fire from Burnt Hill and Crow's Nest respectively; and the Camerons suffered 1 sergeant killed and 3 men wounded before the 21st Brigade deployed.

The enemy's position was well chosen and strongly held. Their guns were well posted on the more prominent features. The Zarps, or Johannesburg police, who had already in the war given proof of their fighting qualities, manned the crest of Crow's Nest. Everything seemed to signify a more determined resistance than Ian Hamilton had yet encountered—

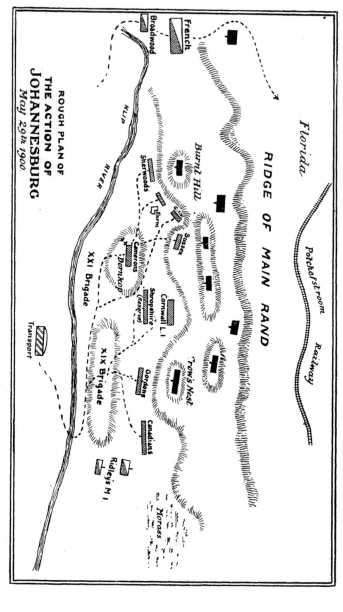

ROUGH PLAN OF
THE ACTION OF
JOHANNESBURG
May 29th 1900

Florida

RIDGE OF MAIN RAND

Potchefstroom Railway

French

Broadwood

NLIP RIVER

Burnt Hill

Sherwoods

Sussex

Barn

Camerons

Domkop

XXI Brigade

Cornwall L.I.

Shropshire (Reserve)

Crow's Nest

Gordons

Canadians

XIX Brigade

Ridley's M.I.

Morass

Transport

[To face p. 57.

both the numbers of the enemy's guns already in action, the position itself, and the fact that Johannesburg lay beyond. Although the smooth slopes of the valley were for the most part destitute of cover, the General had no alternative but to attack from the front. The enemy's left flank rested upon a deep morass, which extended for some miles to the east; and any flanking movement to the west, further than that which had already been accomplished, could be easily cancelled by a corresponding change of position on the part of the enemy along the Witwatersrand at Florida. It solely remained to select the points of attack, and Burnt Hill and Crow's Nest immediately offered themselves as the most feasible and decisive. The latter was at once recognised as the key to the position ; and an attack upon the former could be maintained in touch with General French, who, with the 1st, 2nd and 4th Cavalry Brigades, supported by both Ridley's and Hutton's Mounted Infantry, was advancing upon Florida. A detached attack upon his right rear, similar to that delivered at the Zand River, served to a certain extent to divert his advance. But the cavalry General soon estimated this movement at its proper worth, and ordered his leading regiments to continue to advance.

At about 1 o'clock the infantry all along the line received the order to move forward upon the enemy. The regiment was on the extreme left of the British advance. As they moved down from Doornkop into the valley below, the artillery fire from either side grew fiercer. Half the Battalion were thrust forward towards Burnt Hill; "D" Company (Captain Rigby), supported by "E" (Captain Radford), on the left; and "I" Company (Lieutenant Taylor), supported by "F" (Second-Lieutenant Gilson), on the right. Soon afterwards the remainder of the Battalion reinforced the left, leaving "I" and "F" Companies to maintain their position in a wood in mid-valley at about

800 to 1,000 yards' range from Burnt Hill. The musketry and artillery fire which streamed down from both sides of the valley was now fiercer than anything the 21st Brigade had yet experienced; and General Bruce Hamilton, in order to allow his artillery fire to take fuller effect and to give time to General French to move round the flank, halted the Battalion; while the City Imperial Volunteers moved forward on the right. The Gordons, with the Duke of Cornwall's Light Infantry on their left, were meanwhile closing upon Crow's Nest; but the burghers showed no sign of giving way.

Slowly on all sides the attack developed; and the Sussex Regiment, which had been retained as a divisional reserve, was ordered up to the right of the City Volunteers. But the assault could not long be deferred. The three firing-line battalions of the 21st Brigade were engaging Burnt Hill, which at 3.30 began to show signs of wavering. But further down the valley the engagement was at its height. The Johannesburg Police held desperately to Crow's Nest, while the Gordons lay at a decisive range from their rifles.

At a quarter to 4 Burnt Hill still managed to hold out, although the Inniskilling Dragoons and City Volunteers were rapidly gaining ground on either flank. Still with Crow's Nest uncaptured, Burnt Hill would be little gained: the eyes of the whole division were upon the 19th Brigade. But a few more hours of daylight remained, and it was necessary for the question to be settled. Certain it is that the order did not come from General Smith-Dorrien, who indeed is said to have galloped forward to where the bullets fell thickly to restrain the impulse which led the Gordons to charge. Perhaps it came spontaneously from every man in the gallant regiment; for they had lain for three hours in the open, under a murderous fire, which simply decimated their leading company. But be that as it may, they rose as one man and closed upon their enemy. Some fell at every step, and the Zarps held stoutly to their ground; but at the point of the bayonet, they forced them back, and, crowning the foremost ridge, came upon an even greater fire at the point-blank range. The ground they had so gallantly taken was but a "false crest," and the enemy still held cover close above their heads. And there again they lay for half an hour, until, reinforced, they rose once more, and sending a cheer down the valley, cleared the hill with great loss of life.

They lost 9 officers and 88 non-commissioned officers and men, and the total casualties of Ian Hamilton's Force did not exceed 150 killed and wounded.

The fall of Crow's Nest was decisive. Burnt Hill was soon afterwards evacuated. The Inniskilling Dragoons from the left, the City Volunteers from the right, and the Sherwood Foresters from the centre almost simultaneously occupied the hill: French's regiments to the extreme left had gained the Witwatersrand heights directly south of Florida; and almost immediately the sun set on the battle of Doornkop, leaving the Rand gold-fields, which to some extent had played so important a part in the causes which led to the war, at last in the hands of the British.

The night, though moonless, was everywhere aglow. Long lines of creeping veldt-fires stretched over the field for many a mile, and served in some measure to light the wandering bearer companies, searching the now silent slopes for the dead which lay around. In the 19th Brigade there must have been many a missing man unaccounted for during that night, as daybreak only too sadly revealed. There upon the crest of Crow's Nest, where the whole division had bivouacked, lay many a kilted corpse; some pierced to the heart, a smile upon their sunburnt faces; others shot in the stomach, fists and teeth clenched, and knees drawn upward in the agony of their death. There was one poor fellow who, shot through both knees, had dragged himself with difficulty, leaving a trail with his feet in the soft sand, to the cover of a rock, and there a shell had carried off his head. The sun could never rise on a grimmer spectacle than this. Yet it is upon such scenes alone that the very foundations of all history are laid.

As no sign of the enemy was to be found the following day, the division, leaving the Gordons to their dead, marched to Florida. A stationary train lay on the Krugersdorp railway ; and in every direction rose the tall iron chimneys of the gold-mines and the "headgear" of the shafts, surrounded by groups of ugly tin shanties, and here and there a cheap red villa half-hidden in a clump of poplars or eucalyptus trees ; but all was silent around. The train, the mines, the shanties and the villas were all equally deserted, and no soul was to be seen on what was once, and is again, a busy scene of animation and bustle, as the division marched to its bivouac on the Aurora West claim, between Florida and Roodepoort.

Upon the same day the Commander-in-Chief, after a slight engagement at Germiston, took possession of the city, where for ten years corruption, taxation and injustice had reigned supreme. The clasp "Johannesburg" was awarded to the whole army.

That the Boers played their game to the last a copy of the *Standard Diggers' and Miners' News*, the last of an evil line, dated 29th May, the very day of the battle, fully testified. "Their infantry are even now storming the Klipriversberg," it stated, "and are again and again driven back with fearful loss ! "

The whole division had settled down to rest when the Gordons' pipes were sounded over the hill. They had paid their final tribute to the dead, and as they swung through the brigade lines, cheer after cheer rang out in Florida and went echoing down the empty shafts.

And what of the men who cheered? They were now on half rations; the expected convoys had not arrived; and indeed had Lord Roberts' advance been less precipitate, and had he not secured the line intact, matters might have been truly serious. But with the same determination with which he marched on Bloemfontein, with rations for only twenty-eight days, he had given his Generals three days from the Vaal; and now Johannesburg was his, and it was purely a matter of running stores out to Florida from the city. " I am delighted at your repeated successes," he wrote to Hamilton, " and grieve beyond measure at your poor fellows being without their proper rations. A trainful shall go to you to-day. I expect to get the notice that Johannesburg surrenders this morning, and we shall march into the town. I wish your column, which has done so much to gain possession of it, could be with us. Tell the Gordons I am proud to think I have a Highlander as one of the supporters of my coat-of-arms." So much for their stomachs, and now for the appearance of these men : unwashed, bearded, and in rags; helmets were smashed in, and, in some cases, queerly substituted ; equipment-straps were broken and tied together with string; putties were frayed and filthy, and some men were even without trousers. Since leaving Kroonstad the average rate of marching had greatly increased. In the last sixteen days, which had included only one day's halt, the force, which consisted of four brigades, with more than seven miles of transport, had marched 192 miles. Small wonder if the appearance of the men was hardly prepossessing!

The next day the column moved its bivouac to Goldmines, north of Braamfontein Railway Station, four and a half miles north-west of the city. The march, which was but a few miles, led through blue gum plantations and beneath red sandstone crags. After the open veldt, the country indeed seemed pretty. The men's spirits rose in consequence; and they sang upon the road. They had been silent for many a day; but now Johannesburg had fallen, and they knew that Pretoria lay but a few miles before them.

That evening the much-needed convoy arrived, bringing food and mails from Bloemfontein. Captain Weldon also rejoined with 300 men from East London, warm clothing for the whole Battalion, and 200 pairs of boots. He left again, however, in five days' time, receiving an appointment as D.A.A.G. on General Smith-Dorrien's staff, and afterwards becoming Brigade Major.

As for Johannesburg, in two days it was converted from a " city of the dead " to the scene of the wildest animation. Shopkeepers hastily withdrew their shutters and produced their goods from remote cellars, demanding—and obtaining— the most exorbitant prices for everything. The streets were filled with the dust of transport waggons, and thronged with bearded soldiers, willing to pay any sum for tobacco, clothing, and above all, for a "square meal." Officers crowded the hotels, and, sitting in sixes at tables for two, shouted for food, and wondered that the proprietor could supply them with nothing more when cupboards and cellars were emptied.

But the Commander-in-Chief had no intention of remaining in Johannesburg. He wished to push on to Pretoria as rapidly as possible; and so, after one day's halt, he set his forces again in motion on 3rd June, leaving General Wavell's (15th) Brigade in occupation of the city. Hamilton marched in a north-westerly direction, intending to come upon the Transvaal capital from the west, and by nightfall reached Diepspruit, some fifteen miles upon his way. He had not been long on the march upon the following day, when he received information that Lord Roberts expected little or no resistance at Pretoria. Thereupon the division immediately about-turned, and taking a road to the right, converged upon the main army at Six Mile Spruit towards evening. Early in the afternoon the sound of the naval guns with the Commander-in-Chief's force had been heard to the north, and soon afterwards the Pretoria forts, above which floated Lord Roberts' balloon, became visible.

Though but a rear-guard remained to defend the capital, and the forts had been depleted of their guns, so strong and extensive was the position south of Pretoria that, before the sun set that day, practically the whole army corps had deployed for action. General French, who had not been made aware of the entire change from the original plan, was far away to the west, and somewhat seriously engaged; otherwise the whole British army would have been ranged along Six Mile Spruit.

Colonel Henry, commanding a corps of General Hutton's Mounted Infantry, was the first to come in touch with the enemy, and drove them from an advanced position. Lord Roberts, in order to maintain the ground thus gained, deployed the 14th Brigade, and ordered them to advance; while Ian Hamilton, who by now was well up on the left, thrust the 19th Brigade forward, and holding the 21st in support, ordered Broadwood to move round the enemy's right flank. The ground was favourable to such a movement, and Colonel de Lisle, with the 2nd Corps of Mounted Infantry, cutting in between the cavalry and the 19th Brigade, appeared upon the plain beyond. The enemy immediately turned tail, and De Lisle, pursuing them to the very suburbs of Pretoria itself, captured a machine gun. Taking advantage of the confusion, he then demanded the surrender of the town, which was readily granted; and thus Pretoria fell on the evening of 4th June.

The following morning the three divisions closed upon the capital. Mr. Winston Churchill, then special correspondent for the *Morning Post*, and the Duke of Marlborough were among the first to enter the town; and the latter, making his way to the place where the the British prisoners were confined, called upon their guards to surrender.

At 1 p.m., from the bivouacs scattered around, the whole army marched into the town, and, in column of route, with bayonets fixed, passed before the Commander-in-Chief in Church Square. The three sides of the square, formed by the Banks and Government buildings, over which the Union Jack now floated, were a perfect sea of faces, piled to the topmost storeys. On the 4th, under the shadow of the old Dutch Reform Church where, in days gone by, Kruger was wont to hold forth, sat a little man on a big chestnut horse —the British Commander-in-Chief. There also were Lord Kitchener, Chief of the Staff, and Sir William Nicholson, in whose hands was all the transport, Generals Tucker, Pole-Carew, and Ian Hamilton, the divisional commanders, and all the Generals of Brigade, including General Smith-Dorrien. For three hours the stream of steel flowed past; the brigades of Generals Inigo Jones, Maxwell, Stephenson, Smith-Dorrien, and Bruce-Hamilton followed in quick succession; each battalion to its regimental march, and the guns of the Naval Brigade to "A Life on the Ocean Wave." It was indeed a triumphal hour, and one for which many a brave fellow had fallen in the months gone by.

The crowd looked on in silence with pride or hate, according to their birth; but above all else, there was amazement upon the face of each. Doubtless there were many among them who had undertaken to drive the English to the sea; but here, at last, if never once before, they were brought face to face with the magnitude of the task, and saw that all was lost.

The regiment has not only to be proud that it took part in this historic march-past, but that it passed in the finest style to the tune of the "Young May Moon," the band being one of the few present, and playing nearly the whole army past the Commander-in-Chief.

Though, by the fall of Pretoria, all hope of a "United South Africa" for the Dutch must have vanished for ever, that the war dragged on for another two years is now a matter of common knowledge. The attempted peace negotiations during the next few days came to nothing—perhaps it was for the better that they failed—and the Transvaalers resolved to carry on the struggle.

On the morning of the 6th June the order came to the 21st Brigade to march at once, and what seemed harder—south again. One cannot say cheerfully, neither can one say without a murmur, did the Battalion set out upon the march— fifteen miles through a cloud of dust to Irene—but never a man fell out. If a company officer did hear an occasional murmur of discontent, the soldier at least did not grumble at the order, he grumbled at the necessity, as who would not.

But action was imperative. While Lord Roberts had been driving all before him in the North, Christian de Wet in the Free State was going from success to success. After having fallen upon the detachment of Yeomanry, in garrison at Lindley, he surprised the 4th Battalion Sherwood Foresters at Roodeval, and demolished the line from Kroonstad to the Vaal. Botha, hearing of this a day or so later, refused to consider the offers of peace advanced by the British Commander, and realising the precarious nature of Lord Roberts' position in Pretoria, with the line destroyed behind him and a great scarcity of food, he joined his forces to those of General Delarey, and took up a position in the Schwartz kopjes, running from the north of Pretoria south-east to Bronkhorst Spruit—the scene of the disgraceful piece of treachery at the outbreak of the '81 war—with 10,000 burghers.

E

The 14th Brigade garrisoned Pretoria, General Maxwell having been made Military Governor of the place, and the 19th Brigade was distributed along the lines of communication, General Smith-Dorrien commanding from the capital to Kroonstad. Consequently, only three infantry brigades were at Lord Roberts' disposal—the Guards, Stephenson's and Bruce Hamilton's—while what now passed by the name of a cavalry brigade was barely 500 sabres. Nevertheless, weakened as his great force now was, he was obliged to take the initiative, in order not only to protect his communications, but to secure the safety of the newly-conquered town itself.

The Commander-in-Chief resolved to retain the 11th Division in the vicinity of Pretoria under his immediate command; and by thrusting French and Ian Hamilton well forward on the flanks, to force the enemy to retire. With this object in view Hamilton's Column, which had halted at Irene during the 7th, marched north-east to Garsfontein on the 8th. French, working to the north of Pretoria, found the country swarming with burghers, who, now that they were beyond the reach of the 6-inch guns, grudged the loss of their capital and hung around like jackals.

At this time a certain Mr. Marks of Erste Fabriken, one of the richest and most influential men in the Transvaal— and some time a friend of Paul Kruger's — attempted to arrange a meeting between Lord Roberts and General Botha at his own farm. An armistice was therefore declared upon the 9th. But the news of Roodeval came to Botha's ears on that very day, and he failed to keep the appointment; he could not, he thought, consider terms of peace while the Free Staters held thus manfully on. However, a body of independent burghers took the responsibility upon themselves and opened fire on Broadwood's outposts.

An engagement was now imminent, in which Hamilton's

Column was destined to play the principal part. The 19th Brigade had been replaced by Gordon's (3rd) Cavalry Brigade — the 9th, 16th and 17th Lancers — so that Hamilton's Force was now for the most part a mounted one.

At Pretoria Lieutenant Sadler had rejoined the Battalion from the Bloemfontein Rest Camp, and was placed in charge of the machine gun : Captain Turner-Lee commanding the Volunteer Company, and Lieutenant Webb had been placed upon the sick list.

It was intended that Hamilton, by moving in the direction of Eland's River Station, should threaten the Boer line of retreat along the Delagoa Bay railroad, while French forced back their right flank to the north of Pretoria. It was hoped that thus the enemy would be compelled to retire from the outskirts of the capital. Hamilton, whose column was in itself engaged upon a turning operation upon a large scale, the better to further his object, ordered his cavalry brigades to work well to his right as a supplementary flanking movement. If French succeeded in turning Delarey's position, the result of the operations would be to encircle the entire Boer force.

Matters, however, turned out very differently, and neither French nor Broadwood upon the flanks succeeded in their design. The former, instead of coming unexpectedly upon the enemy's right, as he had hoped, was awakened at daybreak on the morning of the 11th by a vigorous shell fire directed upon his camp, and was obliged to retire. General Broadwood was even more severely treated. He failed to find the enemy's flank ; and although both brigades behaved with great gallantry, charging the enemy's position, two guns of the famous Sanna's Post Battery ("Q"), for the second time, narrowly escaped falling into the hands of the enemy, being only saved by a dashing charge of the 12th Lancers, in which the gallant Earl of Airlie, who had only just rejoined from a wound he had received at Welkom, lost his life.

While these matters were in progress the 21st Brigade, with whom we are mostly concerned, by no means remained idle. They paraded before sunrise and marched off E.N.E. through the hills. The advanced guard was furnished by the C.I.V. Mounted Infantry, the 76th Battery and the Sherwood Foresters, the whole under Colonel Cunningham. This party preceded the column as far as the southern end of Zwavel-poort, and was then directed along the southern slopes of the hills to protect the right flank. The C.I.V. Mounted Infantry were sent well away to the right, and four guns of the 76th Battery were ordered to rejoin the brigade, which continued its march to the south of Tigerpoort, there awaiting orders from the General commanding.

Colonel Cunningham, in the meantime, had found the enemy to the south, and immediately engaged him with his guns. In doing so he not only protected the right flank of the 21st Brigade, but also covered the right rear of the two cavalry brigades, who were operating to his front; Ridley's Mounted Infantry were further to the right, shielding the movements of the cavalry from that flank, under a heavy shell fire. Colonel Cunningham, by advancing his guns, was thus able to relieve the strain upon both the cavalry and mounted infantry. At about mid-day, therefore, he moved on to the hill previously occupied by the Boers, opposing the cavalry, and there retained his position for the remainder of the day.

From this hill, a bird's-eye view of the country, which was the scene of the battle of the 11th and 12th, lay spread before one's feet. The plain below was a vast arena, rectangular in shape, stretching away towards Pretoria in the west. To the front extended the enemy's position, along the heights known as the Donkerpoort and the Diamond Hills, south of the

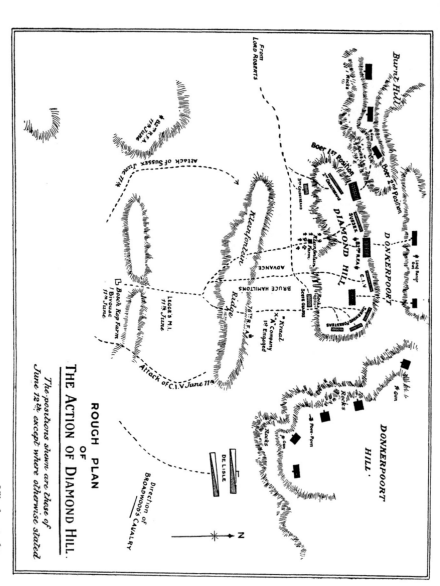

ROUGH PLAN

OF

THE ACTION OF DIAMOND HILL.

The positions shewn are those of
June 12th, except where otherwise stated.

DONKERPOORT
HILL.

Direction of
BROADWOOD'S CAVALRY

DE LISLE

N

Rocks
Pom-Pom
4 Gun
Rocks
"A" gun
Rocks

Burnt Hill.

Boer 2nd Position

Boer 1st Position

W.Y. Rocks
C.I.V. Rocks

D'ONKERPOORT

Long Range
Gun

DIAMOND
HILL.

SUSSEX

SUSSEX & C.I.V.

Derbyshire

3rd Grenadiers

C.I.V.

DERBYSHIRES

BRUCE HAMILTON'S

76th R.F.A.

Scots Guards

Kraal
"X" Company
1st Engaged

ADVANCE

Kleinfontein Ridge

Léger's M.I.
11th June

Attack of Sussex June 11th

R.E.F.A.
11th June

From
LORD ROBERTS

Bosch Kop Farm
Bivouac
11th June

Attack of C.I.V. June 11th

[To face p. 69.

Delagoa Bay line. Before this, and at a distance of some 1,300 yards from it, lay a lower ridge about three miles in length, near the farm of Kleinfontein; to the east a spur, where the Mounted Infantry were engaged on the 11th, ran north to the Boer position; to the south the Tigerpoort and Boschkop heights completely enclosed the plain beneath.

Leaving the Camerons with the guns at Tigerpoort to secure the rear of his brigade—for so great had been the pressure on all sides that it was not known from which direction the enemy might deliver an attack—General Bruce Hamilton advanced north-east against the advanced Boer position upon the Kleinfontein Ridge. It was most necessary to divert the enemy's attention from the cavalry brigades which, shut in on three sides, were severely harassed.

At 1.30 p.m. the 82nd and 74th Batteries came into action ; the Sussex Regiment was ordered to seize the left of the Boer position, and then swing to the right and advance along the ridge. The City Volunteers were to establish themselves as near the enemy as possible from the direct front, and there to throw out an outpost line.

The enemy offered a bold front, and directed a heavy shell fire against the batteries. The movement, however, was entirely successful. The Sussex, under a heavy fire, dislodged the enemy ; and the City Volunteers, supported by " A " Company, under Captain Green, and the Volunteer Company, under Lieutenant Wright, sprang forward and occupied the position upon the front. The Dutchmen held stubbornly to the ridge until the infantry were close upon them, and in consequence received a heavy fire as they galloped back to their main position. The Kleinfontein Ridge was occupied without loss of life, although each of the two regiments which had been responsible for its capture lost seven wounded.

Nevertheless this was but an advanced position, and a more serious matter lay beyond. Indeed the situation at the

close of the day's fighting on the 11th June cannot be otherwise described than as an extremely doubtful one.   French,
far to the north-west, was unable to advance.   Broadwood
had been driven back ; and although the mounted infantry
managed to retain their position, it was still unknown where
the enemy's left flank rested.   Hamilton's Column lay in the
centre of the " arena," facing the bare slopes of the Diamond
Hills, with the enemy's guns still in the vicinity of Tigerpoort
to the right rear.   The Commander-in-Chief sent over two
battalions of Guards to Hamilton's assistance on the following
day ; but the, bulk of the 11th Division were necessary to
safeguard the conquered capital, before which they could do
little more than demonstrate.   The enemy's position, which
extended a distance of about twenty miles, was roughly in
the shape of the figure 3, the curves of which encircled
French and Ian Hamilton's forces respectively, the central
salient angle being on the Delagoa railway line near
Pretoria.

Clearly, this was not a situation to be considered lightly.
Hamilton's force, which by strategy was compelled to adopt
the offensive, was in insufficient strength.   Nevertheless but
one course lay open to the General, and Ian Hamilton
unflinchingly resolved to take it ; selecting Diamond Hill, the
very heart of their position, as an objective, he determined to
drive home a frontal attack.

The morning of the 12th found the situation unaltered,
except that the enemy had probably been reinforced during
the night by commandos from General Delarey.   The
cavalry still maintained their wedge - like position on the
right.   The picquets of Bruce Hamilton's Brigade were in
possession of the Kleinfontein Ridge ; and the enemy held
the Diamond Hills, both east and west of Donkerpoort, in
considerable force.

The 21st Brigade was under arms before   daybreak,

and moving from their bivouac at 6.30 a.m. with the 82nd and 76th Batteries, reinforced the outpost line. The 76th Battery were immediately ordered to shell the enemy's main position, namely, the long, bare ridge surmounted by a rocky " krantz " to the west of the " Poort," which was afterwards known as " Diamond Hill." Although for some twenty minutes this cannonade evoked no reply, the ridges around Donkerpoort appeared to be held in force ; and " A " Company, under Captain Green, accompanied by Colonel Cunningham, was sent forward in that direction to engage, but not attack, the enemy. They immediately came under a heavy shell and rifle fire, but managed to establish themselves successfully within 1,000 yards of the enemy. The Boers had to a great extent reserved their fire and permitted Captain Green to advance 200 yards beyond the cover afforded by a slight rocky rise in the mid-valley. Then, disregarding the shells of the 76th Battery, and openly disclosing the strength with which they held the position, they poured an extremely heavy fire into the exposed company, which suffered severely. Colonel Cunningham immediately ordered Captain Green to retire, and although that officer had received a very severe and painful wound, he not only kept his men in ignorance of the fact, but carried out the retirement to the rocky ridge before-mentioned with the utmost skill. There he maintained his position, and was subsequently reinforced by three more companies. The movement had been entirely successful in forcing the enemy to display his strength and dispositions. From the " Donkerpoort Hill," i.e., the hill to the British right, east of the gap, they had opened gun, pom-pom and heavy rifle fire ; and Colonel Cunningham wrote advising General Bruce Hamilton of the enemy's strength at this point, and suggesting that an attack further to the left against Diamond Hill would more probably succeed.

Meanwhile the 82nd Battery had joined the 76th, in action on the Kleinfontein Ridge. Both were subjected to a heavy and accurate shell fire from the enemy's position, during which General Ian Hamilton himself was struck by the fragment of a shell upon the shoulder. Although it was extremely painful, it did not draw blood, being more of the nature of a severe bruise than a wound, and fortunately did not necessitate the General leaving the field.

So heavy did the shell fire at one time become that both batteries were, for the time being, silenced, and obliged to change their position. The Boer gunners then turned their attention to the half battalion Sherwood Foresters, which was advanced upon the right, in support of "A" Company. This half battalion, which was accompanied by the Commanding Officer, Major Gosset, and the Adjutant, Lieutenant Keller, consisted of the following companies:—

"A" under Captain Green—Colour-Sergeant Murphy.

"D" under Captain Rigby and Second-Lieutenant Wilkin—Colour-Sergeant Girling.

"E" under Captain Radford and Lieutenant Anley— Colour-Sergeant Tobbell.

"F" under Second-Lieutenant Gilson—Colour-Sergeant Randall.

The machine gun under Lieutenant Sadler.

Captain Green, who had been already wounded, was carried from the field, Colonel Cunningham taking charge of his company. These four companies, which till 12.30 p.m. lay in the open, the one behind the other in alphabetical order, drew a considerable fire from the enemy's riflemen throughout the morning, and suffered a few casualties in consequence. The machine gun especially, which came into action in the alignment of "A" Company, became a target from all along the Boer line of defence.

At 12.30 General Ian Hamilton ordered a general advance.

The 1st Battalion Coldstream Guards were ordered to occupy
the Kleinfontein Ridge; the 2nd Battalion Coldstream Guards
to move in echelon on the left of the 21st Brigade, and to
eventually occupy the hill forming the right of the Boer
position. (These two battalions, as already mentioned, were
all Lord Roberts could spare to reinforce Hamilton from the
11th Division.) The 21st Brigade was to attack Diamond
Hill in the following order :—The Sussex Regiment on the
left of the Brigade-line, in advance and to the right of the
2nd Coldstreams, by Kleinfontein Farm; the City Imperial
Volunteers in the centre ; the half battalion Sherwood
Foresters, already half-way across the valley, on the extreme
right, advancing against the eastern extremity of the hill, or
that part overlooking Donkerpoort. The companies of this
half battalion were disposed as follows :—" A " moved to
left, supported by " E " ; while " D," supported by " F,"
advanced upon the right. Colonel de Lisle, with the 2nd
Corps of Mounted Infantry, was instructed to demonstrate
before the Donkerpoort Hill. The remaining half battalion
Sherwood Foresters, under Lieutenant Taylor, advanced in
support of the Sussex and C.I.V., but was not ordered up
the hill until later in the day.

Under cover of a heavy bombardment by the 76th and
82nd Batteries, which advanced to a second position, and the
5-inch guns back at Tigerpoort, the whole line steadily
advanced. " D " and " F " Companies, on the extreme right
of the line, were much exposed to enfilade fire from the
Donkerpoort Hill. As they moved across the valley, belt
after belt of pom-pom shells flew along the lines. The rifle
fire from Diamond Hill slackened from the first, and soon
entirely ceased ; but Donkerpoort Hill remained crowded by
the enemy. Consequently the left and centre of the brigade
were little exposed ; the City Volunteers without difficulty
effected a lodgment on the hill, and almost immediately the

roops all along the line established themselves on the crest of the enemy's position. Then the entire phase of the action changed, and a very different state of affairs came immediately into existence. On the capture of Diamond Hill, even the Commander-in-Chief appears to have considered the victory complete. " When I left the field," he wrote, " Hamilton's Infantry were ascending the heights and the enemy in full retreat." Such, however, was not the case. The top of Diamond Hill proved to be a plateau, swept by the fire of the enemy from the north, east and west ; and far from there being any intended evacuation, the enemy strongly maintained their second position, bringing a deadly fire, at ranges varying from 600 to 1,200 yards, to bear upon the captured hill.

A certain comparison may be made between the actions of Diamond Hill and Spion Kop in Natal. The relationship is more of the nature of an analogy than a similarity, and on that account it may be of interest to consider how it came about that the one was as great a success as the other was a failure. With regard to the conformity of the ground there was this difference : for whereas Spion Kop was situated at the apex of a V-shaped line of hills, running from Acton Holmes and Vaalkrantz on either side, Diamond Hill converted a similar V into an almost equilateral triangle, of which it formed the base. The result of this is obvious : for where, in the case of Spion Kop, in the advance or retirement, the troops were subjected to a cross fire from either flank along *the whole frontage* of the enemy's position, an enfilade fire could only be brought to bear on the attacking infantry at Diamond Hill from the *extremities* of the Boer position. On the other hand, the similarity rests mainly on the fact that the surrounding hills in either case possessed far greater natural facilities for cover than the positions themselves. Once the hills were occupied, therefore, the conditions became practically identical; and the matter became a question of tenability. On Spion Kop large forces were massed upon the smaller area; the "morale" of the army suffered, and the position, in consequence of great bloodshed, was rendered untenable. The plateau of Diamond Hill was more extensive, and but sparsely occupied by troops in widely-extended order. The casualties, therefore, were not severe, and the "morale" was retained. In neither case was it possible to outflank the surrounding hills. At Diamond Hill the right of the enemy's position rested upon a burnt hill, which proved a natural fortress, and from which a heavy fire was brought to bear upon the Sussex Regiment; and the immediate left of the encircling ridges lay on the Donkerpoort Hill, almost equally inaccessible. The enemy's guns were posted along a high ridge beyond their position, which lay to the front, upon the Donkerpoort Hill, the Burnt Hill, and at the mouth of the gap. It was clear, therefore, that even should the enemy be driven from this, their second position, another still remained.

But no such intention could at that time have entered the General's mind. It was sufficient for the time being to retain his grasp on Diamond Hill, which was none too secure.

On the right of the hill the regiment maintained its position and even gained ground. "F" Company, on the extreme right, faced almost due east, and was greatly harassed by the superiority of fire from Donkerpoort Hill; "A" and "D" Companies to their immediate left were scarcely less hardly treated; across the nek of Donkerpoort a line of "sangars" protected the Boer riflemen, and from this position, with artillery, pom-poms and machine guns, they poured a hail of missiles upon the corner of the hill.

This state of affairs existed until 3 o'clock, when General Bruce Hamilton, who had ascended the hill, saw that the tension must be relieved. Although the General had served previously in Natal, as A.A.G. to General Clery's Disvision,

and was present at the battle of Spion Kop, he did not
hesitate to bring guns on to Diamond Hill ; and accordingly
the 82nd Battery were ordered to ascend the " kloof " above
Kleinfontein Farm.

Simultaneously the divisional General decided to settle the
matter one way or the other, and ordered Colonel de Lisle
to advance against the Donkerpoort Hill, at the same time
sending across a staff officer to acquaint the troops on the
eastern extremity of Diamond Hill of the movement. Colonel
de Lisle also took a similar precaution ; and an Australian
orderly crossed the gap between the hills at the gallop.   The
whole force of the enemy seemed to direct their fire upon
him ; but with his helmet on the muzzle of his rifle, raised
high above his head, he rode straight into the British firing
line, where his horse fell dead, and warned Major Gosset that
De Lisle's troops were about to seize the hill.

The 1st Coldstream Guards and the other half battalion of
the Sherwood Foresters were now ordered to reinforce the
firing line.   The former filled up the gap between the Sussex
and the C.I.V.; the latter wheeled to the right on gaining the
hill, and moved to the assistance of their own regiment.   The
appearance both of these reinforcements and of the 82nd
Battery upon Diamond Hill was a signal for the enemy to
redouble their fire, and the constant rattle of musketry
swelled into one continuous roar.

And beyond doubt the decisive moment had arrived.
Hitherto the advantage had lain with the enemy : an
advantage of position and of numerical strength, which it
had required courage to overcome.   The latter evil was now
abolished ; though, for all that, the situation of the troops
was none of the pleasantest.   For four hours they had lain
upon the plateau without cover and under the fiercest fire ;
and now but a few rounds of ammunition remained upon
the hill.

But the final issue was destined to remain little longer in the balance. The 82nd Battery, under a galling fire, struggled manfully to the crest, opposite the Burnt Hill to the right of the Boer position. Eight of their horses fell, and the bullets spread themselves upon the guns; but by hand they brought their battery into action, and opened fire upon the position.

The first shot was answered along the line with something very like a cheer. The strain was relieved; men cried angrily to one another for ammunition, and exposed themselves to get it. Private Smith of "C" Company and Private Alton of "D" passed coolly down the firing line with their helmets filled with rounds. Both received the Distinguished Conduct Medal for their *sang - froid*, for the fire at that time was very heavy. Their appearance was welcomed by the men, who snatched greedily from their helmets; and, loading in haste, fired hotly back into the hills in something like the spirit of revenge.

At 4 o'clock Ian Hamilton himself ascended the hill and ordered up the Scots Guards, who had arrived from General Pole-Carew, to support the right. The firing line had been by now greatly increased, and the heavy fire which streamed from Diamond Hill to a great extent served to protect Major Conolly's gallant Battery, which, although 1 officer and 8 men were killed, and many wounded, continued to ply the enemy with shell.

Also Colonel de Lisle had by now gained the southern edge of the Donkerpoort Hill, and although the Boers fought manfully, was forcing them back before him. The enfilade fire slowly abated and finally ceased. The last hour was one of retribution. Feeling themselves at last masters of the situation, the British troops increased the rapidity of their fire; while the Boers held the closer to their cover. It is to be feared, however, the enemy's casualties were but slight;

for they were well protected on the hills they held by
the many boulders which lay about and their admirably
constructed sangars. The presence of these latter seems to
suggest that Diamond Hill was a trap into which they fully
intended to draw the bulk of the British Force, and towards
this the operations of the 11th certainly tended.

The General did not order an assault; the sun was now
low in the heavens, and the casualties would have been
severe. But a plain lay beyond the Boer artillery position,
cavalry were close at hand, and never were men more in the
mood. It is probable that with another hour of daylight
General Ian Hamilton might have risked it, in which case
there would without doubt have been slaughter—Elandslaagte, where the same General commanded the infantry
and a victory worthy of the name—all over again. But this
was not to be.

As the sun sank the fire of the Boer marksmen upon
Diamond Hill became but desultory; although the fight
continued for some time on the Donkerpoort Hill, where one
of De Lisle's Maxim guns was busily engaged in clearing the
way before him. But when darkness set in all was still once
more. The engagement had lasted since 6 o'clock in the
morning until 7 in the evening, during which the rattle
of musketry and the thunder of the guns had continued
without a pause. From 10 until 5, " A," " D," " E " and
" F " Companies had been under an incessant fire, which for
four hours after the taking of the hill had been exceptionally
severe.

Generals Ian Hamilton and Pole-Carew decided to continue
the action upon the morrow by moving Hamilton's Force to
the right and occupying Diamond Hill with the Guards.
But there was no need for such a conference : for when day
broke the enemy had gone.

At nightfall a strong wind sprang up from the west ; and

the veldt, which as usual had been lighted by the lyddite, became ablaze, and the regiments set to work carrying their wounded through the fire. Had such a wind risen earlier in the day, Fate would have dealt hardly with the British soldiers : their only cover from view would have been destroyed ; they would have been left in their light khaki upon the blackened ground, a clear mark for the enemy's riflemen, and the result of the action could not have been the same.

That evening, on reaching their bivouac upon the southern slopes of Diamond Hill, near the farm at Kleinfontein, the men of the regiment were heartily cheered by the men of De Lisle's Australian Corps. It appears the advance of the half battalion upon the right called forth applause from all quarters. Colonel de Lisle, Colonel Rimington, and General Ian Hamilton himself were unstinting in their praises, and a few days later the following telegram arrived from General Smith-Dorrien :—

"General Ian Hamilton speaks most highly of the behaviour of the old battalion in the actions of 11th and 12th. I warmly congratulate you all, and hope the wounded are doing well."

Although the conditions upon the plateau of Diamond Hill were the least comfortable, the advance was the more dramatic. With sloped arms, and taking their dressing by the right—the threatened flank—under rifle fire and a heavy enfilade from the guns and pom-pom from above Donkerpoort, the Companies had marched forward as if on parade. Neither the fire of the enemy nor our own lyddite shells, from five thousand yards in rear, had served to shake the steadiness of the men, who, extended in column of sections, marched fearlessly across the valley. This discipline, which they retained throughout, was of the greatest service in the accomplishment of the somewhat complicated manœuvres which became necessary upon the plateau; for there "E" Company changed direction half-left, and "A" and "D" half-right; the leading section of "F" Company, under Second-Lieutenant Gilson, wheeled completely to the right towards the enemy across Donkerpoort, while the remaining sections, under Colour-Sergeant Randall, moved to their direct front, filling up the gaps in the firing line. It was the coolness and intrepidity with which Colour-Sergeant Randall led these sections to their places that gained for him the Distinguished Conduct Medal.

The casualties suffered by the Battalion, considering the severity of the fire, were extremely slight, the majority falling to "A" and "F" Companies—of the 10 men, comprising the leading section of "F" Company, under Second-Lieutenant Gilson, 2 were killed and 6 wounded. The total casualties of the Battalion were as follows:—3 men were killed; 2 died of wounds; and 2 officers—Captain Green and Lieutenant Murray, 3 sergeants and 16 rank and file were wounded. The casualties in the 21st Brigade amounted to:—Killed, 3 officers and 5 men; wounded, 4 officers and 77 N.C.O.'s and men. The total casualties in the two days' action did not exceed 200, including the large percentage of 9 officers killed.

The regimental casualty list gives but a vague idea of the part the Battalion played. Had it not been for the discipline by which the men were kept in hand, and the widely extended formation adopted from the first, the butcher's bill would have been an entirely different matter. Wonderful though it may be that so many men came through the ordeal untouched, the amount of narrow escapes were almost more marvellous. The following day there were few men who could not show a bullet-pierced haversack or water-bottle or a torn puttie.

The Commanding Officer, Major Gosset, had a bullet which passed through his helmet, grazing the top of his skull, and another through a pocket-book he carried in his left-hand breast pocket ; Colonel Cunningham escaped with the loss of the heel of his boot, and a bullet through his pony's neck : whereas, most marvellous of all, Captain Rigby received one in the midst of £35 Company money he carried in his belt. The sovereigns, which were wrapped up in a "rouleau," were nearly all dented, the top one being telescoped into the shape of an egg-cup ; the bullet, beyond giving him a severe blow in the stomach, did no harm, falling down to his knee, covered with gold—indeed, a golden bullet. Lieutenant and Adjutant Keller also received a severe shock, a shell, bursting in the ground under his feet, threw him bodily into the air in a cloud of dust, without so much as scratching him. These serve for a few instances, but there was hardly an officer or man of the advanced half battalion who had not similar experiences, and they are only mentioned here to account in part for the slight casualties in the regiments which played the leading part in one of the fiercest battles of the war. Though it would be unfair not to say that every man played the part allotted to him with the utmost gallantry, the following is a list of those whose behaviour was especially conspicuous :—Major Gosset, Captain Green, Captain Rigby, Colour-Sergeant Randall, Sergeant Jackson, Sergeant Gilham, Private Alton and Private A. Smith.

The troops engaged were awarded the clasp, " Diamond Hill." The action was undoubtedly of considerable importance, closely connected as it was with the capture of Pretoria. It had the desired effect of clearing the country for forty miles around the capital of the largest and most organised Boer Force at that time in the field.

On the following day Hamilton's Column followed on the enemy's line of retreat, marching to Eland's River Station on the Delagoa Bay Railway. There the information was received that the enemy's big gun, mounted on a truck, had gone east that very morning. Indeed, the enemy themselves were not so very far distant; for a corps of Australians, moving forward on the right flank, came unexpectedly on their convoy, crossing the drift over Bronkhorst Spruit. Unfortunately, however, their enthusiasm got the better of them; they neglected to send back and inform the cavalry of their "find," and after firing away all their ammunition, they had no alternative but to retire, whereas a large capture might have been effected.

After halting a day at Eland's River, Hamilton's Column received orders to return to Pretoria. Owing to the same reasons which caused the Bloemfontein delay, and in some measure to the Free State mishaps, Lord Roberts was unable for the time being to continue his march in the wake of the Transvaal Army. Accordingly, on the evening of the 15th, the Brigade set out eastwards, bivouacking at Mossplaatz, the farm of the celebrated Mr. Marks—before-mentioned with regard to the attempted peace negotiations, and whose property in consequence was held sacred. There is a legend in connection with this Mr. Marks which, if true, may be of some interest here, as showing both the bigotry and absolute absence of a sense of humour in the character of the late Mr. Paul Kruger. This Mr. Marks, as his name suggests, was of the Jewish persuasion, and as has been already stated, was at one time on intimate terms of friendship with the President, whom he ventured to ask to be so good as to open a synagogue, which he (Mr. Marks) had erected. Kruger did so; but solemnly in these words: "In the name of our Lord Jesus Christ, I declare this synagogue open!"

After Diamond Hill some alteration had by necessity taken place in the distribution of officers to companies;

and although the regimental staff remained the same, it may
be as well here to renumerate the company officers. They
were as follows :—" A," Second-Lieutenant Wilkin ; " C,"
Lieutenant Morley ; " D," Captain Rigby ; " E," Captain
Radford and Lieutenant Anley ; " F,"Second-Lieutenant Gilson ;
" H," Lieutenant Sadler ; " I," Lieutenant Taylor ; and the
Volunteers, Lieutenant Wright. Seven company officers,
therefore, who left Glen were no longer with the Battalion,
and the numbers were destined to be still more diminished ;
for the work which lay before the regiment was not of
an encouraging nature. With Pretoria as a goal, and
with the excitement of constant touch with the enemy,
the month of May had passed rapidly enough ; but during
the greater part of June, July, and the first two weeks of
August such was by no means the case. The vast reaches
of waste country in the Free State—now the Orange River
Colony—the weariness of the war, the lack of an objective
and the invisibility of the enemy only spelt monotony
to all. Even the most sanguine came to think that the
war would never end, and everyone, with the sole
exception, perhaps, of Lieutenant Wilkin, refused to see
anything either of interest or beauty in the illimitable
brown veldt, intersected here and there by mile upon
mile of barbed wire fence. For more than a hundred
days and more than a thousand miles the same long march
was destined to continue.

CHAPTER V

HEIDELBERG AND THE PURSUIT OF DE WET

AFTER two days' rest in the capital, the same force that fought under Hamilton at Diamond Hill received orders to march south again on the 18th, ostensibly to occupy the town of Heidelberg, in reality to swell the great force which was so secretly gathered round the large bodies of Free Staters, collected on the Basuto Borderland, under Prinsloo, Crowther, Olivier and De Wet.

As the column passed Lord Roberts' villa in Sunnyside, the Field-Marshal came out and watched the troops go by ; this was the last the regiment saw of the Commander-in-Chief. A little further on lay an old stage coach, labelled " Mafeking-Buluwayo, Salisbury "—a symbol of the past, which British troops, in the name of Progress, were there to change. And yet another link of the days gone by awaited the regiment on the way. The march lay again along the road to the Irene Estate, winding in and out through a closely-wooded country, past spruits almost entirely hidden by willows. In this picturesque district, Lieutenant Popham, who was foraging far on the left flank, came upon a solitary homestead, in which he found an old man of eighty-eight years of age, who said he had once been a sergeant in the old 45th. He was one of the few remaining who, under Sir Harry Smith, had so gallantly driven Pretorius from his position at Boemplaatz, in the year '48. The incident is pathetic. He had lived to see the " Orange River Sovereignty " become the

" Free State," to hear tales of Majuba and Laing's Nek, and, at a time when, long buried from his old country, he must have thought her former glory gone, her armies flood the Transvaal, and Fate carries his old regiment past his very door. He asked if the Battalion could be marched past his farm, for he himself was now too old to move ; unfortunately, by the time the request reached Major Gosset, the Brigade had nearly reached their camp, and it had to be refused.

The column bivouacked at Doornkloof, and thence to Vlakfontein, a few miles beyond Irene, where Colonel Bullock's "Battalion of Pioneers," the liberated prisoners from Waterval and Pretoria, garrisoned the line, under General Smith-Dorrien's command. And surely, since Harold marched south to Senlac, and raised the Militia of Essex, a more motley crew never bore arms for England. They wore all uniforms—or none—and were for the most part armed with Mausers, though anything from a rook rifle to an elephant gun sufficed. They were mightily thin, however, after their imprisonment, and their skins, compared to the bronzed faces of the 21st Brigade, were passing pale. The Battalion relieved them of its only representative—Private Wheeldon—who had been captured by Piet de Wet outside Lindley. The following day, June 21st, the Brigade reached Springs, the terminus of a small branch line to Elandsfontein, that supplies the Rand with coal. This place had been the scene of a sharp action some days before, and the enemy were reported still in the district. However, Lieutenant Sadler, who lost his way on patrol that night, and did not return to camp until 10 a.m. the following day, as the column was moving off, fortunately escaped falling into their hands.

The march of the following day carried the Brigade to Spaarwater, within striking distance of the town of Heidelberg. Viljoen's outposts had been discovered on the road, and the cavalry patrols, throughout the day, had been busily engaged.   An exceedingly high hill rose to the north-west of Heidelberg, and appeared, on telescopic examination, to be held by the enemy in some force.   The General therefore ordered his big guns to shell this position from the bivouac at Spaarwater; and, as it was afterwards ascertained, their accurate firing induced the enemy to shift their laager to a more secure position, south-east of the town.   On the following morning—that of the 23rd June—the 21st Brigade, making a wide detour round this formidable hill, marched in an easterly direction, and came upon Heidelberg soon after mid-day, from the north-east.   The enemy, in the meantime, who were in considerable force, opposed the mounted infantry on the hills south-east of the town.   During this engagement General Ian Hamilton fell from his horse and broke his collar bone; and it is doubtless on this account that the cavalry received no orders, for they certainly gave no assistance to the mounted infantry, who threw themselves upon Viljoen's commando single-handed.   The 5th and 7th Corps—Dawson's and Bainbridge's—did especially well, Roberts' Horse and the Burmah M.I. (officered by the Durham L.I.), bearing the brunt of the matter, and suffering severely in consequence, losing 5 officers killed.   The enemy's position lay along the most northerly of two ridges; the valley between these terminated abruptly in a vast plain, which extended far to the south. It was clear that the infantry brigade—who were by now marching triumphantly into Heidelberg, to the tune of "Soldiers in the Park," whilst the pom-poms hammered on the hills beyond—could be of little assistance.   They would not only take too long to reach the scene of the action, but their approach would become visible to the enemy from the moment they left the town, situated as it is upon a hill. The cavalry brigades, however, lay under cover of a small kopje at the western end of the valley, and took no part in the action; though the ground to the south was well suited to cavalry operations. General Broadwood undoubtedly waited for orders, unaware that his Chief had been placed *hors de combat*. The incident is to be regretted, as the mounted infantry carried both ridges by a dismounted frontal attack; and whereas, had the cavalry manœuvred on their right, their casualties would not have been so severe.

The Brigade was billeted in the houses around the Railway Station; and, as the weather was now exceedingly cold, the shelter was not unwelcome. The officers of the Battalion were allotted to the "Kantoor" of the District Mining Commissioner, in which were found several official documents, signed by Kruger, Steyn, Reitz, Leyds and others. Many of these proved of great interest and value; and not the least among them in these respects may be mentioned the "Staats Courant" official list of Boer casualties, from 3rd January to 25th May. The dates, of course, would exclude the battles of Talana, Elandslaagte, Lombard's Kop, Willow Grange and Lord Methuen's victories in the west, but embraced Wagon Hill, the actions on the Tugela, and those during Lord Roberts' advance to Bloemfontein (Paardeberg, etc.). In spite of the fact that the lists solely contained the names of burghers, and did not include those of foreigners and mercenaries, the numbers were greatly in excess of those officially reported. The totals amounted to: Killed, 721; died of wounds, 104; wounded, 2,414; total, 3,239. In addition to the above, there were a proportionally large number who had died of disease. The Office was also packed with circulars and proclamations, in which Mr. Reitz ranted against the "Murderers and Treaty-Breakers," and Mr. Kruger conjured his followers to read the eighty-third Psalm, where the *English* (!) have unrighteously cried that "this people shall not continue; but its name shall be rooted out," and generally identified his own cause with that of the Almighty.

On Monday, 25th June, General Sir Archibald Hunter, who had crossed the Southern Transvaal from Warrenton, entered the town, with General FitzRoy Hart's Irish Brigade, which had gained such laurels in Natal. The arrival of Sir Archibald Hunter, at the moment when Hamilton's Column had lost its indefatigable leader, was indeed fortunate; he immediately received orders from Army headquarters to take over the command, and it was thus that General Ian Hamilton lost the lion's share of the spoils of Prinsloo's surrender. One cannot but sympathise with the General, for such a misfortune was not without precedent in his career; for when in command of one of the Brigades of the Tirah Expeditionary Force, in '97, he was thrown from his horse at the head of Kohat Pass, breaking his leg, and the command had passed to another before the first shot was fired.

On the morning of the 27th June, the force continued its march south, under its new Commander; and camping at the Oceana Coal-Mine, General Hunter reached the Vaal at Villiersdorp two days later. The greater part of the 30th was devoted to getting the troops over the River by ferry; and although the waggons crossed at the drift, it took seven and a half hours before the whole column was across and was camped, for the first time, upon the soil of the Orange River Colony. The country between the Vaal and Frankfort, which was reached on 1st July, was quite treeless; a more barren and deserted waste-land could hardly be imagined. The fence posts, which had previously supplied the troops with fuel, were here of stone; and the men were reduced to cowdung, as the only combustible material in the district. The march, however, was little interrupted by the enemy, the majority of whom were collected around Bethlehem, which was the centre upon which several British columns were now converging. Rundle, Paget, Clements and Brabant were already in the neighbourhood; and on 3rd July, Macdonald, with the Highland Brigade, marched into Frankfort and joined Hunter's force. As a large quantity of supplies would be required by these columns, an empty convoy from Frankfort was despatched to Heilbron, and the City Imperial Volunteers were, at their own request, detailed as escort.

On the following day, with Bruce Hamilton's and Macdonald's Brigades marching in parallel columns, Hunter set out to the south. Bivouacking at Rietfontein, Sahie and Stompkop during the nights of the 4th, 5th and 6th, he reached Reitz on the 7th, where the Battalion was immediately ordered to escort another empty convoy to Heilbron.

The strength of the Battalion, in both officers and men, was now fast diminishing ; and though at Frankfort a colour-sergeant and twelve men of the 4th Battalion, and at Reitz, a sergeant and another twelve—all of whom had been taken prisoners at Roodeval—to a small extent helped to swell the numbers, the Regiment was by this time a very different unit to that which had marched out of Glen.

At Reitz, as only 600 infantry were required as escort to the convoy, Captain Radford, Lieutenant Popham and 113 N.C.O.'s and men remained with the Brigade. This party were fortunate ; for, as will appear from subsequent events, the Regiment were not destined to again rejoin the 21st Brigade ; and Captain Radford and his men took part in the operations which led to the surrender of Prinsloo, gaining the clasp, " WITTEBERGEN." An account of their share in the action is to be found elsewhere.

The convoy, consisting of the infantry escort and 300 mounted infantry, under the command of Colonel Cunningham, left Reitz on 8th July ; and, with intermediate bivouacs at Rustfontein, Blau Krantz and Wellust, rushed Heilbron on the 11th. On the following day, the waggons were reloaded ; and Colonel Cunningham left for Pretoria, where he was granted the temporary rank of Brigadier, and took over the command of a newly-formed brigade for the Lydenburg advance, Colonel Ewart, of the Cameron Highlanders, relieving him in command of the convoy.

On the 13th the convoy, the escort having been increased by two field guns and the volunteer company of the Camerons, proceeded along the well-remembered Heilbron-Lindley road, now strewn with the whitened bones of the animals of Hamilton's Army and the many columns that had since traversed it. Some little interest was now awakened by the sight of familiar kopjes. On the night of the 14th the Battalion camped on almost the identical spot where it had passed the never-to-be forgotten night of 20th May; and the bivouac of the following day was none other than Vaalbank, the former scene of Piet de Wet's attack upon Hamilton's rear-guard. But the road was now deserted, and the continuous sound of distant guns, which had, day after day urged Hamilton's Column forward, was no longer to be heard. Most assuredly all the enemy were surrounded at Bethlehem !

On the 16th the convoy reached Lindley, garrisoned by the Bedfordshire Regiment and the Malta Mounted Infantry, under Captain Marshall of the Second Battalion. In those days, Lindley, according to its own lights, was the most ill-used of all the smaller market-towns, which lay scattered over the veldt. Its inhabitants, peace - loving people, suffered much from repeated stings of conscience. When a British Column entered the town, they would sing " God Save the Queen " and hoist the Union Jack ; when the English had departed—as they invariably did—and, as the burghers cantered into Lindley, no less lustily would they sing the " Volkslied " and shake their fists at the dust of the departing column—Lindley was capable of this once in a way ; but sixteen evacuations were more than its tact could manage, and resulted in disorder to the mayor and a few of the choicer spirits; while the remainder of the inhabitants lived on, in grave misdoubt, between the *sjambok* and the Provost-Marshal.

Colonel Ewart's little force was no exception to the general rule; for that officer not only marched out of the place on the 17th, but took the entire garrison with him. The loyal inhabitants were distressed—they overdid it in fact; and yet they thought it strange; for they had received word, they said, that Christian de Wet would enter Lindley that night. They were ill-informed, of course; for everyone knew that Christian de Wet was surrounded at Bethlehem.

Now there is but one road which runs from Bethlehem to Lindley, and this, as far as guns and waggons are concerned, is somewhat in the nature of a defile, since the country on either side is intersected with innumerable dongas and watercourses. Early during the march, Captain Marshall had reported large parties of Boers to the front; and before Sterkfontein was reached, it became apparent that Christian de Wet, with 1,500 men, guns and waggons, had escaped through Hunter's cordon, which was as yet not complete, and was advancing north along the same road.

On the night of the 17th the Boer laager lay only a few miles from the convoy at Sterkfontein, and there appeared every likelihood of an engagement on the following day. It was primarily necessary, however, to acquaint Army headquarters with the position of De Wet's commando; and Lieutenant Gilson volunteered to ride into Kroonstad that night with the intelligence. The task was, however, given to the Convoy Transport Officer, who had previously traversed the road seven times. He got through in safety, and received the D.S.O. in consequence. It was of the utmost importance that the presence of so large a force of the enemy in the very centre of the Orange River Colony should be known to the Commander-in-Chief; but unfortunately there were at that

time no troops available; and, a few days later, not only
was the main line destroyed and a train captured, but the
person of Lord Kitchener himself nearly fell into De Wet's
hands. Had Colonel Ewart known what De Wet must most
certainly have been aware of, namely, that a large force of
mounted troops was already in pursuit, he undoubtedly
should have attacked without delay; but when day broke,
the opportunity had gone, and across the whole veldt, as far
as the eye could reach, there was no sign of De Wet, though
after a few minutes the 2nd and 3rd (Lancer) Brigades and
General Ridley's M.I. came upon the convoy from the south.
General Broadwood, who commanded this force, resolved to
push on immediately in pursuit, and, hearing that the enemy
was in considerable force, and, gathering from this that he
would require every mounted man in his firing line, resolved,
on his own initiative, to take the Regiment with him as
escort to his baggage, since "he knew what hardened
marchers they were." It was a compliment; but it deprived
the headquarters of the Battalion of the Wittebergen clasp,
an l called upon them to make one supreme effort, by which
they covered, first 75 miles in four days, and then 238 miles in
16—that is to say, a total rate of marching of 16 miles a day,
as the completion of a march of more than a thousand miles.

On the 19th Broadwood closed with De Wet, near
Riversdal, his column losing 31 killed and wounded. But
it was with the greatest difficulty that the cavalry General
could keep in touch with the enemy, who crossed the colony
by a route in the shape of a large S. Bivouacking at
Reitpoort, Riversdal, Roodepoort and Vaalkrantz, the
Battalion hurried forward, in the wake of the cavalry,
and reached Horning Kopje, on the railway, the scene of
the Roodeval disaster, on the evening of the 22nd. De Wet
had crossed the line at Roodeval, but was now nowhere to
be found.

The following day the Battalion was ordered down to Serfontein, but the order was cancelled; and on the 24th it rejoined Broadwood at Vleispruit, where he had again run De Wet to earth. It was beyond doubt that if the march had told on the men and horses of the British force, the Boers were also equally exhausted and unable to move further. Troops were therefore ordered towards Vredepoort from every direction. Lord Methuen came down from Potchefstroom and held the Vaal drifts to the north; the 2nd Cavalry Brigade remained at Vleispruit, while the Battalion marched to Wonderheufel on the 27th; Ridley's Brigade changed their position to one to the north-west of Broadwood. Later General Knox moved out from Kroonstad, and De Wet was enclosed on every side.

Both on the 23rd and 25th Broadwood engaged the enemy, who showed every appearance of meaning to hold to their position, which was tolerably secure, until the British were more strongly reinforced.

For two weeks the Boer force was invested, and every day it seemed that its chances of escape diminished. General Hart's Brigade, consisting of the Northumberland Fusiliers, Dublin Fusiliers, R. Canadian Regiment, Shropshire Light Infantry, and half the Somersetshire Light Infantry, arrived and camped to the east of Wonderheufel; and, finally, Lord Kitchener appeared and assumed the supreme command of all the columns.

For ten days no movement was made by either side; but during this period the Battalion did not remain idle. Patrols, generally under Captain Rigby, were almost daily engaged. On the 31st a sharp artillery duel took place, the Boer gun being subjected to long range volleys from "A" Company; and on the same day a party, under Lieutenant Gilson, came under a heavy fire, suffering 2 casualties.

On receiving the news of Prinsloo's surrender General

Broadwood sent his A.D.C. under a flag of truce, acquainting De Wet of the fact, and recommending the Boer General to follow suit, as he most certainly was entirely surrounded. He showed no inclination to do so, however; and on the night of 6th August disproved the latter fact by slipping through Lord Kitchener's outposts and crossing into the Transvaal by an unmarked drift.

The following day the whole of Lord Kitchener's forces set out in pursuit; crossing the Vaal on the 10th by a series of forced marches, and bivouacking at Vaalkraal, Grosterland, Driefontein and Heilsfontein—that is to say, the route lay *via* Vredepoort, Parys and Lindique Drift — reached Welverdiend on the 12th.

But the pace was killing; 20 men, unable to keep up, had fallen out upon the road, and at Welverdiend 170 were left behind, under Lieutenants Taylor and Gilson. Captain Phelps, who had joined at Wonderheufel with a draft of young soldiers, was now in command of "A" Company; and, as Captain Rigby was acting as second in command, Lieutenant Wilkin commanded "D." The strength of the Regiment was now reduced to little more than 500, and of these a great number belonged to the newly-joined draft.

But Lord Kitchener, openly sanguine of success, was determined to push on without delay. De Wet had crossed the Gatsrand at Buffelsdoorn Pass, General Smith-Dorrien, marching to Welverdiend, and leaving his camp fires still burning at Bank, only just failing to cut him off on the Krugersdorp—Potchefstroom line. Lord Methuen, with a small mounted force, which he handled masterfully, kept persistently on the enemy's left flank, continually checking his advance and, at the same time, preventing his escape down the Mooi River Valley to Klerksdorp. General Ian Hamilton held the Magaliesberg Passes, and General Cunningham marched his brigade westward from Commando

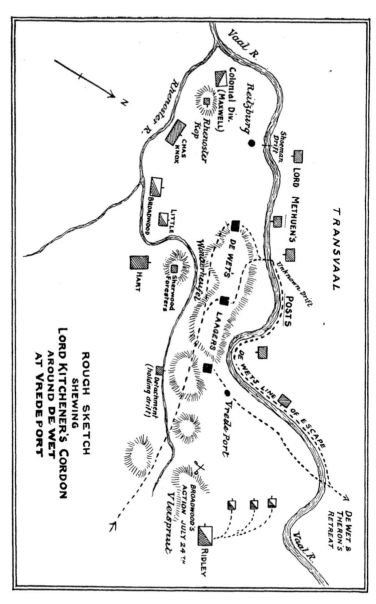

ROUGH SKETCH
SHEWING
LORD KITCHENER'S CORDON
AROUND DE WET
AT VREDE PORT

Nek. Indeed it seemed as if De Wet had little chance of escape.

On the 12th Lord Kitchener's Infantry marched to Cypherfontein, and on the 15th reached Rietfontein, by way of Klip Krantz Drift. In the meantime General de la Rey, north of the Magaliesberg, had not been idle, and his operations saved De Wet. Firstly, he laid siege to General Baden-Powell's force in Rustenburg, to which place General Ian Hamilton was ordered to proceed. Secondly, he surrounded Colonel Hore's force at Eland's River. Ian Hamilton's absence from Oliphant's Nek gave De Wet his chance, and on the evening of the 15th Lord Kitchener sent the following wire to the Commander-in-Chief:—

"De Wet has escaped through Oliphant's Nek. I thought it was held by our people. I am hastening to the relief of Hore."

On the 17th the cavalry reached Eland's River, the infantry marching twenty-eight miles to a point close to the position. De la Rey, on the approach of so powerful a force, immediately broke up his laagers; and thus the defenders of Hore's camp—for the most part Australians and New Zealanders, who had so gallantly held a vastly superior force at bay for ten days—were eventually relieved.

Both De la Rey's and De Wet's commandos having broken up in the bush-veldt, there was no further necessity for so large a force in the vicinity; and the Battalion received orders to march to Krugersdorp by easy stages—a boon which supplies would not admit of. After a day's halt at Waterval, the force marched to Leeufontein, where a veldt-fire swept through the camp, destroying a great deal of equipment, stores, etc., belonging to the other regiments. On the 18th another long march of twenty-eight miles carried the regiment to Vlakfontein, the scene of the battle of the following year, and a Scotch cart was filled with oranges, probably from the same grove in which "E" Company repleted themselves just before the action commenced. Finally, marching by way of Cypherfontein and Reitvlei, the Regiment reached Krugersdorp on 22nd August.

Major Gosset had the misfortune to fall from his horse, breaking a rib, but he managed to lead his Battalion into the town, now only 370 strong, with Captain Rigby and Captain Phelps, Lieutenants Sadler, Morley, Anley and Wilkin, the sole remaining company officers, of whom only the last three had marched the whole way from Glen on foot. The Transport Officer, Lieutenant Rhodes, and the Quartermaster, Lieutenant Tyler, had also covered the entire distance, besides the Commanding Officer, the Adjutant, and the Second in Command.

In estimating the accomplishment of this march at its proper value, it may be well here to look back upon some of the local conditions under which it was performed.

In the first place, a great scarcity of fuel pervades South Africa, more especially the north-eastern Orange River Colony. It was found that the men preferred to cook their own rations on getting into camp, and this system, no doubt, had its advantages, but was exceedingly expensive in fuel. Nearly every man carried a bundle of wood strapped in his blanket, and the spectacle of a man bearing a huge log upon his shoulder, while a messmate carried his rifle, was not uncommon.

Secondly, the great extremes of the South African climate, ranging from 130° in the mid-day sun to sometimes as much as 8° of frost at night, severely taxed the more delicate constitutions. The way often led across the uneven veldt, where there was neither road nor track, where marching was difficult, and no two steps were by necessity of equal length. Not until the Regiment reached Johannesburg was a fresh supply of boots obtained. Few men could by then show a serviceable pair, and there were even cases in which officers were partially bare-footed.

Since the Brigade moved for the most part well away from the railroads, supplies were scanty, the men being generally on three-quarter rations, and sometimes half. Officers, of course, fared well enough as to quantity, though both whisky and jam, to one teaspoonful of which per *diem* each officer was confined, were coveted luxuries. Minced trek-ox, rice and dried peaches were the daily fare. As long as the route lay northward, with Pretoria for a goal, each man stepped forward with the sense of an object to be attained; afterwards there was a seeming aimlessness in it all. The continual fighting during the advance northwards entailed frequent deployments to widely extended formations, thereby at the same time diminishing the distance traversed in the day, and greatly increasing the fatigue. On account of all this—for the actual battle casualties were but few—the Battalion of 370 rank and file which marched into Krugersdorp was indeed but an example of the survival of the fittest; and, without in any way attempting to compare the work they did with deeds of greater historic importance, it is but just to say that the Regiment has, at least, a cause for pride in the many miles they covered during those days. It is impossible to give the exact distances traversed throughout, as all accounts necessarily vary; but the following total may be taken as nearly approximate :—1,026 miles were traversed in 81 marching days, extended over a total period of 116 days, of which two weeks were spent in the vicinity of Wonderheufel—and during which time the Regiment took part in nine general actions and the capture of ten towns including Johannesburg and Pretoria.

G

CHAPTER VI

PRINSLOO'S SURRENDER

IT is here necessary to break off for a while from the chain of continuous narrative, and to follow the fortunes of the large party of men under Captain Radford, which, it will be remembered, remained with the 21st Brigade when the Battalion marched away from Rietz on 8th July, 1900.

Great columns of British troops were at that time closing around the Wittebergen. Hunter and Macdonald came from the north; Clements and Paget from the west; and Rundle and Brabant, with the Colonial Division, from the south. Large bodies of Free Staters, under Prinsloo, Crowther, Olivier and Christian de Wet, lay beyond the passes.

Prinsloo, the General-in-Chief, must have fallen into a similar error to that made by Cronje at Paardeberg; for the district lay well away from the main lines of communication on the Orange River Colony side—Heilbron, the terminus of a small branch line, and Kroonstad being the nearest points— and beyond doubt the Boer General found it difficult to believe that a British force, sufficient to invest the mountains, could be massed *and supplied* within so comparatively small an area. For one knows that he must have had ample warning of the movement. Viljoen , for instance, had engaged th mounted troops of Hamilton's Column at Heidelberg, and certainly saw that the great force went south.

Of the Boer Generals, De Wet and Olivier were alone cognisant of their danger until it was too late, and the great *khaki* arms had folded around the greater part of the Boer force.

The Detachment, left under Captain Radford's command, numbered 103 N.C.O.'s and men; and Lieutenant Popham was attached for duty, so far as it did not interfere with his duties as Brigade Foraging Officer ; or, in other words, Commandeerer and lawful appropriator of cattle, food, forage and all that came within his way.

For four whole days General Bruce Hamilton remained halted at Reitz, and, on the 13th and 14th, moved a further distance of twenty-six miles southward, which carried his Brigade to within four miles of Bethlehem.

On the 16th, as already mentioned in the previous chapter, De Wet broke out, and, on the evening of the following day, came across Colonel Ewart's little force, returning to Bethlehem, along the Lindley Road.

General Bruce Hamilton, on hearing the news, rode hurriedly into Bethlehem, and ordered his Brigade to follow with all speed.

Here, as at Reitz, a section of the outpost line was allotted to the Detachment. On the third day, the Heilbron convoy arrived ; but the infantry escort was found to consist of the Bedfordshire Regiment, the Battalion being by that time well across the Orange River Colony, on the heels of De Wet.

But the famous Free State General had escaped only in the nick of time ; he was as fortunate in this as he was at the conclusion of the self-same flight, when, by a stroke of chance, he found Oliphant's Nek, his only exit, unguarded. However, it is possible that, finding Prinsloo oblivious to his warnings, he may have hoped to divert a large number of troops from the Bethlehem investment to the attention of himself upon the Vaal ; for he seems to have remained there an unnecessary length of time, while the columns closed around him. If this was ever his idea, it failed in its main conception: for there were at that time sufficient troops under Lord Roberts' command to surround both places simultaneously, and on the very day after his escape General Hunter's cordon was all but completed on an outer semicircle, and it alone remained to close in upon the inner passes, with his infantry and guns.

On the 16th the Sussex Regiment, with the 81st Battery, in accordance with the general plan, had marched to Macskop, on the Senekal Road; and, on the 20th, General Bruce Hamilton, leaving his convoy to follow in charge of Captain Radford's Detachment and the City Imperial Volunteers M.I., marched to Spitzkrantz, with the Camerons and another battery.

The weather among the mountains was now bitterly cold; and, on the night of the 22nd, a snowstorm fell, and buried the bivouacs in snow; so that the great Wittebergen range rose white above the yellow plains.

The following day was the day of Retief's Nek. There were many other regiments engaged in the action, but the main credit rests with General Bruce Hamilton, who, with the Sussex, beat off the enemy, but without loss of life, and closed the Pass.

From day to day the firing continued. The Camerons had already seized the heights in the vicinity of Spitzkrantz; and, on the 24th, General Hunter ordered Bruce Hamilton and Macdonald to join forces and advance against Davel's Rust, six miles north of Naauwpoort Nek.

Early on the morning of the 26th, the united brigades advanced against the position, the Detachment holding the high ground covering the right flank of the advance.

The position was captured with but little resistance, and was subsequently occupied by the Black Watch, the Seaforth and the Argyll and Sutherland Highlanders.

Bruce Hamilton and the Highland Light Infantry, the remaining battalion of the Highland Brigade, bivouacked some five miles south of Spitzkrantz, and, the following day, moved four miles to the east, still within easy distance of support of Davel's Rust.

Of the passes through the south of the Wittebergen, the Golden Gate now alone lay open, and thither General Bruce Hamilton was ordered to proceed. The Harrismith Commando was, unfortunately, already through the outlet, and endeavoured, by opposing the British force, to cover the escape of the remainder of Prinsloo's men.

Fighting commenced early on the morning of the 28th; and across twelve miles of country Bruce Hamilton drove the enemy back, in his advance towards what had now become the key of the whole position. On the next day the Force, Captain Radford's Detachment acting as Advance Guard, came under range of the Boer guns on Mount Bessie.

The Mounted Infantry on the left flank captured the plateau; and then, with the Camerons on the right and the Detachment, supported by the Sussex, in the centre, General Bruce Hamilton cleared the enemy from the mountain, scattering them to right and left.

On the 30th Captain Radford relieved the Mounted Infantry in occupation of Mount Bessie, while the remainder of the Brigade marched against the Golden Gate before orders to move could be transmitted to the mountain-top, owing to the signallers' view being obscured by the clouds. Accordingly, when the order was at last received, the Detachment followed as best it could, a party under Lieutenant Popham protecting the exposed flank; but Captain Radford was unable to overtake the main force, and that night bivouacked in its tracks. For Bruce Hamilton had pushed on with great rapidity, and seized the Golden Gate in the nick of time, as a force of some 1,300 Boers were about to break away.

These unconditionally laid down their arms; they were caught like rats in a hole; and, the same day, the main Boer force, under Prinsloo, nearly 3,000 strong, surrendered to Sir Archibald Hunter, the General-in-Chief who had conducted the operations.

But the pick of the enemy, with all their guns and best horses, had escaped in two bodies; De Wet on the 16th, and Olivier on the 31st. Of De Wet's movements we know; and the last-named General—who, it will be remembered, was at one time in command of the Stormberg laagers at the outset of the war—moved south into the Doornberg, where he immediately began to cause trouble, until his enterprises shortly came to a sudden and untimely end in St. Helena.

Lieutenant Popham, acting as Provost-Marshal, was charged with the destruction of the captured arms and ammunition; after which General Bruce Hamilton immediately set out for Winburg with the prisoners.

He marched on the 3rd through Harrismith back to Bethlehem, and thence to Winburg, *via* Senekal, where he arrived on the 12th, and whence his captives were despatched to Cape Town.

Thence he marched north again to Kroonstad, passing Ventersburg Road, where Lieutenant Attfield, with his Mounted Infantry, was stationed, and near which place he was so soon to lose his life—camping at Kroonstad near by the same place where Ian Hamilton's Army had bivouacked in May, after the capture of this town.

Late on the 21st Bruce Hamilton left for the south by train, with the Camerons, a Field Battery, and his mounted troops, to move against Olivier, leaving Captain Radford's men and the Bedfordshire Regiment to follow with his transport.

The whole force reunited at Ventersberg Road Siding, whence the Camerons and four guns moved down to

Smaldeel, half the Sussex Regiment to Winburg, and the remainder of the force out to the east, to Ventersberg town.

On the 27th, Olivier himself, with a small party, fell into General Bruce Hamilton's hands near Winburg ; and the Detachment, which had been joined by Lieutenant M. B. Webb and Lieutenant Wright of the Volunteer Company at Kroonstad, after taking part in a reconnaissance on the 26th, returned to Ventersberg Road Siding, where it remained under the command of Major de Moulin of the Sussex Regiment, who afterwards was killed near Reitz, until it was finally sent down to the rest - camp at Bloemfontein on 3rd September.

General Bruce Hamilton, on the following day, marched the remnants of his Brigade east towards the waterworks and thus the last link of the Battalion's connection with the. 21st Brigade, except in the fact that Major Shaw remained Brigade-Major and afterwards A.A.G., was severed, once and for all.

The Detachment remained at Bloemfontein until 11th September, when it was sent to Einsgevonden, fourteen miles north of Brandfort, where the 2nd Company Derbyshire M.I. was at that time quartered.

Here Captain Radford and his men remained for nearly two weeks, living for the first time since Edenburg under canvas ; until, on the 25th, he received orders to join the headquarters of the Battalion at Krugersdorp.

The Detachment had been separated from the unit to which it properly belonged for eleven weeks, in which time, if they had not *walked* as far, they had at least taken part in a more extensive and infinitely more successful set of operations, for which they gained the clasp, " WITTEBERGEN."

CHAPTER VII

THE WESTERN TRANSVAAL

At Wonderheufel, Lord Kitchener had congratulated Major Gosset on the excellent marching of his battalion, and promised the men a much-needed rest as soon as opportunity occurred. " Until the end of the War," the Commander-in-Chief had said, little expecting that that date was even then two years distant. But if circumstances, which no doubt no one had greater reason to regret than himself, did not hereafter admit of his literally fulfilling his promise, the Regiment were at least granted seven months, from August, 1900, to April, 1901, for comparative rest and a chance of reorganisation, on the lines of communication along the Krugersdorp-Potchefstroom railway.

Of reorganisation there was a sad need. Throughout the long march of' the previous months, sick, wounded and stragglers had been scattered about the country as torn paper in a paper-chase ; and, when once left by the Battalion, they had little or no chance of again rejoining during the line of march.

But at the halt at Krugersdorp, these swarmed into the headquarters from all directions—some even came from Sterkstroom, where they had been left in hospital when the Regiment moved forward from Cyphergat to Bethulie Bridge—and the ranks of the Battalion visibly swelled daily. Lieutenant de Pledge from the Base, joined with a hundred of these men ; and soon afterwards Lieutenant Newbold, with a draft of twenty-three Volunteers. Two subalterns—

Lieutenants Armstrong and Mayall—joined on appointment
Lieutenant Murray—who had been wounded at Diamond
Hill—and Captain Radford and Lieutenant Popham with
the details who had taken part in the Wittebergen
operations.

Captain Keller was sent down to take over command of
the Base Company, which had moved from East London
to Cape Town, Lieutenant Popham temporarily taking his
place as Acting-Adjutant; and Lieutenant Rhodes left
Krugersdorp early in October, with General Barton's Column,
as Transport and Ammunition Column Officer, and did not
rejoin until twenty-three months later.

At first the Battalion headquarters remained in Krugersdorp; but on 28th August, "A," "D," "E," "I" and the
Volunteer Companies proceeded down the line to Bank
Station. The Volunteers shortly received orders to return
to England; but the other companies, under Captain Phelps,
remained in garrison at Bank.

On 1st September "H" Company, under Captain Sadler—
for there had been much promotion of late, seven steps having
gone during the period the Regiment was on the march—
proceeded to Welverdiend, where, it will be remembered,
a large party of men had been left behind on 12th August.
These were afterwards returned to their proper companies,
and the garrison of Welverdiend, which comprised companies
of the Dublin and Northumberland Fusiliers, and other details,
was reinforced by "F" Company.

On 7th October the Battalion was ordered to entrain for
Bank under sealed orders; and, on arrival at this place,
Major Gosset was ordered to occupy a post about half-way
between Bank and Welverdiend. This station proved to
be a solitary Ganger's Hut, with a sign-board on the line
bearing the announcement "Oberholzer," which, it was
immediately apparent, was nearly two miles from water.

But by means of the Battalion water-carts this difficulty was daily overcome during the many months the headquarters remained at this place.

The three posts along the line, viz. : Bank, Oberholzer and Welverdiend, respectively under the command of Captain Phelps, Major Gosset and Major Wilmot, of the Northumberland Fusiliers, were put into an almost impregnable state of defence. The strip of country in this district through which the railway runs is exceedingly flat, and except for the ant-heaps —which were easily demolished—barren of cover and little favourable to attack. Five miles to the south, well beyond effective artillery range, the Gatsrand runs parallel to the line ; the principal passes lie at Bank and Buffelsdoorn, opposite Welverdiend ; but unlike the great range to the north, the Magaliesberg, these hills are accessible along their entire length. At distances varying from two miles to a few hundred yards to the south, the Mooi River—the original of Allan Quatermain's underground river to the land where the White Queens dwell—flows through its picturesque and fertile valley ; at one time disappearing beneath the low hills ; but this again, except at its open *vleis* or marshes, is for the most part fordable, and a barrier alone to guns and transport. As these posts were some eight miles apart, they in no way served to bar the way from the Mooi Valley to the Vaal ; indeed, after De Wet's commando split up in the Magaliesberg, large numbers of the enemy must have crossed the line between the detachments during September. Afterwards smaller intermediate posts, not exceeding 25 men, guarding bridges, important culverts, etc., were scattered along the line at distances from two to four miles.

As for the period we are now embarked upon, being in the middle of a three years' war, and in a district so near to the happy hunting-ground of one of the most audacious of the Transvaal leaders, one Kemp to wit, whose proximity no doubt must have served in some measure to inspire the local chieftains, the ensuing months could hardly have passed without event. Upon those events it is solely necessary to dwell here.

Smaller expeditions and escapades there were in plenty; in the earlier months, shooting parties after buck in the Gatsrand, or along the open *vleis* of the river valley, where coot, duck and snipe mingled with bittern and weaver-birds in a jungle of reed and marsh plants, amid clustered poplars on the drier banks — scenes to delight the heart of any naturalist; to the Gatsrand Caves where Rider Haggard found " King Solomon's Mines," or out on the open veldt after the lesser bustard for the pot. With these we are not concerned, any more than we are with periodical visits of officers to neighbouring detachments with clothing, beer, etc., or perhaps to Johannesburg with " toothache "; though, when the Boers came back to the district, there were occasions when an officer was surprised some way from home, with only a shot-gun, and had to gallop for his life. But there were many minor incidents along the line, unimportant in themselves, yet woven minutely in the threadwork of the War. On 29th September Captain Phelps, with a strong party with a machine-gun, had reconnoitred by train between Bank and Welverdiend, and when near Oberholzer had come under a heavy fire from a party of the enemy, hidden in the dry dongas on either side. The Maxim, unfortun-ately, jammed at the third round, and Private Hook, one of the details who had only joined on the previous day, was killed.

In October the news reached the Battalion of the death of Lieutenant H. K. Attfield, of the 2nd Battalion, near Ventersberg Road Station—a loss which was greatly felt by his brother officers who knew him. The official summary read as follows:—" Lieutenant Attfield is a great loss, he having been more than once brought to the notice of the Commander-in-Chief for gallant conduct."

In November Lieutenant Ritchie joined with a draft from the 2nd Battalion; Lieutenant Wilkin left for Cape Town, he having been selected for employment with the West African Field Force; soon afterwards Second-Lieutenants Napier and Rimington joined on appointment, and Captain Keller returned from Cape Town and reassumed the adjutancy. About this time a smaller detachment, under Lieutenant Anley, was posted at Rietfontein Bridge, west of Bank, and remained there for some time.

General French, who was then in command of the entire line, was well pleased with all the defences, and after his inspection gave the command from Bank to Welverdiend to Major Gosset. The Detachment Commanders, however, continued to have a free hand in the matter of their own defences and patrols, and were enabled to reap full credit for any subsequent local successes; both Captain Phelps and Major Wilmot gained brevets.

Early in October Welverdiend was bombarded from the Gatsrand: forty-eight shells fell in the little camp in twenty minutes; but fortunately the shell-proof shelter for the horses had been completed on the previous day, and little or no damage was done, beyond a relapse of nervous exhaustion on the part of the local Jew—a storekeeper. On the following day General Barton's Column encamped around the station; and, in spite of the warnings of the Commandant, pitched a quarter-column camp on the Gatsrand side of the rails; sure enough the enemy again opened fire, and the General was obliged to bring his long naval guns into action and occupy the hills.

On 27th December a party from Bank were surrounded in the hills, and Private Westwood was mortally wounded.

In the meantime "C" Company, under Captain Morley,

having first occupied Buffelsdoorn Pass for a short time, was railed to Potchefstroom, the old Transvaal capital, which had been taken by General Barton after his engagement at Frederickstad. With this action we are not concerned, but it had been a desperate affair; at one time the advantage lay with the enemy; and the relieving force, which was mobilised at Welverdiend, arrived only in the nick of time, completely turning the tables on Liebenberg's Commando, which suffered severely in consequence; the more so since De Wet deserted the Transvaalers as soon as the numerical superiority rested with the other side.

Towards the end of the year the Gatsrand from end to end was again over-run by the enemy, and continual reports came into the line that Bank Station was in danger of attack. On the 31st a patrol of about 15 men of the Battalion and 18 of Marshall's Horse from Oberholzer, under Second-Lieutenant Rimington, moved towards De Villiers' farm at Driefontein, in the Gatsrand—Captain Phelps, the Commandant of Bank, assisted by sending out a party of 30 men under Second-Lieutenant Mayall. The patrols met in the hills, south of Oberholzer, and occupied a ridge above the farm, the Bank party to the east. But in the meantime Second-Lieutenant Rimington saw cattle being driven down the hillside towards the farm, and seven Boers upon the ridge above. Suspecting a trap, he left six men to hold the kópje on his right flank and advanced with the remainder down towards a wood, which extended about 600 yards north of the farm. With 12 men he advanced; and, on getting round the corner of the wood, about 50 yards from the farm, the Boers opened a terrific fire from a steep, bushy ridge to the south, shooting one horse: the rest of the patrol took shelter behind the farm, and at once opened fire, but Acting Corporal Cunningham was shot dead through the head, and Trooper Northeast, of Marshall's Horse, through the right knee. Orders were then

given to burn the place ; and this was done, the ammunition
stored in the barn going off in the fire.   The Boers, who,
on seeing the smoke, began yelling like savages, appeared
to be in some force.   Orders were therefore given for a
retirement, which was carried out most skilfully—singly—
through the wood, the horses going over two enormous
jumps like birds.   The patrol then, with the covering
party left behind the wood, galloped back through the
open, about a mile up hill, and over very rocky
ground ; but fortunately the horses made no mistakes,
and the Boer marksmanship was none of the best, their
nerves being a little upset by Lieutenant Mayall's party on
the left flank.   Both patrols now quitted the ridge on to the
plain, Lieutenant Mayall, one of whose men—Private Isaacs
—was thrown from his horse, and subsequently died from
cerebral hæmorrhage, retiring on Bank, and Lieutenant
Rimington on Oberholzer.   When Lieutenant Rimington
had got about 800 yards from the ridge, Private Radford of
the Regiment also fell badly, breaking his pelvic bone ; and as
he could neither walk nor ride, a man got on each side of him
and helped him along.   The Boers now lined the ridge and
fired more accurately than before, so that it was necessary to
place Private Radford under cover and to get the horses out
of danger ; then a dismounted party returned, and, whilst
they kept up a fire on the Boers, Lieutenant Rimington and
Private Bullous assisted Radford—a very long and tedious
job, as the man was in considerable pain, and the Boer fire
far too good.   However, they got him out of range, and
finally safely back to camp.   One man of Marshall's Horse,
although he had been ordered back directly, insisted on
searching for his rifle—which he seems to have lost at a
somewhat inopportune moment—and was overlooked in the
retirement.   He hid in the wood during the night, and was
an anxious witness of the savage imprecations of the Boers

around the demolished farm. The dead and the wounded men were brought into the lines on the following day. Trooper Northeast appears to have been treated very well by the enemy, who could hardly, under the circumstances, have been in the best of moods. Indeed, this enemy had a strangely complex character, at times greatly at variance with itself; at one time—such as this—kind and clement; at another, brutal and barbarous. There are many instances of such in the annals of the War; they are for the most part accounted for by an exact discrimination between the character of the town and veldt Boer. No such exact line of distinction, however, can be drawn; for these Boers were town-men under Commandant Boshof; and, on the other hand, it was the veldt Boers who usually ill-treated and often murdered the natives; and again, Kemp's men, who shot the wounded at Vlakfontein, were the original Krugersdorp Commando. But to continue, in connection with this reconnaissance, the following message was received from General Hart, commanding in Krugersdorp, by Captain Rigby, the Commandant of Oberholzer :—" Received your report of your action against De Villiers' farm. I think you have done it very well, and that Lieutenants Mayall and Rimington, and the troops under your command, acted very well in execution of your plan. Please express my opinion to all."

On 9th January a patrol, under Captain Rigby, became hotly engaged, but escaped with no casualties; and on the 15th a sentry at the Ganger's Hut near Bank was wounded by a Boer sniper. Another patrol, under the command of Captain Rigby, reconnoitred to Buffelsdoorn Pass on 2nd February, and again engaged the enemy, effecting the capture of several horses, and confirming the report that the hills were full of Boers.

At Welverdiend, in the meantime, a large number of sheep

and oxen, sent up the line from Frederickstad, fell into the hands of the enemy. A wounded man galloped into Welverdiend with the news, and Captain Sadler's Company, a section of Field Artillery under Lieutenant MacDougal, and a party of Marshall's Horse under Captain Andrew, were immediately sent out in pursuit. Two miles out from camp, Lieutenant Gilson, with four advanced scouts, rode into a large party of the enemy, who sprang up suddenly from the long grass and opened fire at a range of less than fifty yards. Two horses were wounded, and one man was hit through the nose, a queer wound, resembling the hole for a nose-ring. The scouts fell back somewhat hastily, and, joining the main party of Marshall's Horse, then rushed the hill, only to find the enemy well in retreat and firing from the saddle, with sloped arms, as the Turks did at Plevna. From this position the sheep were visible, but safely gathered under a commanding position, while the enemy showed up on every side in appreciable force. Being two miles from camp, with no chance of further reinforcement, it was not considered advisable to risk the safety of the guns, with the practical certainty of loss of life, in an attack upon the position, for the sake of a flock of sheep which had in the first place been insufficiently escorted; and the party returned to Welverdiend.

On 5th February Lieut.-Colonel H. C. Wylly arrived from the 2nd Battalion at Malta, on appointment, and took over command of a somewhat scattered regiment.

At the end of February the officers under his command, and the different detachments where they were stationed, were as follows :—

At Rietfontein Bridge—Captain Anley.

At Bank—Captains Phelps and Radford, Lieutenants Webb, Mayall, Armstrong and Hodgson.

COLONEL H. C. WYLLY, C.B.

[*Face page* 112.

At Oberholzer—The Officer commanding and the Regimental Staff, Captains Rigby and Taylor, and Lieutenant Rimington.

At Welverdiend—Captain Sadler, Lieutenants Murray and De Pledge.

At Potchefstroom—Lieutenant Popham.

At Ventersdorp—Captain Morley.

Attached to A.S.C. (unseconded)—Captain Ritchie, Lieutenants Rhodes and Gilson.

Not yet joined on appointment—Lieutenants Hext, Shepard and O'Farrell.

Sick—Lieutenants Frend and Manby.

Colonel Wylly had only been two days in command when, on 7th February, he received warning by wire that one Smuts intended to attack either Bank or Oberholzer within the week ; and sure enough about 1.30 on the morning of the 13th, shots were fired into Bank, evidently to engage the attention of the garrison, while a determined attack was made upon the bridge by a hundred picked men.   There was a double sentry at the place with the relief posted close at hand : one of the sentries saw a figure approaching, but hesitated to fire, thinking it might be one of the native scouts, the morning being very dark ; then as he half-rose up to fire, he was himself shot dead through the head, while Corporal Tyers, who was just then about to relieve sentries, was mortally wounded through the stomach, and another man, Private Wildgoose, was shot in the thigh and made prisoner.   The Boers now came boldly on, meaning to destroy the pumping station and mine the bridge, but by this time the picquet furnishing the bridge guard had turned out and doubled down to the bridge, where they at once became engaged at the closest quarters.   Here they were joined by Lance-Sergeant Young and Private Handley, sent by Captain

H

Phelps to gather information; but these were all driven back by superior numbers to their picquet post, where they held out till day broke, when the Boers wrecked the bridge and withdrew.

Private Wildgoose came in next morning and reported having seen at least 20 wounded Boers taken off on horses; three, however, were left behind, and a farmer came in and asked Captain Phelps to send for three more who were lying very severely wounded at his house ; one of these died before he could be fetched in, and both the others within a day or two, while two more dead bodies were found on the field next day, so that, except for the loss of the bridge, the Boers came off second best.   The officer commanding Krugersdorp district wrote as follows in regard to the affair :—" I consider the picquet behaved most gallantly, and shall be glad for my appreciation of their conduct to be recorded." Captain Phelps recommended Lance-Sergeant Young for the V.C.

On 16th March Lieutenant Manby, who had fallen sick with dysentery and pneumonia at Houtnek, rejoined the Battalion, the headquarters of which were moved to Bank on the 23rd.

On the night of 2nd April a party of Boers raided the villages near Bank, and afterwards lay in wait for a Cossack Post, but were driven off by a party of mounted men under Captain Anley; and, on the following day, the Ventersdorp and Potchefstroom detachments were railed into Krugersdorp, where the Battalion was to be concentrated prior to joining a column and setting out once again " on trek."

Two days later the headquarters of the Battalion, relieved by the Border Regiment, moved to the same place. Captain Morley's men had already been hurried out to Naauwpoort to Colonel Dixon's—formerly Brig.-General Cunningham's Column—and had been sniped upon the route.

By the 10th Colonel Dixon's Force was securely

concentrated on the commanding position at Naauwpoort;
and on the evening of the following day, leaving the place
with a garrison of 100 Scottish Horse and the Battalion,
under the command of Colonel Wylly, he set out to
co-operate with General Babington, whose headquarters had
for some time been at Ventersdorp.

The position of Naauwpoort was on a lofty ridge, about
a mile and a half long from end to end, and unfortunately
it was necessary to hold the whole crest, as the firewood had
to be cut below one end and the drinking water to be fetched
from below the other. The Company outposts were consequently rather widely separated, but each post was strong
in itself, and all assisted one another in the general scheme
of defence.

A great expanse of country lay spread around the hill,
which completely dominated the immediate neighbourhood.
To the south rolling downs stretched thirty miles, right away
to Krugersdorp, with which place Naauwpoort was in
signalling communication; to the north the view passed
over low, wooded ridges to the Magaliesberg, some eight
miles as the crow flies. Nooitgedacht, where the Northumberland Fusiliers had suffered so severely some months
back, lay to the north-west; and, to the north-east,
communication by helio was established with Oliphant's
Nek, and thence to Rustenburg, and from there west again,
through to Pretoria, by way of Commando Nek.

According to report, Naauwpoort at that time was
surrounded by some 2,000 Boers, in large and small
commandos, and in independent predatory gangs; but they
remained invisible, in the close sheltered valley to the north
—a valley with an evil reputation, where affairs near upon
disaster had already taken place, and where, as the Battalion
was to learn, other fierce struggles had yet still to come; even
then, let but one small party descend into the valley from

Naauwpoort and the invisible enemy remained no longer so, the soil would seem to produce them—like the buildings of Eden City—"spontaneous." They may have at one time fostered some idea of attack; for a Kaffir spy, who had escaped from previous capture, was retaken—*drunk*—in the British lines ; and the highly versatile explanation that "he had come to see his aunt!" being deemed barely sufficient, he departed for Krugersdorp Jail.

On the 25th General Dixon's Column returned to its base ; and his convoy was escorted into Krugersdorp to refill. He decided to leave the Worcester Regiment in occupation of Naauwpoort during his next "trek," but as this corps was not much over 400 strong, Captain Phelps'Company was ordered to remain with them. Lieutenants Frend and Popham, being on the sick-list, were sent into Krugersdorp on the 28th.

That night Major Browne, D.A.A.G. for Intelligence, in order to execute a plan he had arranged, took Yeomanry, and some forty men of the Battalion, accompanied by Captains Rigby and Phelps, and Lieutenants Armstrong and Mayall, for the work. Their object was to surprise a Boer picquet which every morning at daybreak occupied Slipstein kopje, about eight miles from Naauwpoort, commanding the road by which the General proposed to move out on the following morning. The enterprise very nearly succeeded ; the party reached the place shortly before daybreak, and was in position some ten minutes before the advance scouts of a Boer picquet, thirty or forty in number, made their appearance. The scouts rode close up to the kopje, and then, wheeling round, galloped suddenly away, in order to draw fire from anyone unused to their methods. No one, however, fired a shot, and the unsuspecting burghers returned and rode up to the back of the kopje and into the arms of a yeoman who, most unfortunately, had just been sent back with a message to the remainder of the Yeomanry, hidden some distance in rear. The Boers wounded the yeoman, who, however, wounded one in return ; and a hot fire was immediately opened by the men upon the hill, the Boers retiring in haste ; not, however, before three had been seen to be severely wounded. The Column left Naauwpoort at 6 a.m. on the 29th, and at about 9 relieved Captain Phelps' men, who then returned to camp. The right mounted flankers were more or less sniped at all the way to Vlakfontein, about seventeen miles, but only one horse was killed, though a yeoman was captured. Vlakfontein is on the road by which Dr. Jameson travelled on his famous march from Mafeking, and the first camp lay just beyond one of the so-called hotels or stores— put up by Cecil Rhodes in anticipation of the raid. On the march of the following day to Kleinfontein, there was again a certain amount of firing on the right, but no serious opposition was encountered. On 1st May the column camped at the foot of Tafel Kop—a high, flat-topped hill, whence heliographic communication was established with Naauwpoort, Lichtenburg and Ventersdorp. Here General Dixon remained nearly a week, waiting for news of Lord Methuen and General Babington, with whom he was co-operating.

On 7th May the Battalion, with two guns and fifty Yeomanry and the empty convoy, under Colonel Wylly, set out for Ventersdorp, and reached the place in two marches. After a halt of one day in the town, Colonel Wylly's Force moved towards Leeufontein, where he had received instructions to join the General. Communication was established with the main column at the close of the first day's march, and Boers were reported in the vicinity. From its unsavoury condition the camp was evidently an old laager, and a customary rendezvous for the local Boers ; for two parties of the enemy rode unsuspectingly towards the place, and much wild shooting ensued on both sides, with little or no damage to either. But Colonel Wylly burnt the

farm, barns and outhouses, which appeared to have been a
regular supply depot for the Boers for months past, and
joined General Dixon at Leeufontein on the morning of the
following day.   During this march the officer commanding
Colonel Wylly's Yeomanry reported that he was in touch
with General Dixon's patrols.   As was subsequently proved,
General Dixon had no patrols in that direction, and it is
therefore clear that a party of the enemy, finding themselves
unexpectedly close to a British force, had bluffed the Yeomanry
by passing themselves off as Englishmen !   But it is probable
that they even then had some notion of the ruse they were
to adopt at Vlakfontein a fortnight later, and had a desire
to test the credibility of the Yeomanry scouts.   For how it
was that they came so suddenly upon the main body on that
day is a question which it appears is yet to be decided.
Besides, they were known then to have attempted to deceive
the infantry, and their primary effort may have been more
successful.   Beyond doubt, then, this was practice—a bold
experiment in the monstrous game of " spoof."

During the absence of the convoy at Ventersdorp, General
Babington drove a considerable number of the enemy towards
General Dixon, and thirty prisoners and several waggons,
horses, rifles, etc., fell into his hands in consequence.

On the 12th the force, divided into two columns, the
mounted men and most of the guns under Lieut.-Colonel
Shekleton, and the infantry and convoy under Lieut.-Colonel
Wylly, marched to Kaffir Kraal ; and, on the following day,
crossed the Schorn Spruit to Klipfontein, where it was
reported that the Boers had broken away to the south-west,
Lord Methuen in pursuit ; and the column in consequence
changed its direction and headed for Welverdiend, on the old
familiar railroad.

On the next day an ambush was prepared for a body of
the enemy who had been following up the rear-guard for

some time, and a mounted party, with the pom-pom, was hidden in a farm. Sure enough the usual "followers" appeared, three in front, followed at a distance by nine others. One of the three was the son of the owner of the farm, and he came up telling his companions in English of what he would do to the next soldiers he caught. He died next morning from a bad wound in the stomach, the two men with him were captured, and the others fled headlong, pursued by shots from the pom-pom.

Marching by way of Witpoortje, on the Ventersdorp-Potchefstroom road, and Reitvlei, on the Mooi River, General Dixon's Column reached Welverdiend on the 17th. Here Captain Radford was admitted to hospital suffering from fever; and the 5th New Zealand contingent, which had done such fine work in the past, left the column, homeward bound.

On the 19th General Dixon moved to Oberholzer, where Captain Anley rejoined, and, camping first just across the Mooi River and thence moving by way of Doornfontein, Vlakplaats and Kaalfontein, Naauwpoort was again reached on 24th May.

The little expedition had not been wildly exciting, and was in every way of a different nature from the more strenuous efforts of the previous year. Tents and a variety of other comforts not obtainable in the earlier stages of the War were at hand, and the march, for the most part, was performed in comparatively easy stages. A total distance of 211 miles was covered in twenty-six days, of which the column was halted eight.

CHAPTER VIII

VLAKFONTEIN

GENERAL DIXON'S Force did not remain long at Naauwpoort; but leaving 210 men of the Battalion, under Captain Phelps, a company of the King's Own Scottish Borderers, a hundred mounted men and a 4·7-gun at his base, on 26th May he marched out in command of the following force, viz:—

> 6 Guns Royal Field Artillery.
> 1 Pom-pom.
> 1 Howitzer.
> 240 Scottish Horse.
> 240 Yeomanry.
> 400 King's Own Scottish Borderers.
> 400 Sherwood Foresters (*i.e.*, 4 companies each of a hundred strong).

"H" Company, with one company K.O.S.B.'s, seized the Slipstein kopje, prior to the advance, without opposition; but the column had barely traversed six miles before small parties of Boers showed up on the right flank, *i.e.*, along the southern edge of the Magalies Valley. The Scottish Horse were not altogether able to dislodge them, and the advanced guard guns and the pom-pom were brought into action. In moving to reconnoitre some low, rocky kopjes at Basfontein guarding the approaches to the Valley, a party of Yeomanry came to grief, through skirmishing in close order, with the result that 6 of them fell, and the howitzer and "C" and "D" Companies were ordered up to clear the position. But the enemy, although the hill commanded an excellent field of fire, retired under extreme long range fire from the infantry with probably a casualty or so.

From the camp at Basfontein an excursion was made on the following day into the valley towards Middlefontein — almost opposite Oliphant's Nek — where General Cunningham's Force had suffered severely some months back. But the enemy, who showed up in no appreciable strength, seemed, for the most part, to have broken eastward. A number of barns and storehouses were burnt—for the valley up to that time had been little raided, most of the British columns that had passed among the treacherous kopjes having been roughly handled at one time and another, and by no means anxious to remain in the district —and the expedition returned to camp soon after 1 o'clock.

The next day's march to Vlakfontein—already mentioned in the previous chapter in connection with the Jameson Raid —was a short one of some six or seven miles. There was again desultory firing on the right, and after arrival in camp, the mounted men and some guns, pushing on towards the west, sighted a big Boer convoy moving northwards. The guns opened fire upon the convoy ineffectively, and then the force returned to Vlakfontein, having 1 yeoman wounded and 2 Scottish Horse missing. That night the Padre, the Doctor and an ambulance went out to look for the missing men, but "fell among" Boers who, having some reason to conceal their whereabouts, took them to their laager, where they (the Padre and Doctor) were informed that "they would be much safer on the following day than in the British camp!"

On the 29th the whole force, with the exception of two Companies of the Battalion and two of the K.O.S.B.'s, left camp at 8 o'clock. The General had heard that some Boer guns were buried in a valley about three and a half miles off to the west, and also that a quantity of ammunition was buried in another valley about the same distance to the north of the camp, and he meant to try and recover each in turn. The original advance guard consisted of two guns, 230 Yeomanry and " H " Company, under Major Chance, R.A.— Lieut.-Colonel Shekelton, who was to have commanded, being sick in camp. The main body and rear-guard, under Lieut.-Colonel Wylly (with whom was Brig.-General Dixon), consisted of two guns, the howitzer, " E " Company of ours, and two weak Companies of the K.O.S.B.'s, while a strong flank guard on the right, holding the valley side, a good mile and a half distant, was composed of two guns, two weak Companies K.O.S.B.'s and the Scottish Horse.

When the force reached the ground overlooking the place where the guns were supposed to be, " E " Company sent half a company forward, while the advance and flank guards guarded both flanks and opened fire on small parties of Boers seen within range. Meanwhile the high ground to the left rear of the advance guard was occupied by one of the K.O.S.B. Companies from the main body. No guns were found, and the order was then and there given to retire in a north-easterly direction to search for the ammunition. The K.O.S.B. Companies, with the main body, were withdrawn and sent off first—probably half an hour at least before any retrograde movement by the other units of the force commenced. These had gone about two miles, and had reached the hill overlooking the spot where the ammunition was said to be, when by a lucky chance General Dixon changed his mind and said the troops could return to camp.

In commencing to retire, " E " Company, which was under the command of Lieutenant Gilson, with whom were Lieutenants Hodgson and Milward, now became the leading unit, followed by the two guns and a howitzer, then the two Companies of the K.O.S.B.'s, and finally, at a further distance,

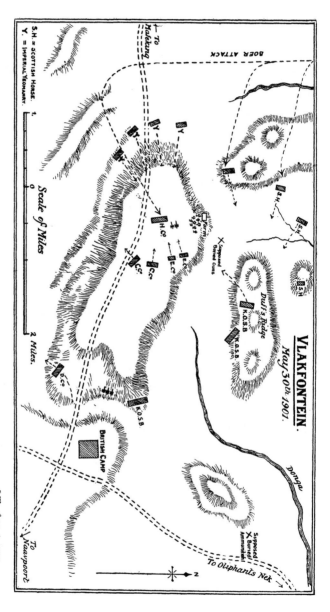

VLAKFONTEIN.
May 30th 1901.

BOER ATTACK

To Mafeking

Scale of Miles

0   2 Miles.

S.H. = SCOTTISH HORSE.
Y. = IMPERIAL YEOMANRY.

Duff's Ridge

K.O.S.B.

K.O.S.B.

Supposed Buried Guns

BRITISH CAMP

Donga

Supposed Buried Ammunition

To Naauwport

To Oliphants Nek

[To face p. 123.

the old right-flank guard. The former advanced guard should by now have reached camp, but it seems to have been followed up almost as soon as it began to retire and came into action about 2,600 yards to the west of the camp. But at this time Major Chance does not seem to have anticipated any real attack, for the Yeomanry were still covering his rear, and especially his unguarded left-*right*, as he retired. Just now, however, a big veldt fire—lighted of course by the enemy—began to come down on the guns and infantry with great rapidity. Behind the smoke were seen the figures of mounted men and men leading their horses, and everyone seems naturally enough to have taken these to be the Yeomanry covering the retirement.

The country to the left was open veldt, which to an inexperienced eye might have appeared flat. Earlier in the day large bodies of the enemy had been seen moving north-west, into the heart of the Magalies Valley; but, beyond doubt, these riding under cover of a supplementary valley or minor depression, running from north to south, crossed the front of the advanced guard unnoticed. They probably deceived the Yeomanry by means of their khaki—as has been already suggested—and came upon " H " Company with a suddenness and determined courage, which gave an ugly aspect to the engagement from the very first.

The bulk of the Yeomanry came back at the gallop, leaving the south wholly unguarded. Kemp's 1,500 men followed fast through the smoke of the burning veldt fire, decimating the Yeomanry as they retired by a fire which burst instantaneously from the whole commando.

The opening phase of the action was as much to the credit of the enemy as its close was to their disgrace. It ranks, with Nooitgedacht and Moedwil, as one of Kemp's most daring enterprises; and even if he had all Delarey's Commandos behind him, and though the portion of the

British force attacked numbered but four hundred, he charged deliberately, in practically open country, into the very heart of a British column, relying upon suddenness for success.

And sudden indeed it was. Captain Sadler, who commanded " H " Company, had barely time to grasp the situation, face about to the south-west and partially extend. The two guns under Lieut. MacDougal—who at one time had been one of the old Welverdiend garrison, and was greatly popular with the officers of that detachment—immediately unlimbered and sent two case-shells into the oncoming Boers before the whole body was upon them.

The next few minutes are such as a man is apt to remember, yet of which he can afterwards give no definite account. It must have been now that the bulk of the casualties occurred. They were surprised, outnumbered, and all the odds—moral and physical—were well on the other side. Captain Sadler, with his subalterns — Lieutenants Armstrong and Rimington—kept their men steady, and Lieutenant MacDougal coolly gave orders to his gunners up to the very last moment; but no courage, individual or collective, could serve to turn the scale.

" H " Company were outnumbered by at least five or six to one; and for the first few seconds the men must have fallen like flies in a trap. Captain Sadler seized a rifle from a dead soldier and fired into the enemy; and, in drawing back the bolt, a bullet carried away his thumb. " Look at your thumb," cried Rimington, very excitedly, and shortly afterwards had to look to himself, with a badly fractured thigh. Another bullet pierced his foot, another his calf, and another the other thigh. Captain Sadler, besides losing a thumb, was hit in the back, the arm and the upper part of the thigh; and Lieutenant Armstrong was also wounded in the leg. Of the 100 men in " H " Company,

Colour-Sergeant Herrod brought only *twenty-eight* out of action at the close of the fight.

And all this was but an affair of minutes. " E " Company at once extended and advanced from the northern edge of the camp ridge, while the remaining guns and the howitzer came into action on the left of the infantry.

Owing to the fact that the ground along this ridge was exceedingly broken, and also that, owing to the suddenness of the order, the three officers of the company found themselves on the same flank, " E " Company line became divided in the advance, the Colour-Sergeant being in command on the left.

As Lieutenant Gilson was about to halt in order to re-establish touch with the remainder of the company, the Royal Artillery guns to the front wheeled about and opened fire upon the British lines. Whereupon, not considering it a time suited to delay, he continued to advance, with Lieutenants Hodgson and Milward and the handful of men on the right of the company, and soon came under a heavy fire. As the guns were obviously even then in the hands of the enemy, this party moved forward at the double, thereby increasing their distance from the remainder of the company.

What had actually happened was this : The enemy had passed through Captain Sadler's Company and come upon the guns, which, of course, were unable to offer any resistance. Nearly all the men and horses of the section were down, and Lieutenant MacDougal lay between the guns mortally wounded. The story goes, that when Kemp's men first seized the guns, desiring to open fire without delay upon the British, and being at a loss as to how to set the fuses, they ordered the wounded officer to do so for them, or at least to show them how : this MacDougal gallantly refused to do ; whereupon they threatened him, with loaded rifles levelled at his head. But he even then stoutly defied them—as indeed it was within him to have done—and, if the story be true—and two of his men afterwards testified to its accuracy, else it would never be here—he met his death as heroically and in as good a cause as it was possible for any man to do.

In the meantime Lieutenant Gilson's men had closed with the enemy; and considering the severity of the fire, they had lost few enough during their advance. But on ascending the higher ground, occupied by the Boers, the fire in that quarter suddenly ceased, and a large party of men, dressed in khaki, advanced towards them, calling out that they were Yeomanry and telling them in English not to fire—"the confidence trick" again! For some time Lieutenant Gilson was deceived, and the two parties drew nearer and nearer. But when within only a few yards of each other, some black-coated figures came up in rear of the alleged Yeomanry and joined the same party, and when the Commandant, a man of immaculate appearance, and standing a good head and shoulders above his companions, turned and ordered these back, he no longer had any doubt, and immediately ordered his men to open fire. But so convinced were the majority that it actually was the Yeomanry who were before them, that all hesitated to obey the order; and it was only an individual command to Lance-Corporal Hook, who fell dead almost immediately he had dropped the Boer leader, that commenced the firing. In two or three minutes nearly every man on either side lay dead or wounded; seven dead Boers were afterwards found upon this spot, and others may have been carried off.

Then those who remained wounded or alive fired at each other through the long grass at a point blank range. It is difficult to say how long this lasted, probably only an additional few minutes — it seemed more — for the position, the majority being badly wounded and unable to fire or move, was hardly an enviable one. It was at this time that Lieutenant Milward crossed to Lieutenant Gilson, who was wounded, at the latter's own request, and gave the order in stentorian tones for the men to fix bayonets. Probably four men remained capable of doing so ; but the command might have been given to a division, and the order had the desired effect ; for the enemy's fire immediately slackened and finally ceased ; and to crawl, broadside on, across the front of and at a hand's-breadth from a line of Mauser rifles, was an act of sufficient gallantry in itself.

While all this was in progress, a combined attack was made on the south and south-west sides of the camp. Everybody who could handle a rifle, from the prisoners upwards, was turned out ; and " C " Company, from the western picquet, advanced in the direction of the captured guns, while " D " moved to the south-west towards a farmstead, in occupation of the enemy. Also the right-flank guard were by now fast approaching the camp from the north, and the tide of the action began to turn.

Major Browne, the Intelligence Officer, was with " C " Company, and it was he who organised the advance and final rush, led by Lieutenant Manby, which induced the enemy, with the help, no doubt, of the heavy shelling they were now experiencing, to fall back ; and this was the signal for a general retirement all along their line, leaving the guns once more in British hands.

Much to the dishonour of the Commando, which it cannot be denied had behaved very gallantly in the first instance, the close of the scene is marked by acts of the direst disgrace. It can never be urged that each burgher participated in the villainy, and neither is it to be supposed that Commandant Kemp sanctioned the deeds ; yet the depositions of many men upon their deathbeds cannot but be accepted as true :

dying men do not lie, and the large proportion of officers killed only goes to corroborate what is more than mere suspicion, that many wounded—especially the Yeomanry Officers—were shot upon the field.

The casualties were very severe, and in the case of the original advanced guard amounted to over fifty per cent. Of the 13 officers with this party, 8 were killed and 4 wounded—two in several places ; Major Chance, the commander of the force, alone escaping unhurt. Seven men only remained of the gun section and 29 of " H " Company, while the total casualties among the Yeomanry amounted to 58. In all 61 were killed or died of wounds. The Battalion suffered 20 killed, 59 wounded and 5 missing. Many of the wounded had narrow escapes from the fire, which rapidly spread across the ground ; and Captain Keller was very badly burnt at the close of the action in attempting to get a wounded man away from the danger.

The Boer casualties were roughly estimated at 57 dead, with a proportionately large number of wounded.

The wounded men were not all brought in until after dark, and a few of the dangerous cases were very wisely left out on the field all night, having tents pitched over them and blankets provided. The killed were buried on the afternoon of the following day—the dead of the Artillery and of the Regiment in one grave, and the Yeomanry in another.

The whole of the 30th the vedettes on either side watched each other across some 2,000 yards of neutral ground, about which the stretcher-bearers went to and fro. But as General Dixon had reason to believe that De la Rey's main body was rapidly approaching to support Kemp, and as his column—isolated as it was in a difficult country—had already suffered severely, he that night marched back to Naauwpoort by a circuitous route, leaving his crowded field hospital upon the veldt to find its own way into Krugersdorp.

After a week's halt at Naauwpoort, General Dixon's Column again set out, on 7th June, across the Magalies River towards Oliphant's Nek.

Naturally enough he met with much petty opposition upon the flanks, etc., when crossing the Valley; but eventually he reached Oliphant's Nek, late in the day, having suffered only 4 casualties in all.

The following day, acting in conjunction with several other columns, under the command of Colonel Fetherstone-haugh, General Dixon's Column was ordered to seize Boschhoek; but as this *Nek* was nearly twenty-three miles to the north-west, the mounted troops were sent on alone and seized the place by night, when they captured one of Kemp's despatch riders. The Infantry marched through Rustenburg to Boekenhoutfontein, and thence on to Boschhoek the following day.

After three days halt at this place, the Column moved, *via* Magato's Village to Selons Kraal, whence Captain Rigby and a party of men participated in a hazardous expedition to Ratsegai's Kraal, capturing three or four prisoners. Two days later, the Boers had their revenge. The General had taken part of his force out about six miles from Selons Kraal, when a small body of Scottish Horse became sur-rounded in a house. The remainder of the expedition went away, not knowing what straits they were in, until finally one of their men got through, who reported that they were still holding out, but could not do so much longer. Never-theless, it was decided to leave the party to their fate; they held out until all their ammunition was expended and then surrendered.

On the 27th the Column marched back again to Magato Nek, where it remained until 1st July. On the night of the

I

30th Captain Phelps seized the Nek at Boschhoek with thirty men, and the remainder of the force arrived at the same place on the following day. On the 2nd a long march carried the Column to Brak-kloof, on the Eland's River, where it came in touch with a small commando under Van Tonder—the same man who had previously cut off the party of Scottish Horse. General Dixon halted here for two days to allow the other columns, under Colonels Fetherstonehaugh, Williams and Hickie, to close up. On the 2nd he moved along the Eland's Valley, but was not opposed, though Williams' troops near at hand were heavily engaged. A halt for one day was made at the next camp, during which the Scottish Horse again became engaged ; and, on the 7th, the Column crossed the Marico River and reached Zender-ling's Post on the 8th, and Zeerust, where the other three columns were already camped, two days later.

The Column halted two days at Zeerust, during which time it lost twenty-two gun horses, and had eleven more seriously ill, through eating a most poisonous bulb, called "tulp," which grew around the town. On the morning of the 13th the Column lost its way, and finished up about sixteen miles east of Mafeking. The march continued through Lichtenburg without any event of greater import than an engagement on the 17th, when a party under Captain Rigby, Lieutenant Manby and a Yeomanry officer was very nearly surrounded, and lost 1 man wounded and the Yeomanry officer killed. Halting a day at Ventersdorp, on the 19th, General Dixon again reached Welverdiend on the 21st, many of his men being by then practically bootless. Thence the Column moved along the line to Waterval, near Krugersdorp, and thence north again once more to its mountain home at Naauwpoort, which was reached on the 30th. Here several officers joined—Major Watts, Captains Green (wounded at Diamond Hill), Radford, Morley and

COLONEL C. N. WATTS.

[*Face page* 130.

Anley; Lieutenants Frend, Popham and Harvey, and Second - Lieutenants Mott and Becke on appointment. While Lieutenant Armstrong (wounded at Vlakfontein) and Second-Lieutenant Mills (on appointment) had previously picked up the Column at Welverdiend, and Dr. Worth—who at Naauwpoort had succeeded Major Duncan as Regimental Medical Officer—at Waterval.

Colonel Kekewich, C.B., the defender of Kimberley, who had taken over command of the Column from General Dixon at Waterval, did not remain at Naauwpoort, but moved across the old valley to Oliphant's Nek the following day.

Nevertheless, as Naauwpoort was the base from which the force had operated at its return to the place, a summary of the march is not here wholly out of place, especially as the Column was now entering upon a new set of operations and under the command of a new General.

The march had lasted from 7th June to 30th July—in other words, a period of fifty-five days—and had carried the Regiment round in a large circle, across the Magaliesberg to Rustenburg and back again to Zeerust; out towards Mafeking and back through Lichtenburg to Ventersdorp, and thence from Welverdiend along the well-known line to Krugersdorp, and finally back to Naauwpoort; in all, a total distance of about 320 miles.

CHAPTER IX

MOEDWIL

On 31st July Colonel Kekewich crossed the Magalies Valley with a large convoy, and received the usual attention from the local Boers as far as Oliphant's Nek; whence the Battalion and convoy proceeded to Rustenburg, its destination, under the command of Colonel Wylly. But by 3rd August the whole force was again back at Naauwpoort.

On the 5th the Column once again crossed to the Nek, and on the following day advanced eastward, north of the range, in two columns: the left one, with all the transport, under Colonel Kekewich; the right, composed of four companies, two squadrons, a gun and a pom-pom, under Colonel Wylly.

The latter column marched close under cover of the hills; and, for the first five miles, was accompanied by a party from the garrison of Oliphant's Nek, who came out to remove some families. The enemy, of course, were active in the neighbourhood; and the evicting party experienced some difficulty in getting away, and it was not until infantry had been deployed and guns brought into action that they were finally able to withdraw.

As the march progressed eastward, the country became even more difficult; when Colonel Wylly's Column debouched into a thickly-wooded basin, surrounded by low and rocky hills. The scouts immediately reported the ridges, 1,200 yards to the front, to be held by the enemy; and, soon afterwards, two or three hundred Boers were observed coming down the slopes of the Magaliesberg on the right. Under these circumstances there did not appear to be much time to lose. Major Watts, with "H" Company, under Captain Green, rushed the ridges in front, accompanied by the advance scouts of the Scottish Horse; while two more companies moved forward on the right of the road, the whole covered by the fire of the two guns—one of which was chiefly directed on the right of the ridge to keep off the advancing body above-mentioned. "H" Company gained the hill in a marvellously short time, capturing one prisoner on the top, who said that five of his friends had been wounded by the shell fire. After this, the enemy, having been forestalled in occupation of the higher ground, withdrew altogether; and the two columns again united in camp at Kroomrivier.

On the following day Colonel Kekewich seized the pass across the mountains, known as Breedt's Nek, without opposition, and, leaving four companies of the K.O.S.B.'s with a gun to hold the place, marched to Eland's Drift on the 8th.

Here the mounted troops collided with a small commando, driven north across the Magaliesberg by Colonel Allenby. Both parties were equally surprised; and, in the skirmish which ensued, the Boers lost 2 killed, 2 wounded, and 1 prisoner; and the British, 1 man killed and 1 officer wounded.

On the following day Colonel Kekewich marched to Boschfontein, where he remained until the 15th, when he suddenly doubled back and co-operated with Colonel Allenby.

Each column held the lower slopes of the Magaliesberg, and, at the same time, seized the crest-line of the precipitous range by night, at points seven miles distant. Major Watts, with "A" and "E" Companies, ascended above Boschfontein; and during the whole of the next day the columns closed in, taking over 40 prisoners—including Mr. Wolmarans, the former chairman of the Volksraad—and nearly 200 head of cattle.

On the 12th Colonel Kekewich returned to Boschfontein, and thence crossed again to the south of the mountains, camping at Grootplaatz, near Commando Nek.

On the 14th Captain Radford, with Lieutenants Manby and Mott and 80 men from Naauwpoort, co-operated with a party from Colonel Allenby's Column in an attack upon Basfontein, capturing 20 Boers and 150 head of cattle.

As General Barton, the senior Column Commander in the neighbourhood, desired to keep a force on the northern side of the Magaliesberg, part of Colonel Kekewich's Column marched through Commando Nek on the 16th to Zandfontein, where it was joined by the remainder on the following day, whence the whole pushed on to Bokfontein.

On the night of the 19th the Column, again in conjunction with Colonel Allenby, crept through the hills, along the Crocodile River, in an unsuccessful attempt to surprise Badenhorst's Commando.

From Wolverkraal, on the Crocodile, the force moved to Zoutpan's Drift, where the men of the Regiment, the Scottish Horse and part of Allenby's Column, hotly engaged each other in error, but fortunately with no casualties, though the Scottish Horse were afterwards able to congratulate the Regiment on their uncomfortably accurate shooting.

Thence the two columns marched seventeen miles northwards, down the Crocodile Valley, through the thick bush on either side of the river, and thence turned south, circling to the west, thirty-six miles back again to Boschfontein, which was reached on the 26th. During this march 28 surrenders came in to the Column ; and, on the 27th, Captain Green, in charge of a convoy to Colonel Allenby, captured 2 more.

Leaving Boschfontein once more, on the afternoon of the

30th, Colonel Kekewich covered forty-six miles in fifty-four hours, and, passing through Rustenburg, reached Magato Nek on 1st September. Kemp and Delarey, with 800 men, were reported to be in the district west of Naauwpoort, and large parties of Boers, driven from the north, had slipped through at Boschhoek and joined them. Columns under Colonels Gilbert Hamilton, Fetherstonehaugh, Williams and Hickie were fast closing in from the south and west : Colonel Allenby was to seize Boschhoek, and stop the northern exit, while Colonel Kekewich marched south to Selons River, and Lord Methuen, with a large mounted force, held himself in readiness to pursue any Boers who might succeed in breaking back across the mountain range.

When Colonel Kekewich had reached Doornlaagte, it did not appear that the cordon was complete, for Allenby's guns were heard in rear, whereas he should have been on Kekewich's right, closing in on Roodeval, where Delarey's laager was said to be. And such, unfortunately, proved to be the case; the bulk of the enemy, under Delarey and Steinkamp escaped north-west, and the remainder, under Kemp, westward; all then turned back towards Pretoria, to meet the Commandant-General, Louis Botha, on the 15th, the date from which Lord Kitchener's latest proclamation threatened the Boer leaders with exile.

On 3rd September Kekewich's and Gilbert Hamilton's Column lay camped at Roodeval, and on the following day three parties went out in the same direction to try and " round up " any dismounted Boers who might be hidden in the bushy kloofs and dongas, scattered all over this part of the country. The left party, which consisted of two companies, under Major Watts, took 20 prisoners, the other two only 4 between them. The majority of these were caught in thick bush, though a few had emulated Charles II., of happy memory, and had sought to hide themselves in trees.

On 5th September the mounted men went far afield, and returned in the evening with 28 prisoners: 4 more were brought in that morning; and Captain Anley's company captured an additional 3: so that in three days the Column had taken 59 in all.

The following day Colonel Kekewich marched to Kopperfontein, filling his empty waggons on the way with families, amongst whom was a Dutch maiden — Susannah Meyer, the betrothed of General Kemp—and another, the sister of Delarey.

On 7th September the Column reached Basfontein, the camp of 28th May—the day before the action of Vlakfontein. Here they stumbled across Mrs. Smuts—wife of the General of that name, whose happy hunting-grounds, it will be remembered, are on or about the Gatsrand—who had come out from Pretoria with a white flag to try and find her husband.

Capturing 8 more prisoners on the 9th, the Column again reached Naauwpoort on the following day, completing another trek, in which a total of 144 prisoners had been taken, and nearly 600 women and children collected for the refugee camps.

After a halt of a day the Column again marched out of Naauwpoort, on 12th September. A violent wind was blowing, and the road to Oliphant's Nek was ankle-deep in dust; and in consequence the march was none of the pleasantest. The force camped that night within the *Nek;* and, early on the following morning, "E," "F" and half of "H" Companies, under Colonel Wylly, passed out of the Nek again and climbed, by the steepest possible ascent, to the top of the Magaliesberg. Meanwhile "A," "C" and the other half of "H" Companies, under Major Watts, moved along the foot of the northern slopes, parallel to the party on the top; while Colonel Kekewich

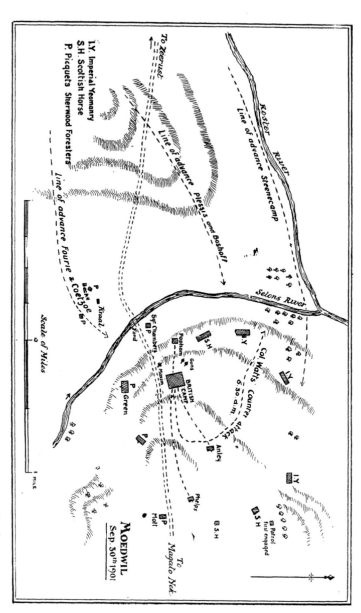

I.Y. Imperial Yeomanry
S.H. Scottish Horse
P. Picquets Sherwood Foresters

To Zeerust

Line of advance Steenecamp

Line of advance Plessis and Bosthoff

Line of advance Fourie & Coetzee

Koster River

Selons River

Col. Watts' Counter attack 6.30 a.m.

Sgt Chambers
Popham
Pond
S.H.
Y.
Guns
BRITISH CAMP
Green
Anley
Mann
Phelps
Mott
S.H.
I.Y.
S.H.
P = Kraal.
Bezhe &
Coetzee

Patrol first engaged

To Magato Nek

Scale of Miles

MILE

MOEDWIL
Sep. 30th 1901

[To face p. 137.

marched the remainder of the force seven miles on to
Rhenosterfontein.   The Battalion captured in all 36
prisoners, including Field-Cornet Kloppers, 24 being
taken by "F" Company, under Captain Anley.

Thence Colonel Kekewich's Force moved to Waagfontein
against Commandant Else, and when about to leave this
place to go north to the Crocodile River, he was ordered
south again by Lord Kitchener to participate in the
usual Delarey - Kemp drive, and thereupon returned to
Rhenosterfontein, where the K.O.S.B.'s discovered 7,000
rounds of ammunition hidden in the kloofs.

On the 22nd the Column reached Magato Nek, by
way of Rustenburg, where Colonel Kekewich was ordered
to give up one of his Infantry Battalions for the Frederickstad block-house line : as the Regiment was just then
luckily the stronger battalion, the Brigadier sent the
King's Own Scottish Borderers.

On the 23rd the Column, now greatly diminished in
strength, marched to the Selons River, within earshot of
Colonel Hickie's guns, and heard a rumour that Kemp
had fled.

But the Boers were still in the district ; and on the
next day's march to Waterval, through a country and
along a road which did not appear to have been previously
traversed by any column, Captain Rigby, in charge of
the rear - guard, was attacked and obliged to bring the
machine-gun into action to induce the enemy to retire.
Marching by way of Brak-kloof, Colonel Kekewich reached
Lindley's Poort on the 26th, and there received the
information that Kemp and Delarey were only eight
miles off, at Vrede, and had just been joined by Van
Tonder, with 200 men from the Dreierberg.   That night
the mounted men reconnoitred towards this place but
failed to locate any of the enemy.

Colonel Kekewich was now made aware that the other two columns had turned back; while there were no tidings at all of Lord Methuen, who had been expected to co-operate; and Kekewich was marching leisurely back towards Rustenburg, stopping here and there to destroy the crops which were coming on very abundantly, when he reached Moedwil, on the banks of the Selons River, on 29th September. It was not an ideal position for the river, which, on the north and north-west, ran round the better part of two sides of the camp, was hidden in broken, and in places precipitous, ground, covered with thick bush. The mounted troops were picqueted along the river - banks, the other two sides—where there was also a good deal of low scrub—being guarded by the Regiment.

On the evening of the 29th about 60 mounted men and "F" Company, under Captain Rigby and Lieutenant Murray, were sent on into Naauwpoort, *via* Rustenburg, with the empty waggons to refill.

At 4.30 on the morning of the 30th, when the moon was waning and dawn had not yet appeared, a picquet of the Imperial Yeomanry on the river - bank, at the extreme north-west of the camp, sent out a patrol, which had only gone a few yards when it came upon a number of Boers advancing through the scrub from the front, and upon others who had evidently approached along the front of the picquets found by the mounted troops, by way of the river-bed. This patrol and the picquet to which it belonged were at once overpowered and nearly all shot down. However, the noise, of course; immediately alarmed the camp, and the men came tumbling out from under the flies of the tents; but the Boers were already well advanced, and the fire became at once very heavy indeed, several men being hit before they could leave their tents.

The companies under Captain Phelps and Lieutenant Popham were at once sent off through the camp towards the enemy. Captain Phelps' company shortly afterwards returned for their bayonets, and then for the rest of the fight held the east face of the camp itself. Lieutenant Popham, with whom were Second-Lieutenants Milward and Mills, advanced his company on the other flank, followed by Major Watts and Captain Keller, carrying a box of ammunition. These two officers then returned to the camp and there separated, Major Watts going to the east and Captain Keller towards the Maxim at the south-west corner of the camp, where he fell, dangerously wounded, with a bullet in the abdomen.

Meanwhile Captain Anley had taken another party towards the north-east side of the camp, which was not strongly picqueted, and where he too was severely wounded in the leg.

Small parties of the enemy, attempting to make their way along the front of the camp, were held in check by two small picquets, under Second-Lieutenant Becke, established in two houses some distance out.

The Column was now entirely surrounded; for, shortly afterwards, musketry fire broke out on the southern side, where " H " Company were on picquet. The overwhelming of the Yeomanry picquet had enabled the Boers— who were here led by Kemp in person—to penetrate to the very heart of the Column and to within short range of the guns, which were with great difficulty kept in action ; but this had also left a gap in the picquet line, of which the Boers were quick to avail themselves; and they established themselves on the flank and within a short distance of " H " Company's right picquet, among some rocks overlooking the drift.

This post consisted of 12 men under Sergeant Chambers.

The Boers called on him to surrender, but he told them to "go to hell," and called to his men, "Stick to it, men, stick to it!" This became a sort of rallying cry among them, and as each was hit, the survivors passed on the word. Of these gallant 13, 9 were killed or died of wounds, 3 were wounded, and only 1 man, Private Picard, was untouched. (The Boer prisoners, who were taken during the action, acknowledged the services of this picquet in checking their advance, and declared that Sergeant Chambers must have had at least 100 men under his command.)

The three guns had come early into action in front of the centre of the camp; they were, however, quite out in the open and terribly exposed under a hail of bullets—as indeed was every part of the camp. The Colonel commanding the Column, Colonel Kekewich, was twice wounded near the guns, about half-way through the action, and the command therefore devolved upon Lieut.-Colonel Wylly. The A.D.C. and Captain Baldwin, the D.A.A.G., were also hit. One of the guns was silenced early in the action, owing to so many of the detachment being down: 2 of the 3 artillery officers were wounded — 1 mortally. Later the pom-pom jammed; and Sergeant Naylor, R.A., though badly wounded in the leg, kept on returning under a heavy fire to his gun to try and get it again into working order.

The Maxim, under Corporal Simpson, had early come into action, and maintained its ground right well, until 6 of the 9 men composing the detachment were wounded. Here Private Bees, who received the Victoria Cross for his gallantry, and Private Brierly greatly distinguished themselves: the former, hearing his wounded comrades asking for water, went down to the river, running the gauntlet of a number of Boers, who were firing from

within a hundred yards; Private Brierly went sixty
yards under a hot fire to fetch water for the gun from
the officers' mess—the kettle he carried being hit several
times. Poor young Second-Lieutenant Mills was killed
alongside Popham in the advance towards the river:
he showed the greatest keenness and disregard of danger.
Even the men of the company, when advancing, cautioned
him not to expose himself too much, and he replied:
"Never mind me, men; there they are—shoot, shoot!"
He was himself shot through the head and died about
midday, never regaining consciousness. He would have
made a fine soldier had he been spared. Afterwards
the men of his company sent a deputation to Captain
Green, asking that their sympathy and regret might be
expressed to poor Mill's people.

By 6 a.m. the fire had appreciably lessened, and the
men of the Regiment had mastered the enemy in the
river-bed, where several were bayoneted and shot at the
closest quarters.

By 6.15 the Boers were in full retreat, availing themselves equally skilfully of cover in their retirement as
they had done in their advance. They left on the field
6 dead, 7 wounded, and 3 unwounded prisoners; but
they acknowledged losses mounting up to nearly 90.
Of their dead, one was Commandant Boshof, the leader of
their scouts; Kemp himself led the main attack, and at
one time actually had penetrated almost into the camp.
One of the prisoners, the Private Secretary of Commandant
Van Heerden, was tried and convicted of treachery under
the white flag, and shot on the morning of 2nd October.

The total losses of the Battalion amounted to 63, of
whom 21, including poor young Mills, were killed or
died of wounds. In addition to those officers already
mentioned, Second-Lieutenant Hodgson was also hit; a

spent bullet just penetrated into the flesh of his thigh, but he operated upon it himself on the ground, with the assistance of Second-Lieutenant Milward, with a rusty pen-knife ! The casualties among the force totalled 191 ; of these 57 were killed or died of wounds, while 27 officers were hit and 5 died. The Column suffered also very heavily in horses and mules, 307 horses and 185 mules being either killed or so seriously wounded that they had to be destroyed.

From Boer accounts it seems that the enemy, become desperate from shortness of food and ammunition supplies, had for some time been concentrating, in view of attacking an isolated column. Throughout the previous week they had been holding Fetherstonehaugh's two columns with a weak screen, while they lay in wait for Kekewich at a spot a little way north of the main road. They thought he was making for Zeerust, and their intention was to rush the camp by night, trusting to their screen in front of General Fetherstonehaugh to prevent his coming north to Kekewich's assistance. Unfortunately for the success of this well-conceived scheme, Colonel Kekewich did not go to Zeerust, but marched back late one afternoon to a previous camp, and then, fairly rapidly, to Moedwil, which the Boers attacked on Monday morning, after having made a forced march of twenty-three miles on the previous Sunday. One thousand two hundred men are said to have come on under Delarey, who, however, does not appear to have taken any very leading part in the action, the conduct of which he left to General Kemp and Commandants Van Heerden and Steinkamp ; General Beyers, who had daily been expected from the north, is also believed to have been present, if not actually actively engaged. This force was to have attacked instantaneously on three sides. All engaged were very confident, and there is little doubt that had Van Heerden and Steinkamp acted as vigorously as did Kemp, things might have gone badly indeed with the British force.

Since the retrograde movement after Vlakfontein had had so encouraging an effect upon the enemy, it was decided to remain at Moedwil, in spite of the fact that Colonel Williams' Column alone was within easy supporting distance.

While the action was in progress, helio messages had been sent off to Rustenburg asking for ambulances and medical officers. Civil-Surgeon Worth, who had served for nine months with the Battalion, had only left on the previous evening, on the termination of his engagement under Government. He had reached Rustenburg—fifteen miles distant—early on the morning of the 30th, and then learnt how greatly medical aid was needed; for the only two doctors then with the Column had themselves been wounded. Dr. Worth at once asked leave to return: this was refused; whereupon he promptly turned his pony's head and galloped off to Moedwil to lend assistance. One pony dropped in the first seven miles, whereupon he borrowed another one and rode it to a standstill just outside the camp. It will be long before the Battalion forgets this act of prompt devotion on the part of Civil-Surgeon Worth.

Colonel Williams moved quickly to the help of the crippled Column; and as General Fetherstonehaugh was also on the move, by 1st October, the anxiety of a second attack was removed.

On the following day the remainder of the wounded went into Rustenburg, some 90 or more having been sent in on the evening of the day of the fight.

The dead of the Battalion were buried on the field; not so many miles away from Vlakfontein, across the Magalies

Valley, where a similar trench lies near the scene of the other action.   Tombstones have long since been erected in both these lonely cemeteries, and stand to-day, not only in memorial to those who fell, but also in testimony of the honour of the Regiment, in whose service they gave their lives.

CHAPTER X

RUSTENBURG

AFTER the action of Moedwil, the Regiment was ordered to relieve the Norfolk Regiment in occupation of Rustenburg and the adjacent passes through the Magaliesberg.

The Battalion were all unfeignedly sorry to leave Colonel Kekewich's command—though all had been continuously on the march for the last six months, and were glad enough of the rest—and when, a week later, Colonel Kekewich, after a marvellous recovery from his wounds, went out from Rustenburg to resume the command of his Column, all ranks parted from him with the greatest regret ; for the Battalion can seldom have served under a more charming and more considerate or more appreciative Commander. He was escorted as he left the town by an escort, composed of the subalterns of the Regiment.

The Regimental Headquarters remained in Rustenburg for the concluding six months of the War. Colonel Wylly was made Commandant of the Rustenburg District, which comprised an area of ten thousand square miles ; and the Commandant's pay — the lordly sum of eighteenpence a day—seems absurdly inadequate for the administration of a realm the size of the Netherlands.

Lieutenant Popham acted as Staff officer to Colonel Wylly. The troops under his command were distributed as follows :—

K

At Magato Nek—Captain Green, with "H" and half "A" Companies, a gun and a few Yeomanry.

At Oliphant's Nek — Captain Radford, with "E" Company, two guns and some Yeomanry, the whole under Major Young, R.A.

At Breedt's Nek—Captain Morley with 70 men.

At Groblaar's Pass—(Temporarily occupied).

On the Naauwpoort-Oliphant's Nek Block-house Line— Lieutenant Frend, with "F" Company.

At Rustenburg — Colonel Wylly, the Regimental Headquarters and Staff, the remainder of the Battalion, one gun and 50 Yeomanry.

During all this long period, practically nothing of an exciting nature occurred. Columns occasionally visited Rustenburg, under Colonel Kekewich or Colonel Colenbrander, who operated most frequently in the neighbourhood, for choice. But as a general rule there were hardly any troops to the north of the Magaliesberg, west of the Pretoria-Pietersburg Railway line. The "horse-sickness" kept the Boers from the "bush-veldt" district; in fact, the Rustenburg Commando had lost over a hundred animals by February, and it was found necessary to abandon the South African Constabulary posts along the Rustenburg-Pretoria Road during the "horse-sickness" season.

Still a few dismounted Boers continued to wander about the country; and Captain Morley captured one near Breedt's Nek, and had one of his men slightly wounded in trying to catch another on the following day. On one occasion one of the block-houses at the same place was sniped for half an hour; and on another, Private Paget narrowly escaped falling into the enemy's hands.

Late in October the 2nd Volunteer Company, under

Captain Goodman, with Lieutenants Webb and Marsden, arrived.

In December Captain and Brevet-Major Phelps left for the Orange River Colony to take over command of No. 2 Mounted Infantry Company; and Captain Radford went to the M.I. a few months later. In February Major Gordon Cumming and Lieutenant French arrived from England.

Soon after this Schalk Burger, with the remnant of the Transvaal Government, was reported to have moved west, in order to confer with Delarey; and Colonel Colenbrander's Column was despatched to seize the party. But as no trace could be found of the President and his men, Colenbrander — who was celebrated for the rapidity with which he moved — disappeared as quickly as he had come, and retired, across the Magaliesberg, into the "high-veldt" beyond, away from the "horse sickness."

Two days after they had gone, news came that a party, suspiciously like the so-called President and his Government, had been sighted at a place called Veekraal, forty-five miles north-east of Rustenburg. Lord Kitchener wired that he thought these must be the "expected guests"; and it was resolved to try and block the passes without any outside assistance.

By great exertions about 150 Infantry and 45 mounted men were scraped together, the command being given to Major Watts. It was an awful night, rain had been falling all day, and as the men stole quietly from their posts to rendezvous on the north side of the town, rain was coming down in torrents. No waggons accompanied the party, for it was intended to forward rations, blankets, etc., the next day. By 6.30 on the following morning all passes up to the Eland's River had been seized and occupied, and considering the awful state of the roads and the fact that Boschhoek — the furthest pass — was some twenty-four miles off, the march was a most creditable one.

Lord Kitchener had wired for Colenbrander to return, but he was some way off, and the roads were so bad that he was not able to lend support till the fourth day, so would have been too late to catch Schalk Burger had that astute gentleman attempted to break through. On 9th March the troops came in, after being out just over a week, it appearing that the Veekraal party was either not the Government at all, or that Schalk Burger had left it and gone east again.

In April a magnificent draft of 107 old soldiers from the 2nd Battalion, together with 23 volunteers, under Lieutenant Blackwell, arrived at Rustenburg; and, on the following day, the 2nd Volunteer Company, which had served some time in the country, before joining the Battalion, left for England.

Soon after this, sniping occurred on the Naauwpoort-Oliphant's Nek Block-house Line; and in consequence a drive was arranged along the valley. No Boers were seen or captured; but Major Watts had the misfortune to be shot through the left foot by some of the Middlesex M.I., who were co-operating, and took Major Watts and his party for the enemy.

On the morning of 1st June peace was declared; the good news reached Rustenburg when the Battalion was in church, and was given out at the close of the service. In the afternoon the band and drums played up and down the main street, before a crowd of beaming faces, finishing up with "Rule Britannia" and the "National Anthem," followed by three cheers for the King, which were given with tremendous heartiness.

On the next day a message was received from the Quarter-Master General, asking for 1 officer, 3 N.C.O.'s and 7 privates, to be detailed to attend the Coronation of King Edward VII.

The following party was specially selected, and, four hours after the order had been received, was on its way to Krugersdorp :—

Captain and Brevet-Major Rigby.

Sergeant Gilham	-	" A " Company.
,, Bishop -	-	" E " ,,
Lance-Sergeant Lymn -		" H " ,,
Private Graham -	-	" A " ,,
,, Radborne	-	" C " ,,
,, Hartley -	-	" D " ,,
,, Pawson -	-	" E " ,,
,, Cunningham -		" F " ,,
,, Gould -	-	" H " ,,
,, Yeomans	-	" H " ,,

This party were not actually destined to take part in the Coronation Procession, however ; for, on 25th June, the news reached Rustenburg of the King's serious illness and the consequent postponement of the ceremony.

A week after the declaration of peace a mounted party, under Lieutenants Mayall and Hodgson, were sent as escort to Lieutenant Popham, who represented the Government, and had received orders to visit all the native chiefs for miles around, as far as the Pilansberg, and to warn them on no account to molest unarmed Dutchmen.

On the afternoon of 8th June the first batch of the 11,000 Boers, who had surrendered to General Walter Kitchener at Doornkom, came into Rustenburg. This was the Pretoria Commando, under Liebenberg, and numbered

72 all told. Liebenberg himself was decently dressed, and
Kemp's secretary, who accompanied him also; but the
others of his Staff seemed to take little or no pride in
their appearance.

The A.D.C. was garbed in a suiting such as is worn in
the engine - room of an ocean tramp: he wore one spur
(the Adjutant wore its fellow), and on his head was a
toy straw hat, such as the comic man *might* wear in a
transpontine pantomime; this was kept on his head by
means of a chin-strap, obviously fashioned from an aged
boot - lace. The Adjutant, bearded like the Pard, wore a
red handkerchief round his neck, the slouchiest of slouch-
hats on his head, and boots like waders. This Commando
was patchy as to its nether-garments, but the Rustenburg
Commando, which came in the following day, under Field-
Cornet Breetz, was clothed *entirely* in patches of the most
gorgeous hues, [causing it to present the appearance of a
parterre of rather wilted flowers. But they were, for the
most part, good, simple fellows; and each was under a
mistaken impression that Colonel Wylly, as Commandant
of Rustenburg, was personally cognisant of his wife's latest
address.

All these men had to be disarmed, which was rather a
long job, in spite of the fact that all were anxious to get
off to Pretoria, and few would even wait for the rations
they were offered. Nevertheless their demeanour was, on
the whole, most excellent: some few of course were surly;
but the majority seemed even then to recognise that they
had fought a good fight and had been beaten, and actually
said that they would for the future be as loyal to King
Edward as they had hitherto been to their own Government.

Now, at the date of writing, four years have passed since
then, and a Liberal Government is about to trust these men
so soon with the government of the great country, on which,

throughout the period with which this record deals, so many millions of pounds and so many thousands of lives were spent to make a British Colony. One can only sincerely hope and trust that Lord Milner's judgment is, at least, for once at fault.

CHAPTER XI

WITH NO. 1 ("B") COMPANY, DERBYSHIRE M.I.

No. 1 Company, Derbyshire M.I., which afterwards was incorporated with the 10th Battalion of Mounted Infantry, was raised at Philip's Farm, near Cyphergat, Cape Colony, on 25th January, 1900. It was commanded by Major Godley, with whom were Lieutenants Casswell and Watson. Colour - Sergeant Ewin, was made Sergeant-Major; and Sergeant Dodd, Quarter - Master Sergeant. The sections were commanded by Sergeants Heapy, Seaton, Storer and Caudwell. All the men were volunteers; and, with a few exceptions, all had previously been through an M.I. course. They were mounted, for the most part, on Argentine horses—a breed of animal which proved far from satisfactory throughout the campaign — and were supplied with English - made Colonial saddles. The total strength of the Company at the time of its formation was 3 officers and 103 N.C.O.'s and men, with separate transport complete.

As will be remembered, the Company at first formed part of General Gatacre's Division, and up to the end of April served with the same force as the Infantry Battalion itself. One of Colonel Smith - Dorrien's final duties, before leaving Philip's Farm to take up the ommand of the 19th Brigade, was to inspect Major Godley's newly-formed body of men and wish them the best of luck; and a few days afterwards General Gatacre visited the Company for the first time, and expressed great satisfaction at the workman-like appearance of the men.

When the advanced camp, under Colonel Cunningham, was formed at Cyphergat, the enforced inactivity, which it was the lot of the Infantry Battalion to bear, was not shared by the Mounted Infantry Company. On 14th February a strong mounted reconnaissance, with guns, was made to Pope's Farm; but without encountering the enemy's patrols. A similar movement in the direction of Stormberg itself, on the 16th, succeeded, however, in drawing the enemy's artillery fire; and thus, a few days after its formation, the Company received its baptism of fire. Four days later another expedition was made to the north of Pen Hoek, where De Montmorency had reported 250 Boers off-saddled at a farm. The mounted troops galloped eight miles to surround the place; but the enemy had already received notice of their coming, through the British scouts themselves, who had foolishly opened fire, and only 2 prisoners were taken.

Thus it will be seen that during the occupation of Cyphergat, as the advanced post of the Third Division, the Company were sufficiently employed to gain some knowledge of the kind of work which lay before them; and, as time went on, that work gradually became of a more serious and determined character. The 23rd was the day of the great reconnaissance in force, during which De Montmorency lost his life. As this has been dealt with fully elsewhere, it is only here necessary to repeat that the Company advanced in the centre of the long line of mounted troops, which moved that day against the Rooikop. Being in the first line of the British advance, and knowing that General Gatacre's idea was to entice the enemy from their position, they were at first overjoyed at the success of the plan, when the enemy showed themselves bold enough to follow up their guarded retreat upon the hidden Infantry and Artillery. They were, therefore, astounded at the sudden disclosure of their position by the British guns, at the very moment when the retirement was well in progress; and it was not until later on that memorable day that they heard of the sad catastrophe on the right, and of the death-trap into which De Montmorency's Scouts had fallen, that so altered the very head and front of the whole action. As for the rest of the fight, the Company played its part in covering the general retirement, which, however, was not followed up by the Boers; but it must be borne in mind that during the earlier part of the day they had come under a severe shell and rifle fire, and had had a greater taste of the meaning of war than the Battalion itself experienced until three weeks later at Bethulie Bridge. They had two horses killed and six wounded, and were lucky to escape with no other casualties.

After this the Company were almost daily employed in reconnoitring uneventfully the surrounding country; as the Boers, already preparing to evacuate Stormberg, had unscientifically drawn in their outposts and patrols, leaving the country to the south in peace.

On 2nd March the 10th Battalion of Mounted Infantry was officially formed, the command being given to Lieut.-Colonel Sitwell of the Northumberland Fusiliers, and Lieutenant Watson becoming Adjutant. The Battalion was composed of the following Companies:—Royal Scots, Northumberland Fusiliers, Royal Irish Rifles and Sherwood Foresters.

The first operation, which was conducted by the M.I. Battalion, as a whole, was the reconnaissance of the 5th, which discovered the Stormberg position to be evacuated. The mounted troops, with the exception of the Royal Scots Company, returned to camp at Cyphergat, and preceded the Infantry Battalion to the occupation of the place on the following day.

Though small patrols were almost daily sent out from Stormberg, it was not until the 8th that the information was received from the north that the Cape Police and De Montmorency's Scouts had gained touch with the enemy's main body. Leaving their tents behind, the 10th M.I. hurried forward, reaching Burgersdorp only two hours after the last train-load of Boers had left the place. On the following day they pushed on to Osfontein, where the advanced scouts reported 400 of the enemy still south of the Orange River, and the remainder strongly entrenched on the northern bank. A twenty-five-mile march on the 10th to Knapdaar hustled the enemy's rear-guard over the river, without giving them time to completely demolish both bridges.

The next day, the 11th, the action of Bethulie, which has been fully dealt with in Chapter II., took place. The opportune arrival of the 10th M.I. was of valuable assistance to the Cape Police, who, being in very inferior numbers, could hardly have been expected to hold the entire Boer force in check for an indefinite period. Though unattended with any human casualties, the part played by the 10th M.I., throughout the 11th, was of the greatest importance in keeping the enemy from the Road Bridge. Lieutenant Casswell, with the right half Company, was on the extreme British right, Major Godley in support, and for forty-eight hours, until relieved by the Infantry of the Battalion on the morning of the 13th, they held to the southern bank, under a continual shell fire, keeping the Boers in check. Then, leaving the Infantry to complete the work they had so ably begun, the Company fell back; and the next day left the scene of the action altogether, moving to Venterstad, thirty miles to the west, where

Major Godley received surrendered arms in the Court-House.

But as General Gatacre had by then established himself on the northern bank of the river, the Company received instructions to return immediately. This they did with all haste; but they did not rejoin the headquarters of the Third Division until the latter had reached Springfontein Junction; for the advance of the Infantry had been greatly accelerated by means of the train captured by Captains Pope-Hennessy and Gordon-Turner.

But the Mounted Infantry had moved with great rapidity, and the pace had told on their horses, the Argentines especially having given out almost daily. Fortunately, however, several Cape ponies had been commandeered on the line of march, and by means of these, the Company was again brought up to its full mounted strength.

The first days at Springfontein were occupied in patrolling the surrounding country, and in collecting arms from the outlying homesteads, in accordance with Lord Roberts' proclamation. As afterwards became only too apparent, the majority of rifles given up at this time were either of obsolete pattern or of a kind for which there was a lack of ammunition in the country: to this an "Ex-Lieutenant of Colonel Villebois de Mareuil," who served with the Boer forces, fully testifies, dwelling sympathetically in his book upon the elasticity of the Boer conscience in accepting the oath of neutrality without the slightest intention of adhering to it. The majority of rifles issued originally to the burghers were *Mausers*, with a plentiful supply of ammunition, and it is — or rather, should have been — significant that the patrols from Springfontein collected absolutely no rifles of that pattern. The Mausers were everywhere retained; and, in some cases, even flint-locks were meekly handed over as tokens of submission.

On the 21st, owing to the simple fact that the 5th Fusiliers' Captain was late for breakfast, Major Godley's Company was ordered to occupy Philippolis, in order to issue Lord Roberts' proclamation and receive arms and ammunition, and was so saved from participating later in the Reddersburg disaster. Arriving at that place at 7 p.m. they were heartily welcomed by two Englishmen—a Mr. Mildman and a Mr. Davis—who affirmed that during the past months of continued suspense and depression they had been insulted on every possible occasion by the Dutch inhabitants. They reported that a commando of 600 of the enemy lay only a few miles from the town. On this account the five days, during which the Company garrisoned the town, was a period of natural anxiety to Major Godley, isolated as he was from the divisional headquarters, in close proximity to a large Boer force, and among people openly hostile. Fortunately, General Clements, with 7,000 men, was close upon the place ; and, taking the Company for a supported advanced party of this force, the Boer Commandant hesitated to attack. To that fact alone the Company owed its safety ; for it is difficult to consider their position in any other light than that of a decidedly precarious one. At Reddersburg, a few days later, an exceedingly superior force found itself in a similar situation, with disastrous results. For at this period the Boers still moved in large bodies with guns and transport, and had not yet learnt the great art of dissemination.

Clements occupied Philippolis on the 23rd, and for the next four days the patrols carried the proclamation around the district. On the 27th the Company had the good fortune to fall upon General Groblaar and his brother, the Commissary-General, and to effect their arrest. The following day the Boer General was taken into Springfontein by an escort under Captain Casswell—for that officer had on the previous day received his promotion. The meeting of the Generals was of some interest, for it was the same Groblaar who, with Olivier, had defeated Gatacre at Stormberg on the fatal morning of 10th December.

At this time the Company hoped to join the main army for the advance on Pretoria; for they were not ordered to rejoin Colonel Sitwell's Battalion at Philippolis, but were sent north, and in consequence had some expectations, based no doubt upon the influence of General Smith-Dorrien, who never forgot his old Battalion. But on reaching Bethanie events occurred which necessitated a change in the arrangements. At 10 p.m., on that day, Lieutenant Percival, of the 9th M.I., informed General Gatacre that his detached columns, consisting of half the Irish Rifles and two Companies of Mounted Infantry, had been surrounded by the enemy at Reddersburg, and was sadly in need of assistance. Captain Casswell, with fifty men, was immediately ordered to seize a nek, overlooking the town of Reddersburg, through which the relieving troops would have to pass. He arrived in position at 4.45 a.m. on the morning of 4th April, where he remained until 9 a.m., a helpless witness of the engagement, and beyond keeping General Gatacre constantly informed of the gravity of the situation, powerless to act or lend assistance. The story of the disaster can be stated briefly. The British held gallantly to their post; all their officers were killed; the relieving column arrived too late—after the whole force had surrendered, and had been ignominiously led away, in full view of Captain Casswell's picquet. A half-hearted advance was made by the mounted troops; but no real attempt was made to recapture the surrendered column, and on the 5th, General Gatacre's force fell back again to Bethanie. Five days later General Chermside took over the command of the Third Division, which on the 11th readvanced on Reddersburg, leaving the

Sherwood Foresters Infantry Battalion to guard the line. On the 14th General Chermside's force moved six miles to Rosendal Farm. Hundreds of troops had now joined the column, and fighting was expected nearly every day; for, owing to the investment of Wepener, a large majority of the enemy's commandos were in the South-Eastern Free State, at this period the only theatre of really active operations. General Brabazon arrived and took over command of all the mounted troops, composed chiefly of Imperial Yeomanry, and, on the 18th, the advance commenced in earnest, driving in the enemy's patrols towards Wakkerstroom, though Dewetsdorp was evidently the main objective.

On the following day the force, covered by the advanced patrols of the 10th M.I., came into contact with the enemy. Captain Casswell, who had been sent forward by General Brabazon to reconnoitre, coming suddenly upon a dismounted party of Boers, who opened fire upon him at eighty yards, narrowly escaped falling into their hands. Soon afterwards the rifle fire became general along the whole front, and the mounted supports were brought into the firing line. The 10th M.I.—Major Godley's Company on the extreme right—seized a kopje affording very little natural cover, which they held for five hours under a heavy rifle and shell fire, until relieved by the Gloucester Regiment. This kopje subsequently proved to be the key to the position, and was held by the infantry during the next five days. But the tenacity with which it was defended in the first instance, before any artificial cover could be improvised, and the manner in which the repeated attempts of the enemy to recapture it had been frustrated, was noticed by General Rundle, whose division co-operated, and who congratulated the 10th M.I. on their behaviour.

On the following day, as General Chermside was anxious

to ascertain how far the enemy's left flank extended, he ordered General Brabazon's troops to move in the direction of Dewetsdorp, where they came upon three guns and 600 of the enemy moving towards Wepener. After two hours' fighting this force attempted to work round General Brabazon's right flank. In order to check this movement De Montmorency's Scouts, under Captain McNeill — yet still retaining the title of their first commander's name— were sent off to occupy a high ridge on that flank ; but the Boers arrived there first and opened fire. The Scouts fell back : and Mr. Winston Churchill—who had gone out with them—in trying to mount, fell to the ground, his saddle slipping round and his horse galloping away. One of the Scouts immediately returned, put him on his horse and carried him safely out of fire, when his horse, riddled with bullets, fell dead. This gallant action was rewarded by the V.C.

The engagement of Dewetsdorp was in some way perhaps one of the most unsatisfactory of the whole War, inasmuch as absolutely nothing was accomplished by either side. It was the object of the Boers to surround the British column as they had done at Wepener and Reddersburg; it was the object of the British to hold the enemy's force in the neighbourhood, until the large bodies of troops sent out from Bloemfontein had cut off their line of retreat northwards : and both completely failed. Had either side ventured to attack, the issue might have been more decisive ; but as the fighting throughout was of a more or less desultory character, and for the most part confined to the mounted troops, nothing whatever was accomplished. On the 21st Brabazon's troops fell back with great difficulty under a heavy fire ; but on the following day they again advanced, and, after a repulse, managed eventually to dislodge four guns and about 200 of the enemy from their advanced position. On the 23rd

General Brabazon, reconnoitring well to the enemy's right
flank, gained touch with General French's cavalry; and, on
the next day, the Boers, finding themselves in imminent
danger of being surrounded by 15,000 British, retired along
the Wepener and Thaba 'Nchu roads, which had been left
unguarded.

On the 25th the 10th M.I., as part of the force under
General Brabazon, marched to the relief of Wepener, where
they arrived at 8 a.m. on the following morning, only to
find that the Boers had again retreated during the night.
Two days later the enemy again returned to Dewetsdorp;
and it was reported that General Chermside's convoy had
been captured on the Thaba 'Nchu road. Accordingly, on the
29th, General Brabazon set off in pursuit. But it was
doubtless only a small detached party of the enemy; for
the escort had already beaten them off, and Brabazon
returned to Dewetsdorp on 1st May—the day of the action
of Houtnek—where the commandos, which during the past
month had given such continual trouble in this district,
succeeded in breaking through the British columns to the
north of Bloemfontein.

Throughout May and the greater part of June the bulk
of the Boer forces, under the Commandant-General, fell back
before the advance of the main army and the army of the
right flank; but when Lord Roberts crossed the Vaal,
large bodies of Free Staters, notably the celebrated
Commando under Christian De Wet, remained in their own
territory, operating for the most part in the vicinity of
Kroonstad and around Lindley; while the south-eastern
corner of the Free State—or rather Orange River Colony
—which had been the scene of so many fierce engagements
in April, remained comparatively tranquil for the time
being.

In the early part of May the Mounted Infantry Company

L

went into garrison at Wepener, and busied themselves in accepting surrenders, collecting arms and patrolling the district, which had been methodically divided into sections for that purpose ; and it was not until the end of July that Boers in any appreciable force were again reported in the neighbourhood.

On 1st August the Company set out for Edenburg, and reached the place on the 4th, where they were immediately ordered to return whence they came, leaving half the Company at Dewetsdorp under Captain Casswell. But such orders and counter-orders—seemingly useless though they may be—have the invariable significance that the authorities are not without reason for apprehension. But the backbone of the Boer defence was now broken; and after Lord Roberts' occupation of Lydenberg, the aspect of the War completely changed; the commandos spread themselves over the whole country, and the Orange River Colony to the south-west of the capital again became overrun by the enemy's patrols.

On the 27th Thaba 'Nchu was evacuated ; and on the same day, Captain Casswell, at Dewetsdorp, received a wire from Lord Kitchener to be prepared to burn all stores, and retreat to the Basuto border at a moment's notice. Boer patrols were almost daily reported in the neighbourhood, and the inhabitants of the town were beginning to get alarmed and leave the place in large numbers. Lord Kitchener instructed Captain Casswell to do his utmost to reassure the people ; and that officer ordered a large Variety Entertainment to be given, which had the desired effect.

On 1st September the telegraph wires were cut, and Dewetsdorp became isolated. But on the following night an advanced patrol of Malta M.I. entered the town and reported that a column was at hand, and the enemy had been driven off. The news was a great relief, for, as the Company had been on picquet every night for a week, and on patrol by day, both men and horses were thoroughly exhausted by the work. Major Godley at Wepener had had a hardly less trying time, and had been prepared, by order of Lord Kitchener, to cross into Basutoland in case of attack by a superior force.

On the 3rd Captain Casswell's half Company rejoined Major Godley at Wepener. But on the 24th the town was evacuated, and the Company returned to Dewetsdorp. Thence they moved to Bloemfontein; but were ordered to return with a flying column, under General Allen, as Dewetsdorp was again in the hands of the enemy. The continual evacuations and reoccupations of the principal South African towns was the main feature of the War about this time; and this was in part due to the fact that the British never imagined that the campaign had not yet assumed the entire nature of a guerilla war. For this the authorities were to some extent to blame; for a few large commandos still remained in the field undispersed, causing considerable anxiety regarding the safety of the smaller garrisons. With united commandos the Boers were enabled to retain what little discipline they possessed, and combined attacks remained feasible as long as the Commandants held organised bodies under their immediate control. But guerilla tactics mean dissemination, and continual dissemination means disorganisation beyond repair, as far as combined operations are concerned. Such a state of things was soon actually to come into existence; but the commandos had not yet thoroughly learnt the art of dissolving on the approach of superior British forces; for such is the chief essential of guerilla warfare, in which harmonious combination is impossible. Rapidity and secrecy are all-important factors in guerilla warfare; and in order to maintain them, smaller commandos are essential: and as a general rule with smaller commandos, unable to combine—except through the medium of a happy chance—trained troops in permanent fortifications are unassailable. As in all other problems of war, it is a question of numbers alone. At this period, commandos combined and, by numerical strength, forced the weaker garrisons into either evacuation or surrender. On the approach of the relieving columns, they fell back cautiously to beyond striking distance, but did not *disperse*, they merely *separated*, remaining in immediate call of one another. These were not true guerilla tactics ; though the majority of writers upon the subject are ready to assert that with Prinsloo's surrender and the battle of Bergendal on the Delagoa Line the guerilla war began.

General Allen's force occupied Dewetsdorp on 3rd October, but the enemy showed no signs of quitting the district. On the 6th Private Page, when on patrol, suddenly rode on to a party of 5 Boers, 1 of whom—who subsequently proved to be Commandant Fouret himself—beckoned to him to approach, and then fired, hitting his horse in the neck. This seems to have paralysed the animal, for it did not move, and Page, jumping off, ran for his life and escaped without being hit, though Fouret was not forty yards away. On the 8th the Dewetsdorp column was divided into two—one half for Dewetsdorp, and the other for Wepener. Major Godley, asked which column he would prefer to join, selected the latter, and his decision was a lucky one, for the whole of the force left behind under Major Massey, R.A., fell into the hands of De Wet.

The Wepener column consisted of the headquarters and three Companies of the Highland Light Infantry, two guns, 68th Battery and the M.I. Company, the whole under Colonel Kelham. Their destination was reached in a day's march, and the place was immediately put in a state of fortification, as the surrounding country was found to be alive with the enemy's patrols, moving south to the invasion of Cape Colony. Six weeks later, 19th November, the enemy's main force, under De Wet and Steyn, surrounded Dewetsdorp on their way south, and after four days' severe fighting, the town surrendered. Colonel Kelham at once wired the news of the disaster to General Macdonald, who informed him that "the information was unfounded"; whereas the Chief Staff Officer at Bloemfontein was almost uncourteous on the subject, replying briefly, "Don't believe it." In both cases the wish, no doubt, was father to the thought. But the fact, nevertheless, remained unaltered.

All through the month of November De Wet carried his invasion of Cape Colony far to the south, stirring up the disloyal element to join his forces. But at the beginning of December he found himself hard pressed on all sides, and was obliged to retreat north again. On the 9th of that month a detachment, consisting of two companies H.L.I., the M.I. Company and one gun, under Major Godley, were despatched to the Caledon Bridge, to prevent the enemy crossing. On the 11th De Wet's patrols were well about the place, and Sergeant-Major Ewin, with 12 men, surrounded a party in a farm, and badly wounded and captured a Field-Cornet. But finding the Caledon Bridge held, De Wet crossed at Bastard's Drift, eighteen miles to the south, and moved north towards Daspoort, where General Knox was encamped. On the 14th Sergeant Heapy, in command of a patrol, narrowly escaped being captured. After fighting for some time, he very cleverly managed to get away, only losing one man wounded and two horses. The next day Major Godley's detachment returned to Wepener. On arrival there, 40 Boers were reputed in laager, in the direction of Rouxville; and Captain Casswell, sent out with 40 men, attacked and forced them to retire.

But soon afterwards the country again filled with larger bodies of the enemy. De Wet, who had gone as far north

as Winburg, turned, and again moved against Wepener.
Colonel Kelham was immediately ordered to burn his stores
and retreat — somewhat ignominiously — to Aliwal North
through Basutoland ; and during the first two weeks of
February, the garrison marched through Mafeking, down
the Caledon Valley followed by Haasbrock's Commando, 600
strong, moving as a parallel column on the other side of the
river, and reached Aliwal North on the 14th, whence they
moved to Commissie Drift on the Orange River.

Major Godley was left in command of a detachment at this
drift, which, by the way, is an exceedingly difficult one to
hold, and parties of Boers, already on the Free State side of
the river, were able to fire into the camp.   In order to put a
stop to this state of affairs, and in pursuance of a plan
arranged by Lord Lovat and Captain Casswell, a party,
under Sergeant-Major Ewin, was sent to Venter's Drift,
which had been reported fordable.   To prove this a man of
the H.L.I. walked across, and a Kaffir boy on a horse was
sent over to test the strength of the stream, and left
stationary, as a point for the men to march upon.   Sergeant-
Major Ewin then formed up the men, and, explaining the idea,
pointed out the ford and the mounted man on the opposite
bank ; he also told them that in case they got off the ford
and were obliged to swim, to take hold of their horses by the
mane, tail or stirrup-leather, taking care to get into the
water *up* stream.   The Scouts were started off at three
horses' lengths distance, Corporal Bradshaw leading, as he
was a powerful swimmer.   All went well for three-fourths of
the journey, when it was noticed by those on the bank that
the men were going too far to the left.   Several called out,
"Go more to the right !" but as no notice was taken, a man
was sent into the water, and he, almost getting up to the
rear horse, repeated the caution ; this, however, was also
disregarded, the Corporal going more to the left still.   All at

once his horse began to swim; the others closed up, and followed suit. Then the men suddenly losing their heads, threw themselves into the water *down* stream, and were washed away from their horses; nevertheless they struck out bravely for the bank, but had only gone a few yards when they simultaneously called out "Help!" and disappeared. These were Corporal Bradshaw, Privates Murphy, Hull, Costal and Turner. They were never seen again; one body only was recovered, that of Private Hull, found twenty miles down the river. The Detachment of the H.L.I. did everything in their power, the men diving for hours at the place where their comrades were last seen. All the horses swam to the bank and were recovered.

After this terrible episode, all idea of the plan was given up, and only a small picquet remained at the place, the headquarters of the Company moving to Odendalstroom. So the sniping across the river continued for some days, the detachments being unable to prevent it. On 27th March Captain Casswell took over command from Major Godley, who received orders to rejoin the 2nd Battalion as second in command. Other changes had also taken place in the Company. At Wepener, on 23rd November, Sergeant Dodd, who had acted as Quartermaster-Sergeant to the Company since its formation, had died of enteric fever. His loss had been greatly felt by all. On 3rd April, 1901, Sergeant-Major Ewin left the Company to become Regimental Sergeant-Major of the 10th M.I., under Major Marshall, and Sergeant Seaton became Company Sergeant-Major in his place.

Early in April Van Reenan's and Kritzinger's Commandos were reported in the district, driven thither through Cape Colony by the columns under Colonels Herbert Gorringe, De Lisle and Major Massey. An additional column, under Major Garland, H.L.I., was hastily formed, and joined by Captain Casswell with thirty men. But the Boers managed to elude them all, and finding a boat negligently left on the Caledon River, crossed at Ondefontein Drift.   On 7th April the Company received orders to march to Springfontein, which place was reached on the 12th.   A large Yeomanry camp had been formed at that place under the command of General Hart; but beyond a few cattle and horse raids, and an occasional attempt upon the lines of communication, very little was seen of the enemy.

As the War went on their Commandos became smaller and smaller, and spread themselves over the whole theatre of War.   This necessitated similar tactics on the part of the British Commander; and at this period there were as many as eighty flying columns moving backwards and forwards across the country, turning from one Commando to another, separating and then closing around some isolated force of the enemy; only once more to separate again—all controlled by Lord Kitchener in Pretoria.   In fact the whole campaign may be divided in four phases, each with a distinct characteristic of its own.   Firstly, the disastrous frontal attacks, then the period of wide turning movements, followed by the days of flying columns—at this time in full working order—and the final stage of block-house lines and systematic "drives." At this time Companies lost sight of their battalions for months at a time; even single guns became separated from their batteries.   On paper Captain Casswell's Company still formed part of the 10th M.I., which was then commanded by Major Marshall of the Regiment; but they had been for some time entirely detached from the headquarters of their Battalion.

Lieutenant Marshall, Loyal North Lancashire Regiment, served temporarily at Springfontein as Captain Casswell's subaltern: on his return to England his place was taken by Lieutenant W. Beatty, 6th Royal Warwicks.   For more than two months the Company continued to serve at Springfontein, on the lines of communication. General Hart was full of praise for the good work they did, especially upon one occasion, when they recaptured the greater portion of a large quantity of sheep and cattle, taken by the Boers on the previous night. But on 12th June the last of the Company entrained for Smaldeel, where Major Marshall was concentrating the 10th M.I., for more active work in the field.

On the 13th the officer commanding at Winburg ordered Captain Casswell's Company, with the Berkshire M.I., to move on the following night to Tabackberg, in conjunction with other columns. On the 16th the British closed with the enemy, but the operation failed, and Captain Casswell's groom, Private Linally, fell, wounded, into the hands of the enemy, and was disgracefully maltreated. Having fainted from loss of blood, a horse was given him, and, with his wounds still undressed, he was made to do orderly the whole day long to an obtrusive Field-Cornet.

Three days later Major Marshall's Battalion, consisting of the Berkshires, R. Scots, Northumberland Fusiliers and Sherwood Forester Companies, three of which had fought together on the day of De Montmorency's death at Stormberg, nearly a year and a half before, set out in pursuit of Commandant Haasbrock's 150 men. The Commando was soon found and put to flight by the Sherwood Forester Company, under Lieutenant Rostram, Northumberland Fusiliers, and Major Marshall himself, Captain Casswell and Lieutenant Beatty being temporarily on the sick-list; but the Regimental Sergeant - Major Ewin, who, in company with Sergeant - Major Seaton, had obtained permission to ride down a solitary Boer, galloped into a party of twelve and was shot in the chest. Sergeant-Major Seaton, though his horse was wounded in several places, was fortunately not touched, and finally managed to reach cover under a perfect hail of bullets. But soon afterwards both sides were strongly reinforced, for the Officers and Sergeant-Majors, being better mounted, had outstripped the men in the pursuit, and the engagement became serious. By the time the other three Companies had arrived upon the scene, and the enemy been driven back, 2 men had been killed, and Major Marshall, Lieutenant Rostram and 2 others wounded.

Major Marshall and the other wounded were subsequently sent to Bloemfontein Hospital, while his battalion moved on to Winburg. From this centre the Company was engaged in several minor operations, and was continually in touch with the enemy. On 16th July Captain Casswell attacked a Boer convoy, sending parties under Lieutenant Beatty and Sergeant-Major Seaton around either flank, and riding straight for it himself. They captured in all 3 Boers, 8 waggons and 300 head of cattle. Lieutenant Beatty captured one of the men himself, and this fellow, on the officer riding up to him, immediately held up his hands; but as Beatty was in the act of dismounting, he rapidly slipped a cartridge into his rifle, with the evident intention of shooting him. Fortunately the cartridge jammed, and Lieutenant Beatty, who would have been fully justified in killing him, contented himself with a few kicks and a punch on the head. But in the meantime a party of 150 Boers, with ten waggons, had been located at a farm; and Captain Casswell sent back word to Colonel Barker, commanding in Winburg, asking for reinforcements. Two guns and 200 men, under Major Marshall, who had recovered from his wound, were immediately despatched to the place; but the position was found to be too strong to attack, without risking a great many lives.

At the end of July the 10th M.I., accompanied by Captain Leveson-Gower of the Regiment Intelligence Office of the district, made a detour to Brandfort, via the Vet River, hoping to surprise a party of the enemy reported to be at

Einsgevonden. The operation failed, however ; and the Battalion took up a position extending from Brandfort to Einsgevonden, for the purpose of guarding that portion of the railway line. But the Boers, divided before General Eliot's Columns, managed to break through ; and in doing so, captured a small Cossack Post belonging to the Company.

On 7th August the Company—then stationed at Karree Siding—received its first and only reinforcement since its formation, of thirty men, under Lieutenant De Pledge, which was greatly needed, as the wastage up to that time amounted to 50 per cent. of their original strength.

A few days later a strong flying column, under Colonel Barker, consisting of the 9th, 10th and 15th M.I. Battalions, 400 Yeomanry and 4 guns, set out to the Tabackberg after Haasbrock's Commando, which was reported to be in the Doornberg. They fell upon the laager soon after daybreak on 16th August, and effected a complete surprise. The Boer camp lay in the hollow of a horse-shoe-shaped line of hills, which were immediately seized by the mounted troops. Unfortunately the Yeomanry were late at the entrance of the Kloof ; and three-fourths of the enemy managed to escape. Major Marshall endeavoured to rectify the mistake, and sent the R. Scots Company to the gap ; while Captain Casswell's Company fixed bayonets and charged down the slope. Thereupon the laager became a perfect pandemonium ; rifles were thrown away, horses were mounted bare-backed, with no time for saddling, and Boers were pulled out of their bivouacs before they were fully awake. Had not Haasbrock himself left the laager the night before with 90 men, and had the Yeomanry not failed him, Colonel Barker would have obtained a much more important " bag." But as it was, 12 Boers killed and 40 captured—many of them wounded— 40 saddles and several horses, waggons, oxen, etc., with no casualties on the British side, was in itself a useful day's work

From 22nd August to 8th September Colonel Barker's
Column operated in the Brandwater Basin, in conjunction
with General Eliot's columns.   The Company, under Captain
Casswell and Lieutenant Beatty, numbered 76 N.C.O.'s and
men.   On the 29th an attempt to capture a convoy, sighted
by Major Pine-Coffin's Column, failed, and on the following
day Lieutenant Beatty, with a section, extricated a Yeomanry
patrol which had been surrounded.   Fighting was at this time
of almost daily occurrence ; and on the 31st a convoy
was captured after a determined resistance, during which
Lieutenant Drysdale, R. Scots and 10th M.I., lost his life.
After this the greater part of Colonel Barker's Force remained
at Stalbert's Nek, while Major Marshall's Battalion was sent
on to Retief's Nek.   There they were severely harassed from
all sides ; and, on 2nd September, Lieutenant Beatty, with 80
men, narrowly escaped capture, coming unexpectedly upon a
position held by two or three hundred of the enemy.   The
Boers fortunately were off-saddled at the time, which gave
the patrol a good start, but the Boers, firing from their saddles,
pursued for eight miles, when Captain Casswell, on patrol
with 12 men, was able to check their advance from the cover
of a donga.

But in the meantime the position of Major Marshall's troops
at Retief's Nek was daily becoming more serious, for the
enemy had by now completely surrounded the place.
Sergeant-Major M'Gregor, R. Scots, volunteered to ride
through to Colonel Barker for assistance ; and on the 3rd
reinforcements, including a gun, arrived at the place, and on
the following day Major Marshall was enabled to rejoin the
Column.   The Sergeant-Major received the Distinguished
Conduct Medal for his action.

Colonel Barker's Column left Stalbert's Nek on the 5th,
and engaged the enemy on that day, killing 4 and
capturing 6.   Marching on half rations, they reached

Winburg on the 8th, where the Company immediately entrained for Pretoria, "to have a couple of months hard-earned rest on garrison duty"; so, at least, said General Alderson, the Inspector - General of M.I. Lieutenant De Pledge remained in Winburg Hospital; the officers of the Company being Captain Casswell and Lieutenant Beatty, 6th R. Warwicks, who had done such good work during the past weeks.

The Company crossed the Vaal into the Transvaal for the first time on 9th September, and, on arrival at Pretoria, were met by General Alderson. The General, in a speech, said that he had heard of the excellent work that the Company had done, and that he soon hoped to be able to give them a rest, but at present this could not be managed. It appears that a column, consisting of 2 Horse Guns, 2 Field Guns, a Pom-Pom, 4 Machine Guns, 1 Company of the Camerons, 200 Canadians, under Major Ross, and some Imperial Yeomanry, the whole under the command of Colonel Hackett-Thompson, had just been formed for the purpose of hunting down Jack Hindon, the train-wrecker, and that Captain Casswell's Company was to join this force at Waterval camp.

Two days out, twelve of the train-wreckers were captured, and the next day another engagement took place—each side suffering a few casualties. After this, Colonel Hackett-Thompson's Column, co-operating with the Columns under Colonel Copley and Sir Henry Rawlinson, remained in the Bokpoort - Balmoral area until 10th October, during which period minor skirmishes—but nothing of an important nature —were of almost daily occurrence.

The Company returned to Pretoria on the 10th, where Lieutenant De Pledge rejoined; and on the 19th proceeded to Klerksdorp and joined a column under Colonel Hickie, consisting of 2 guns " P " Battery, 2 guns 78th Battery, 1 Pom-Pom, 400 Yeomanry, 2 Companies 21st M.I., 1

Company 11th M.I., and 300 S. Wales Borderers, which, together with Colonel Hackett-Thompson's Force, may be taken as fully illustrative of the heterogeneous character of the majority of columns which at this time ransacked the country.

With this Column, being not far distant, comparatively speaking, from Rustenburg, the headquarters of the Infantry Battalion, Lieutenant Napier joined the Company, which was now under the command of Lieutenant Beatty, Captain Casswell having fallen sick at Klerksdorp.

On the 28th the Column, three days out from its base, engaged the enemy upon an occasion in which both Lieutenant Beatty and Sergeant-Major Seaton acted with the greatest gallantry, carrying men out of action under a very heavy fire, and being respectively recommended for the D.S.O. and D.C.M. in consequence.

Upon the Column returning to Klerksdorp, Captain Casswell rejoined, and commanded on an expedition to Ventersdorp, which was for the time being hard pressed. The enemy was successfully driven from the neighbourhood and the Column returned to Klerksdorp, subsequently assisting in covering the construction of a line of block-houses along the Schoon Spruit Valley to that place. Large bodies of Transvaalers, under De la Rey, Kemp, Walmarans, Vermaas and Liebenberg were in the district, endeavouring to oppose the building of the line, which they only too plainly perceived would greatly hamper their movements in the future. Had Colonel Hickie followed his telegraphic instructions from General Barker, and moved from his entrenched position, his whole force would probably have been annihilated ; for, as the men of the Regiment who had fought at Vlakfontein and Moedwil only too well knew, of these Boer leaders, De la Rey and Kemp, at all events, were not men to be despised with impunity. Even as it was, the Column was severely harassed, until Lord Methuen and Colonel Kekewich came to its relief. On 11th and 13th November especially, they were heavily engaged; and the Company was congratulated by Colonel Hickie and mentioned in his despatches to Lord Kitchener for its conduct on the latter day.

But after the arrival of reinforcements, the building continued without interference from the enemy; and the work was completed on 4th December, on which day the Column was able to return to Klerksdorp. There General Alderson again expressed his satisfaction at the good work done by the Company, and said that he would recommend Captain Casswell for the first vacancy to command an M.I. Regiment.

Moving first to Potchefstroom, whence an expedition was made to the Vaal, Colonel Hickie's Column, now consisting solely of mounted troops—for the War, with the erection of the lines of "block-houses," had entered upon the period of "drives"—moved through Ventersdorp to Tafel Kop, over the same ground traversed by the Infantry Battalion on the "trek" before Vlakfontein. Indeed the M.I. Company were now once again in touch with their Regiment, and Captain Casswell was able to exchange compliments and Christmas greetings with Colonel Wylly, by way of Major Rigby's detachment at Magato Nek.

From 6th to 19th January Colonel Hickie's Column covered the construction of the block-house line, continued from Ventersdorp to Tafel Kop. De la Rey and Kemp did their utmost to hinder the work; and at one time these two famous leaders concentrated 2,000 men, with the idea of attack. It is reputed that when De la Rey made the suggestion to his subordinate, Kemp asked how long the Column had been in its present position. When told three days, he is said to have replied: "It is useless; by this time they will be under the ground."

And Kemp was not without experience. He commanded what had once been the Krugersdorp Commando, which had hurled itself against Waggon Hill and Spion Kop. Then as De la Rey's chief lieutenant, there had been no end to his audacity: Nooitgedacht, where he surprised Clements ; Modderfontein, where he flung himself upon Cunningham ; Vlakfontein and Moedwil, in which actions, if finally beaten back, he at least gave his opponents some cause to remember him ; and that final episode of the whole War, when he defeated and captured Lord Methuen, are among the most notable of his exploits. But in no case did he venture against trained troops entrenched, however superior in numbers his commando may have been.

By 30th January, after a trying time of continual outpost duty, almost daily harassed by the enemy, the block-house line was completed, and the Column was enabled to return to Ventersdorp, and, on 1st February, to join Colonel Kekewich's Force at Vaalbank.

On the 4th, in an attempt to seize the person of General De la Rey, a Boer picquet was captured, and Commandant Albert's laager was located five miles distant. The original idea was instantly abandoned, and a scheme was originated to seize the laager. On the morning of the following day, in the execution of this plan, a squadron of the Scottish Horse became hotly engaged, and sent to Captain Casswell for assistance. That officer immediately galloped his Company straight into the enemy's camp, completing a capture of 131 Boers and 800 cattle, besides waggons, Cape carts, saddles, rifles, etc. Eight of the enemy were killed ; the British losses amounted to only 3 officers and 3 men wounded, none of which were in Captain Casswell's Company. Major Leader, of the Carbineers and Scottish Horse, the senior officer present, and the troops under his command were specially congratulated by Lord Kitchener upon their behaviour.

After a series of skirmishes, usually accompanied by a few casualties and the capture of a prisoner or so, Colonel Grenfell took over command of Colonel Hickie's portion of Kekewich's Force, Captain Casswell commanding the mounted troops under Colonel Grenfell's command.

The Column scarcely ever rested ; in every direction were parties of the enemy to be driven from column to column, and finally up against the lines of block-houses. It was a war of fish and fishermen ; the columns were cast about the country as nets, and then slowly drawn in upon the entrenched positions. Nevertheless, especially in this western district of the Transvaal, whenever a convoy insufficiently protected, or a small column for the time being isolated, came within striking distance of their commandos, Kemp and De la Rey seldom missed their chance, but rapidly concentrating their forces, hurled themselves suddenly and unexpectedly upon their victims. It was the warfare of the Chouans in La Vendee, when the watchword was, " Gather, Strike, Disperse " ; than which none is harder to suppress. But Lord Kitchener had the telegraph wires under his control ; the block-houses intersecting the country from the Magaliesberg to the Orange River were an infallible source of information, and, as each cast of the nets proved more or less successful, the enemy's available forces were fast diminishing, and the end grew nearer and nearer at hand.

But in February Kemp and De la Rey moved actively about the area they had chosen as the scene of their operations ; and on the 25th, when camped at Hartebeestfontein, the scene of General Babington's successful action the year before, Colonel Grenfell's Column, receiving the news that Colonel Von Donop's convoy had fallen into the enemy's hands, immediately set out in pursuit. It was characteristic of both De Wet and De la Rey that, in avoiding the pursuit of one force, they frequently inflicted

M

a reverse upon another, and on this occasion, at the beginning of March, De la Rey, lost to his pursuers, defeated Lord Methuen at Barber's Pass.

About this time Captain Casswell was admitted to hospital at Klerksdorp, and was afterwards invalided to England on the recommendation of a Medical Board. He had been with the Company from the very beginning, and was no doubt largely responsible for the high state of efficiency it had shown throughout the War. During the first portion of this period, as Major Godley's only subaltern, he had been almost daily employed upon patrol, and afterwards, when the command of the Company had passed to him, these pages fully testify to the good work he did. He was succeeded in command of the Company—which soon afterwards formed Colonel Von Donop's Column—by Lieutenant Napier.

From 23rd to 29th March, Von Donop's Force was continuously on the move, sometimes covering immense distances, in pursuit of De la Rey and Kemp, at this time the sole remaining Boer force of any appreciable strength. On 11th April Major Roy, of the 2nd Battalion, commanding the advanced guard of the Column, was furiously attacked by 1,500 of the enemy at Roodeval. It was one of De la Rey's final efforts; Kemp charged right through the advanced guard, cutting the Company completely off from the remainder and riding down the 21st M.I. Major Roy was dangerously wounded, and 2 officers were killed and 2 others wounded, and the casualties amongst the rank and file had amounted to about 20, before the main body of the force had come to the assistance of the advanced guard. Thereupon the whole aspect of the engagement changed, and the enemy were beaten back and pursued, losing 3 guns, 48 killed and 68 wounded. Here again the M.I. Company distinguished themselves. At one time they were completely isolated and under a heavy fire, losing 9 men taken prisoners, and 11

horses killed.   But Lieutenant Napier was complimented
upon the manner in which he got them away, and upon the
excellent behaviour of the men under most trying circumstances.   On the 15th the Column again returned to
Klerksdorp, capturing 50 Boers in the neighbourhood of the
town.

After a week's rest the Company entrained for Kroonstad,
to join the 9th M.I., with which Battalion No. 2 Company
were then serving.   On 4th May the two Companies became
linked under the command of Captain Radford.   Both were
by now considerably diminished in strength, and together
they did not exceed 113 rifles.   Peace was not officially
declared until four weeks later, on the 1st of June; but with
the amalgamation of the two Companies, the story of No. 1
Company ("B"), Derbyshire M.I., may be said to end.

CHAPTER XII

WITH NO. 2 ("G") COMPANY, DERBYSHIRE M.I.

ON 1st March, 1900, the officer commanding the Battalion, at that time at Cyphergat camp, a few miles south of Molteno, Cape Colony, received orders to raise a second company of Mounted Infantry.

Though Major Godley's Company had for the most part absorbed all the men with official mounted infantry certificates, many yet remained with a sufficient knowledge of riding and horses to enable them to become efficient mounted infantry men after a very short period of training.

Captain P. Leveson-Gower, who was selected for the command—as Major Godley had already done before him—retained as many men as possible of his original Company—"G." But in order to complete the establishment, several were taken from other companies—not only those with previous experience as grooms, etc., but marksmen and men of exemplary conduct ; and thus, to a very great extent, both Companies of Mounted Infantry may be said to have been largely composed of "picked men." The horses, in the case of No. 2 Company M.I., were nearly all South Africans.

Captain Leveson-Gower's subalterns were, in the first instance, Lieutenants Burnett-Hitchcock and Wybergh. Colour-Sergeant Corrigan went to the Company as Sergeant-Major, the Section Commanders being Sergeants Lovatt, Cooper, Geissler, and Robinson, with Sergeant Musson, Company Quartermaster-Sergeant.

After the occupation of Stormberg Junction by Gatacre's

Force, the newly-formed 11th M.I., consisting of this Company and Companies of the Royal Scots, Northumberland Fusiliers and R. Irish Rifles, commanded by Major Festing, D.S.O., of the last-named regiment, marched hurriedly northwards, *bare-backed*, without waiting for their supply of saddlery, in expectation of assisting at the action at the Bethulie Bridges. For this, however, they were too late, arriving on the 14th—the day before the enemy evacuated the position—when the saddlery was issued, and Lieutenant Burnett-Hitchcock left the Company on being appointed Provost-Marshal at Bloemfontein, his place being taken by Lieutenant Percival.

From Bethulie Captain Leveson-Gower's Company moved on to Springfontein, Gatacre's temporary headquarters, becoming, for the time being, attached to Colonel Sitwell's Battalion—the 10th M.I. At this time they also shared the hopes of Major Godley's Company of joining Lord Roberts' Main Army for the advance on Pretoria, and had reached as far north as Edenburg, when the southern Boer movement east of the railway line—so often referred to in previous chapters—necessitated a complete change in the distribution of troops.

It was well known that De Wet's Commando had moved south after Sanna's Post, and considerable apprehension was felt for the safety of the Wepener garrison. General Gatacre, who commanded the line south of the capital, and who had detached a small force at Reddersburg, had special cause for anxiety. The telegraph lines were everywhere cut, and his sources of information confined to the observations of patrols.

From Edenburg Captain Leveson-Gower despatched 6 men under Lieutenant Percival and 15 under Lieutenant Wybergh in the direction of Reddersburg. Both patrols discovered that the isolated garrison had been completely surrounded by the enemy, and retired at night to the railway-line: the former to Bethanie, Gatacre's headqearters, and the latter to Major Shaw's detachment at the Riet River Bridge. As mentioned in the last chapter, it was Lieutenant Percival who personally apprised General Gatacre of the danger in which the Reddersburg detachment lay; this was at 10 a.m. on the morning of 3rd April; and the relieving force did not leave Bethanie until the following day.

After General Chermside had taken over the command of the Third Division, a second movement was made to the scene of the disaster, and the 9th M.I. accompained the large mounted force, under General Brabazon, which, with the remainder of Chermside's Force, gained touch with General Rundle's Eighth Division at Rosendal Farm, and afterwards moved upon Dewetsdorp.

As far as the general operations are concerned, the histories of the two Mounted Infantry Companies during this period are identical; though during the actions of 20th and 21st April Captain Leveson-Gower's Company played a part of its own in a different portion of the field to that occupied by the 10th M.I.

On the former day the two divisions commenced to move on Dewetsdorp, and immediately the Company which formed the right-flank guard came under fire from the enemy's advanced posts, retiring before the British advance. Captain Leveson-Gower galloped kopje after kopje, clearing the way for the large column of infantry in rear; but no serious opposition was encountered, until the country assumed a less open nature in the vicinity of Dewetsdorp itself. Here the enemy showed up in greater numbers, and the firing became more general along the whole front. Captain Leveson-Gower, in view of the roughness of the ground and the increased severity of the fire, extended his Company and advanced on foot, leaving the horses to follow in rear. Suddenly the 10th M.I. seized the kopje to his left, and a tremendous fire burst forth from both sides. Pushing forward as far as possible with half a dozen men, Captain Leveson-Gower and Lieutenant Wybergh secured a position within six or seven hundred yards of the enemy, but affording indifferent facilities for cover. However, the Boers were strongly entrenched; and, as subsequently proved to be the case, the task was one utterly beyond the capacity of a couple of regiments of Mounted Infantry. Nevertheless, they held manfully to their ground, and Captain Leveson-Gower's left section managed to get the range of one of the enemy's guns and did considerable execution, killing or wounding 7 or 8 of the men serving it.

But the position soon became untenable, as the Boers worked round the right flank and threatened the Company with enfilade fire. A squadron of Yeomanry, sent to reinforce them, almost immediately retired, without lending any material assistance; and Captain Leveson-Gower was left to extricate himself as best he could. With as little delay as possible he ordered a retirement by sections, and the Company fell back under a galling fire from the enemy: shrapnel, segment and pom-pom shells, besides rifle-fire, rained upon them, until they attained a ridge 2,000 yards from the Boers. But a Corporal of Yeomanry, wounded and unable to move, lay upon the first position; so Corporal Beet gallantly returned under a murderous fire, and carried him back to a place of safety, thereby gaining the Victoria Cross. During the action the men must have made good use of the natural cover afforded by the ground, for the Company only lost 1 man killed and 2 wounded; though they were under fire from eight in the morning until nightfall.

The following day the enemy continued the engagement soon after daybreak by shelling the camp. General Chermside immediately deployed his force; and Captain Leveson - Gower's Company, with two guns, returned to the ridge they had held at the close of the previous day. From this place, Sergeant Geissler and Corporal Beet went down to the farm-house, half-way between the British and Boer position, where the latter had left the Corporal of Yeomanry; and placing a board upon an old perambulator, which they found in the house, they wheeled the man safely back to the British lines.

A heavy artillery duel continued throughout the day; but no material alteration in the dispositions of the two forces was effected, neither side venturing to take the initiative.

General Brabazon's reconnaissance with all the mounted troops, to endeavour to discover the enemy's right flank, took place on the 23rd; and the following day the Infantry of both divisions advanced, Captain Leveson - Gower's Company being temporarily attached to General Boyes' Brigade of Rundle's Division.

As will be remembered, upon this occasion no opposition was encountered, the Boers having retired during the night. Touch having been gained with General French's cavalry, Dewetsdorp was occupied that evening.

From this place Lieutenant Percival, with one section, was sent back to Edenburg with a convoy, and did not rejoin until after the Company had arrived in Bloemfontein in May; and Lieutenant Wybergh with another section escorted General Chermside to Wepener, where Major Godley's Company had already established themselves. Thus Captain Leveson - Gower was left with only half the Company; but in the middle of May, the whole Third Division moved into Bloemfontein, and was soon afterwards broken up, General Chermside being placed temporarily in charge of the line north of the capital. The Company took part in the Queen's Birthday Parade before the Governor, General Kelly-Kenny; and soon afterwards, at the reading of the Annexation Proclamation, Lieutenant Wybergh with one section of the Company, besides Lieutenant Burnett-Hitchcock, the Provost-Marshal, and Mr. Goddard, Mayor of Bloemfontein, who had fought in the ranks of the regiment at Bloemplaatz, secured the continuity of the connection between the old 45th Regiment and the Orange River Colony: in 1848, the 45th had formed the escort to the reading of the first Proclamation of Annexation to the Crown of the Orange River Sovereignty, and had been the last to leave the Bloemfontein Fort when independence was granted to the Orange Free State in 1854. And thus History, with no premeditated circumstance, repeated itself.

Soon after this Sergeant Lovatt's Section, under Lieutenant Wybergh, went down to Kaffir River Bridge, twenty-five miles south of Bloemfontein, for the purpose of making a census of that district, and remained there for about six weeks. In July the Company were reinforced by a draft of 20 men, sent out from England. In the meantime Lieutenant Percival had gone permanently to the Army Service Corps; and the Company had also lost the services of Colour-Sergeant Corrigan, who had had the misfortune to break his leg; and, owing to it being improperly set, he was never again fit for mounted infantry work. His place as Company Sergeant-Major was taken by Sergeant Cooper.

From August, 1900, to May, 1901, the headquarters of the Company were established at Brandfort, where Captain Leveson-Gower became District Intelligence Officer — in which capacity he has been already mentioned in the previous chapter, as accompanying Major Marshall's expedi-

tion to Einsgevonden. Half the Company only was retained
at this place, the other two sections being sent to Karree and
Glen Sidings.

The Brandfort half Company were by no means idle
during this period. First they were utilised on patrol duty
along the valley of the Modder River, which at that time
was little disturbed by the enemy. Afterwards they became
temporarily attached to various columns which the operations happened to bring into the district, notably Colonel
Thorneycroft's, the Highland Brigade and General Charles
Knox's Force. But the work in the intervening periods was
even more severe; patrols, reconnoitring parties and Cossack
posts had to be found, and sharp skirmishes with the enemy
were of frequent occurrence, the Company suffering occasional casualties in these little affairs, which are so
necessary for purposes of information in every War, and
yet, after all, count for nothing as far as the issue is
concerned.

It was the custom of the Boers around Brandfort to lie
in wait for the British patrols; and upon one occasion
Captain Leveson - Gower, reversing this order of things,
surprised a small party of the enemy at daybreak, capturing
5 prisoners. Upon another occasion, a "Captain," of "Free
State Despatch Riders," and another man fell into the hands
of Lieutenant Wybergh and Sergeant Lovatt, and Judge
Hertzog himself, whose laager was not far distant, narrowly
escaped capture. Soon after this, Captain Leveson-Gower
and about a dozen men almost rode into Haasbrock's laager.
All, however, got safely away, after a hard gallop of four
or five miles, closely pursued, the sole casualties being two
horses hit. The only expedition extending over a lengthened
period of days which was made from Brandfort, was one
to Bultfontein, about half - way between Brandfort and
Hoopstad, which was at one time attacked, and, having a

garrison of only 16 men fit for duty, was greatly in need of assistance. The Boers, however, taking Captain Leveson-Gower's party for the advanced guard of a column, immediately dispersed on his approach, and left him in possession of the place, which he forthwith entrenched, making the inhabitants assist in the digging, as well as drawing upon them for supplies.

In May, 1901, the headquarters of the Company, under Lieutenant Wybergh, moved to the Eland River, two sections, under Sergeant Cooper, being posted at Doorn River, ten miles to the south. Captain Leveson-Gower remained at Brandfort as Intelligence Officer.

At Doorn River Sergeant Cooper and a patrol were surrounded by a large number of the enemy ; after holding out for some time the party made a dash to get through. Some of them succeeded, but 1 man was killed, 2 wounded, and Sergeant Gregson and 2 men were captured, their horses being shot down. On this occasion Private Hunt distinguished himself by attempting to carry a wounded man of the South Wales Borderers, who had accompanied the party, *through the enemy's ranks*. Private Sheeran also behaved with great gallantry. His horse had been shot under him ; but on Commandant Fronemann demanding his surrender he stoutly refused, and raised his rifle to shoot him ; whereupon Fronemann immediately seized one of the prisoners and, holding him between himself and Sheeran, wounded the latter dangerously. Fronemann's men belonged to Haasbrock's Commando, who had their headquarters— soon to be so successfully broken up by Colonel Barker—in the Doornberg, a few miles distant : they were in greatly superior force, and it was only due to the excellent behaviour of the men and their quickness in seizing favourable opportunities that the whole party escaped capture.

On many occasions the Boers tried to cut off the Company's

Cossack posts; and once they succeeded, capturing a party of 5 privates. Sergeant Geissler also fell into the enemy's hands on another occasion, through no fault of his own, and 2 other men were severely wounded.

On 3rd August the Company—once more under Captain Leveson-Gower—was reinforced by some men from Captain Phelps' detachment at Bank; and a month afterwards they were attached to Major Holmes' Column for a short time, and succeeded one day in capturing 5 prisoners after a ten-mile gallop—covering a total of sixty miles in twenty-four hours.

In October Captain Leveson-Gower's Company, with some Yeomanry (in all some 350 strong), formed a small Column, under Colonel Shekelton, with Eland River Station as its headquarters. The "flying-column period" of the War was then in full vogue; and the work of the Column, which for the most part moved by night, told heavily on both men and horses; on frequent occasions over forty miles were covered in a single night. But this rapidity of movement had the effect of keeping the country tolerably clear of the enemy; though the total number of prisoners—barely a dozen all told—was hardly satisfactory. This was not wholly due, however, to bad luck; for on one occasion, when "lying up" at Kaal Valley Diamond Mines, thirty Boers were about to ride straight into the enclosure, when a few Yeomanry, unable to restrain their ardour, foolishly opened fire, with the result that only two or three of the enemy were taken, while the remainder made off again as fast as they could. Colonel Shekelton's Column operated from Eland River during the whole of October and November, on some occasions being out for a week at a time, on others for only a day or so; but on the whole with indifferent success.

On 4th December Captain and Brevet-Major Phelps took over command of the Company from Captain Leveson-Gower, who proceeded to England on being posted to the 2nd Battalion ; and, on the next day, the Company left Eland River and, marching along the line, reached Bloemfontein on the 8th.

But immediately on their arrival at the capital the Company were entrained to Edenburg, and at 1 a.m. on the following morning were sent out by the Commandant of Edenburg to attempt the capture of Commandant Brand, who was reported to have crossed the block-house line with only a few men.

The Company were well out from Edenburg before day broke ; and soon afterwards Major Phelps divided his men into two parties for the purpose of searching some rough ground, taking one section himself and leaving Lieutenant Wybergh the other three.   Soon after parting, Major Phelps' party saw two Boers in the distance, and instantly gave chase ; after pursuing for some way, they were led right into the centre of a commando of about 150 men, who were lying concealed on some low-lying kopjes and in a donga.   At the first volley nearly every horse was hit, and the men took up a position in a small kraal—the only cover at hand, but commanded by kopjes on two sides.   After holding out for some time the enemy suddenly ceased firing, and some men were seen approaching the kraal, each leading a horse.   Major Phelps did not fire on them, as someone shouted that they belonged to Lieutenant Wybergh's party, and were coming to relieve them : when they got near to the wall of the kraal this party dismounted and suddenly shouted : " Hands up."   As every man in the kraal was covered by at least two rifles there was no alternative, though the party who "held them up" consisted of *natives* dressed in khaki and slouch-hats.   The Boers then appeared from all sides, and proceeded to take the men's clothing—or rather, any that was worth taking. Sergeant Beet, V.C., was wounded, and 17 horses either killed or wounded—the only one not hit being Major Phelps', which had broke away and galloped over to the Boers at the commencement of the fight.   Meanwhile Lieutenant Wybergh's party had lost all trace of their comrades, and being strongly opposed by a large number of Boers in position had been forced to withdraw.   After searching the neighbourhood for some time, Lieutenant Wybergh at last saw a man on foot who turned out to be one of Major Phelps' section, and from him was first heard the news of their capture.   From his account, the Boers, on seeing Lieutenant Wybergh's party, had retired, leaving the men where they were, also nine rifles and some bandoliers with ammunition.   On the whole it was a most disastrous episode; but the blame rested upon the Intelligence Authorities; for Major Phelps' had been informed that the district was clear of any large body of the enemy, and that it would be safe to gallop any party he might encounter; instead of which Judge Hertzog and George Brand had crossed the line unnoticed with a whole commando.

During the following week the Company was exceedingly hard-worked in connection with a big " drive " which took place in the district.   No stragglers, however, came their way; though, in a large tract of broken ground covered with bush and intersected with deep ravines—a favourite place for fugitives — they found the bodies of some unfortunate Kaffirs whom the Boers had murdered a few days previously : and, after burning one or two farms and a large flour-mill, which the enemy were in the habit of using, the Company returned to Edenburg on 13th December. From the 15th to the 18th, in company with a hundred men of the Irish Fusiliers, Major Phelps' Company acted as a " stop " to another " drive " at Bulberg, six miles north of Reddersburg, and returned to Bloemfontein, *via* Kaffir River, on the following day.

On the 20th the Company was again split up for outpost duty around Bloemfontein, Major Phelps with two sections going to Fischer's Farm on the west side, Lieutenant Wybergh and one section to Brand Kop on the south, one section to Mount Pleasant, near the Modder River, a few miles beyond Fischer's Farm, and a small detachment to Springfield, about seven miles to the east on the Thaba 'Nchu Road.

The Company held these posts from 30th December, 1901, to 16th March, 1092, finding the usual patrols. During this period Sergeant Musson left the Company, Corporal Smith taking over his duties as Quartermaster - Sergeant; and, on 1st March, Major Phelps left to command the Base Company at Cape Town, Lieutenant Wybergh again taking temporary command.

On the 16th the Company left Bloemfontein by train and arrived at Kroonstad the following day. On the 19th they joined the 9th M.I., then with Lord Basing's Column, about fifteen miles north-west of the Lace Diamond Mines.

The Column moved northwards by way of Bethulie and Commando Drift; and on the evening of 23rd March the Company crossed the Vaal River for the first time during the campaign, and passed through Wolmaranstad, co-operating in an extensive "drive" towards Klerksdorp. The "drive" itself was entirely successful; though, as was invariably the case in these last days of the War, the troops met with little or no organised resistance, the Boers flying between lines of block-houses and extended columns in a *sauve-qui-peut* panic-stricken fashion. Yet the great exertions demanded of the mounted forces came thereby none the easier, without the stimulating excitement of continual fighting. Lord Basing's Column, for instance, in this case, by the time it returned to Commando Drift had covered

a hundred miles in forty-eight hours, without transport
of any description—only great - coats and a feed or two
for both men and horses carried by each man.   After a
rest of two days the 9th M.I. left Lord Basing's Column
and returned to Klerksdorp, where Captain Radford took
over command of the Company.

On the night of 4th April the 9th M.I. moved to Glencoe
Siding to reinforce the railway block-house line during
another "drive," and on the following morning marched
to Meercatfontein, where the camp was sniped throughout
the night, but without damage.   On the 6th they moved
to Kaalfontein Bridge, about half-way between Kroonstad
and Lindley, where Ian Hamilton's great force, sweeping
all before it on its way northwards, had bivouacked nearly
two years before : and how often since columns had
trudged the dusty roads, the whitened bones along the
wayside gave testimony ; and still the War dragged on !
Boers were even then in that much-beloved district ; and
as the 9th M.I. patrols daily returned to camp they were
sniped by unseen rifles, as surely as Piet de Wet had
sprung out of the ground upon the rear-guard of the "Army
of the Right Flank," not many miles from that very spot.

On the 10th the Battalion moved towards Lindley by way
of Doorn Kloof, and, keeping constantly on the move, arrived
back at Kaalfontein Bridge on the 14th, small parties of
Boers having kept persistently on their heels throughout
with a tenacity true to the neighbourhood.   On the 15th
they finally left the district for good, marching to Amerika
Siding, near which place they came upon a Government
cattle farm, the guard of which—about 70 nervous natives
armed with Martinis—opened fire, at a close range, and
before they had discovered their mistake, wounded a man
of the Munster Fusilier Company so seriously that he
subsequently lost his leg.

On the 17th the 9th M.I. marched to Proclamation Drift on the Valsch River. A laager was surprised at Schotland West, about fifteen miles to the south, at daylight on the 20th. Ten Boers were killed and 20 more were captured after a running fight over seven miles of country. Lieutenant Shea, of the Munster Fusiliers, was treacherously shot by men who had previously laid down their arms, similarly as on a former occasion an attempt had been made to murder Lieutenant Beatty, with the 10th M.I. in the Dornberg. But this tragedy was linked with an incident much in the light of comedy, though unfortunately of a kind only too frequent in these last days of the war. Two men—Privates Harrington and Skelton, through getting out of touch, and losing their horses when covering the retreat of some men of the Bedford Regiment, fell into the enemy's hands. But in those days the Boers had little use for prisoners; but their horses, arms, ammunition and, most of all in winter-time, their serge clothing, were greatly in demand, and Harrington and Skelton rejoined the company, as God first set them in the world—without a stitch of clothing!

On 25th April the Company moved down the Valsch River to Doorn Dali, and then returned to Midden Spruit, about six miles out of Kroonstad. Here the waggons were reloaded with stores and supplies ; and on 2nd May Lieutenant Napier, with No. 1 ("B") Company, joined Captain Radford's Command, thereby bringing the total strength up to 113 rifles.

On 5th May the Company again marched ; and after a movement upon Schotland West, joined a column under the command of Brevet-Lieut.-Colonel Marshall, Derbyshire Regiment. But the Company were not destined to remain long under Colonel Marshall's orders; for during a pursuit on the very first day they received orders to

N

rejoin the 9th M.I. at Doornspruit, on the block-house line, ten miles west of Kroonstad.

Here they remained for a fortnight, and then returned to Kroonstad. During the last week in May the Company patrolled the Rhenoster River Valley, halting at Witkopies until Sunday, 1st June, when the Kroonstad helio blinked the welcome news of Peace.

More than two years had both the Companies served; and in that time such a record as this purports to be tells nothing of the little daily dangers: of scouts beating close scrub and ominous boulder-scattered kopjes, where whole commandos had the wherewithal to hide; of long nights on picquet and longer days upon patrol; of foes disguised in one's own uniform, who did not scruple to use the means to deceive; and, last but not least, treacherous farm-houses, tucked away in inner valleys, that harboured at one period a proclamation protected enemy, who had more than once been known to open fire under the White Flag.

Such had been the unbroken lot of the Mounted Infantry men: a lot of which the men who played their own part in the former chapters of this History—in the great snake-line columns which crawled along the dusty roads—knew nothing. The Great Boer War was fought from start to finish against a mobile mounted enemy; whether in the days when flank reinforced flank against the British frontal onslaughts, or when in the end "the nets" were drawn in upon the "block-house lines," the foe was essentially a mobile force; and on that account alone, if for none other, the Mounted Infantrymen were in themselves a counter-power, whose task was none of the lightest, and whose part —which was at one time new and strange — was none the less ably played.

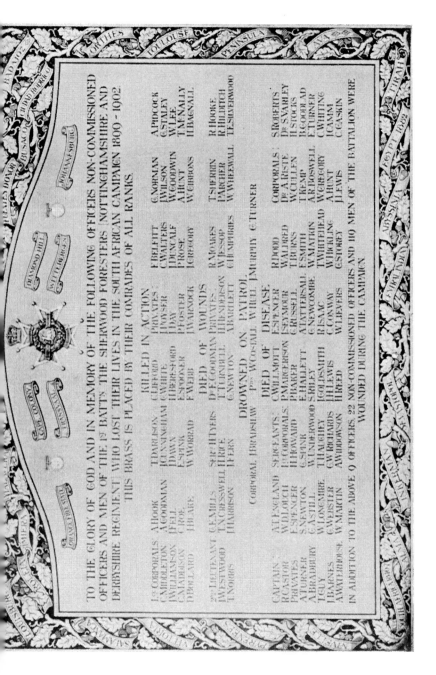

[*Face page* 194

APPENDIX A

CASUALTIES IN THE SOUTH AFRICAN CAMPAIGN.

Killed in Action.

No. 5609.	Lce.-Cpl.	A. Hook,	-	-	Vlakfontein
,, 5258.	,, ,,	T. Darlison,	-	-	,,
,, 3464.	,, ,,	C. Lifford,	-	-	Moedwil
,, 5647.	Private	F. Belfitt,	-	-	Diamond Hill
,, 3525.	,,	G. Norman,	-	-	,,
,, 5791.	,,	A. Pidcock,	-	-	,,
,, 5482.	,,	C. Middleton,	-	-	Dewetsdorp
,, 6118.	,,	A. Goodman,	-	-	Springfontein
,, 3094.	,,	J. Cunningham,	-	-	Gatsrand
,, 5417.	,,	G. White,	-	-	Bank
,, 3328.	,,	J. Poyser,	-	-	Vlakfontein
,, 4792.	,,	C. Walters,	-	-	,,
,, 6177.	,,	J. Wilson,	-	-	,,
,, 4216.	,,	G. Staley,	-	-	,,
,, 2405.	,,	J. Williamson,	-	-	,,
,, 4115.	,,	A. Fell,	-	-	,,
,, 5607.	,,	J. Dawn,	-	-	,,
,, 4428.	,,	H. Beresford,	-	-	,,
,, 2645.	,,	J. Day, -	-	-	,,
,, 5481.	,,	J. Duncalf,	-	-	,,
,, 5651.	,,	W. Goodwin,	-	-	,,
,, 5514.	,,	W. Lee, -	-	-	,,
,, 4778.	,,	C. Maddison,	-	-	,,
,, 5632.	,,	C. Roe, -	-	-	,,
,, 4780.	,,	E. Spink,	-	-	,,
,, 5478.	,,	E. Spooner,	-	-	,,
,, 6448.	,,	P. Foster,	-	-	Doorn River
,, 5190.	,,	P. Rose,	-	-	With No. 1 M.I. Co.
,, 3878.	,,	A. Hunt,	-	-	,,
,, 6535.	,,	T. M'Nally,	-	-	Moedwil

No. 5707.	Private	D. Bollard,	-	-	Moedwil
,, 5347.	,,	J. Blake,	-	-	,,
,, 4311.	,,	W. Worrad,	-	-	,,
,, 185.	,,	F. Webb,	-	-	,,
,, 6518.	,,	F. Warnock,	-	-	,,
,, 6481.	,,	J. Gregory,	-	-	,,
,, 3988.	,,	W. Gibbons,	-	-	,,
,, 2112.	,,	H. Bagnall,	-	-	,,

Died of Wounds.

	2nd Lieutenant	G. E. Mills,	-	-	Moedwil
No. 5210.	Sergeant	H. Tyers,*	-	-	Bank
,, 4875.	Drummer	E. Goodman,	-	-	Vlakfontein
,, 2856.	Private	R. Moakes,	-	-	Diamond Hill
,, 5602.	,,	T. Sherrin,	-	-	,,
,, 4834.	,,	R. Hooke,	-	-	Bank
,, 5432.	,,	J. Westwood,	-	-	,,
,, 5151.	,,	C. Cresswell,	-	-	Vlakfontein
,, 3877.	,,	H. Rice,	-	-	,,
,, 5283.	,,	T. Turnbull,	-	-	,,
,, 5775.	,,	H. Henderson,	-	-	,,
,, 4245.	,,	W. Jessop,	-	-	,,
,, 3212.	,,	P. Archer,	-	-	Moedwil
,, 5386.	,,	R. Hilditch,	-	-	,,
,, 5807.	,,	F. Norris,	-	-	,,
,, 3052.	,,	J. Harrison,	-	-	,,
,, 409.	,,	J. Fern,	-	-	,,
,, 4891.	,,	G. Newton,	-	-	,,
,, 6484.	,,	A. Bartlett,	-	-	,,
,, 2177.	,,	G. Humphries,	-	-	,,
,, 2611.	,,	W. Wheewall,	-	-	,,
,, 4725.	,,	T. Silverwood,	-	-	,,

Drowned on Patrol.

No. 4367.	Corporal	J. Bradshaw,	-	-	Venter's Drift
,, 5794.	Private	W. Costall,	-	-	,,
,, 5413.	,,	W. Hull,	-	-	,,
,, 3357.	,,	J. Murphy,	-	-	,,
,, 5715.	,,	G. Turner,	-	-	,,

* Previously wounded at Wonderheufel.

Died of Disease.

Captain A. T. England

No.	4308.	Sergeant	C. Willmott
,,	3942.	,,	E. Spencer
,,	2894.	,,	R. Dodd
,,	3116.	Corporal	S. Roberts
,,	5633.	,,	R. Castor
,,	4447.	,,	W. Louch
,,	7487.	Lce.-Cpl.	P. Margerison
,,	5756.	,,	J. Seymour
,,	2978.	,,	W. Aldred
,,	4376.	Drummer	A. Riste
,,	1645.	,,	S. Varley
,,	5645.	Private	E. Spencer
,,	5681.	,,	H. Howard
,,	2196.	,,	P. Baker
,,	5727.	,,	G. Russell
,,	3180.	,,	T. Burns
,,	5887.	,,	W. Cullen
,,	5628.	,,	H. Stocks
,,	7360.	,,	A. Turner
,,	5829.	,,	S. Newton
,,	2077.	,,	G. Spink
,,	5740.	,,	E. Hallett
,,	7425.	,,	A. Tattersall
,,	5219.	,,	F. Smith
,,	4804.	,,	T. Kemp
,,	7378.	,,	B. Goodlad
,,	5444.	,,	A. Bradbury
,,	1240.	,,	G. Astill
,,	4122.	,,	W. Underwood
,,	175.	,,	J. Riley
,,	2721.	,,	G. Newcombe
,,	1628.	,,	W. Matkin
,,	5261.	,,	A. Boswell
,,	5757.	,,	E. Turner
,,	6397.	,,	T. Guy
,,	5652.	,,	W. Longmire
,,	6517.	,,	T. Haughey
,,	3131.	,,	J. Goldsmith
,,	2903.	,,	R. Isaacs
,,	763.	,,	T. Whitehead
,,	5335.	,,	W. Gregory

No. 6504. Private   C. Whiting
,, 2536.   ,,   J. Barnes
,, 5605.   ,,   G. Webster
,, 7518.   ,,   G. Richards
,, 7523.   ,,   J. Lewis
,, 5251.   ,,   C. Conway
,, 1308.   ,,   W. Hickling
,, 6088.   ,,   A. Hunt
,, 6435.   ,,   J. Camm
,, 3863.   ,,   A. Waterhouse
,, 5787.   ,,   W. Martin

Wounded.

Captain T. H. M. Green, - -	Severe,	Diamond Hill
Lieut. A. S. Murray, - - -	Slight,	,, ,,
Captain R. P. Sadler, - -	Severe,	Vlakfontein
Lieutenant C. J. L. Gilson, -	Dangerous,	,,
Lieutenant G. D. I. Armstrong,	Severe,	,,
2nd Lieut. M. B. Rimington, -	,,	,,
Captain R. H. Keller, - -	Dangerous,	Moedwil
Captain P. F. R. Anley, - -	Severe,	,,
2nd Lieut. M. K. Hodgson, -	Slight,	,,
No. 4276. Lce.-Cpl. N. Nicholls,	Severe,	Bethulie
,, 2548. Private A. Lenton, -	Slight,	,,
,, 4378. ,, E. Johnson,	Severe,	With No. 1 M.I. Co.
,, 3211. ,, R. Lineker,	Slight,	,,
,, 2709. ,, H. Nicholas,	,,	,,
,, 6106. ,, F. Bradley,*	,,	Dewetsdorp
,, 5772. ,, G. Cope, -	,,	,,
,, 5323. ,, R. Grice, -	,,	With No. 1 M.I. Co.
,, 5534. ,, A. Hollis, -	,,	,,
,, 5880. ,, A. Williams,*	,,	Brandfort
,, 2889. Sergt. E. Rowell, -	,,	Diamond Hill
,, 4566. ,, T. Thorpe, -	Severe,	,,
,, 5531. Corporal G. Roper, -	Slight,	,,
,, 4376. Drumr. A. Riste, -	,,	,,
,, 1281. Private P. Merron, -	,,	,,
,, 3289. ,, T. Tomlinson,	,,	,,
,, 4652. ,, F. Cooper, -	,,	,,
,, 5827. ,, A. Foster, -	,,	,,
,, 2929. ,, W. Goode, -	,,	,,

*Twice Wounded.

	No.				
No.	3218.	Private	J. Holroyd,	Severe,	Diamond Hill
,,	2319.	,,	J. Reynolds,	Slight,	,,
,,	2712.	,,	D. Chambers,*	,,	,,
,,	4803.	,,	W. Cheetham,*	,,	,,
,,	5080.	,,	S. Richards,	,,	,,
,,	5532.	,,	R. Baxter, -	,,	,,
,,	2444.	,,	M. Gill, -	,,	,,
,,	5674.	,,	C. Kingston	,,	,,
,,	5751.	,,	A. Everitt, -	,,	,,
,,	5210.	Corporal	H. Tyers, -	,,	Wonderheufel
,,	2986.	Private	W. Howe, -	Severe,	,,
,,	6226.	,,	C. Bates, -	,,	Bank
,,	6366.	,,	G. Wildgust,	Slight,	,,
,,	4604.	,,	H. Bradbury,	Severe,	Brandfort
,,	4985.	Corporal	T. Wright,-	,,	Vlakfontein
,,	3963.	Lce.-Cpl.	G. Booth, -	Slight,	,,
,,	5784.	Private	J. Gaunt, -	,,	,,
,,	6016.	,,	W. Irenmonger,	Severe,	,,
,,	4136.	,,	J. Porter, -	Slight,	,,
,,	5782.	,,	A. Johnson,	Severe,	,.
,,	2529.	,,	A. Lees, -	,,	,,
,,	4258.	,,	W. Shaw, -	,,	,,
,,	6034.	,,	J. Moon, -	,,	,,
,,	4650.	,,	P. Randall, -	,,	,,
,,	5035.	,,	A. Blood, -	,,	,,
,,	4506.	,,	G. Cresswell,	Slight,	,,
,,	4231.	,,	A. Spencer, -	,,	,,
,,	5747.	,,	A. Allen, -	Severe,	,,
,,	3458.	,,	J. Holmes, -	,,	,,
,,	1794.	,,	G. Wylie, -	Slight,	,,
,,	3475.	,,	T. Bellamy, -	,,	,,
,,	5265.	,,	J. Smith, -	Severe,	,,
,,	5569.	,,	W. Bacon, -	,,	,,
,,	4773.	,,	J. Caroline,-	,,	,,
,,	6466.	,,	T. Adamson,	,,	,,
,,	5422.	Sergt.	C. Chambers,*	Slight,	,,
,,	4770.	Corporal	F. Sargent, -	Severe,	,,
,,	6357.	Private	A. Clarke, -	Slight,	,,
,,	3278.	,,	C. Ager, -	,,	,,
,,	5491.	,,	G. Atkins, -	Severe,	,,
,,	2489.	,,	A. Bednall, -	Dangerous,	,,
,,	6125.	,,	G. Brooks, -	Severe,	,,

*Twice Wounded.

No. 2836.	Private H. Charles, -	Severe,	Vlakfontein
,, 3718.	,, B. Clarke, -	Slight,	,,
,, 3424.	,, J. Collins, -	Severe,	,,
,, 3410.	,, J. Colley, -	,,	,,
,, 6456.	,, A. Enser, -	Slight,	,,
,, 2999.	,, H. Fletcher,	Severe,	,,
,, 5302.	,, C. Girling, -	,,	,,
,, 3433.	,, C. Green, -	,,	,,
,, 6481.	,, J. Gregory, -	Slight,	,,
,, 2812.	,, J. Hickey, -	Severe,	,,
,, 5457.	Lce.-Cpl. J. Morley, -	,,	,,
,, 3234.	Private C. Percival, -	,,	,,
,, 269.	,, J. Redfearn,	,,	,,
,, 6410.	,, J. Sephton, -	,,	,,
,, 3297.	,, T. Shannon,	,,	,,
,, 5205.	,, H. Smith, -	,,	,,
,, 5216.	,, G. Spendlove,	,,	,,
,, 5824.	,, E. Stevens, -	,,	,,
,, 4629.	Lce.-Cpl. F. Ward, -	,,	,,
,, 6518.	Private F. Warnock,	Slight,	,,
,, 3863.	,, E. Waterhouse,	Severe,	,,
,, 2598.	,, J. Wiseman, -	,,	,,
,, 3363.	,, T. Ycomans, -	,,	,,
,, 5487.	,, D. Jackson, -	,,	,,
,, 4768.	,, C. Lowe, -	Slight,	,,
,, 5298.	,, F. Sheeran, -	Dangerous,	Doorn River
,, 5880.	,, A. Williams,	Slight,*	,,
,, 4404.	,, G. Smalley, -	,,	With No. 1 M.I. Co.
,, 2855.	Cr.-Sgt. A. Ewin, -	Dangerous,	,,
,, 3662.	Private W. Ashmore,	Severe,	,,
,, 4159.	Corporal A. Payne, -	,,	,,
,, 5813.	Private G. Ramshay,	,,	Zand River
,, 4538.	,, J. Russell, -	,,	,,
,, 1104.	,, F. Clarke, -	,,	Naauwpoort
,, 4838.	,, A. Hayes, -	Slight,	Orange Grove
,, 6357.	,, A. Clarke, -	,,	Vlakfontein
,, 3646.	,, T. Singleton,	,,	With No. 1 M.I. Co.
,, —	,, W. Fidler, -	,,	Brandfort
,, 5380.	,, A. Galer, -	,,	Moedwil
,, 6140.	,, T. Heap, -	,,	,,
,, 6494.	,, A. Haslam, -	,,	,,
,, 4991.	,, H. Hopkin, -	,,	,,

* Also at Brandfort.

No.	3707.	Private G. Greaves, -	Slight,	Moedwil
,,	6095.	,, R. Baines, -	Severe,	,,
,,	1500.	,, J. Gilding, -	,,	,,
,,	2525.	,, J. Nicholson,	Slight,	,,
,,	4202.	Sergt. J. Roberts, -	,,	,,
,,	4853.	Private C. Greasley,-	Severe,	,,
,,	2492.	,, T. Johnson, -	,,	,,
,,	5339.	,, E. Jones, -	,,	,,
,,	4420.	,, W. Vickers,-	,,	,,
,,	5586.	,, O. Eyre, -	Slight,	,,
,,	1796.	,, G. Simpson,	Severe,	,,
,,	5913.	,, H. Moss, -	Slight,	,,
,,	1120.	,, G. Stapleford,	Severe,	,,
,,	4366.	,, W. Grace, -	Slight,	,,
,,	5906.	,, W. Seymour,	Severe,	,,
,,	1774.	Sergt. J. Beecroft,	Slight,	,,
,,	5580.	Corporal J. Simpson,	Severe,	,,
,,	3656.	Private A. Baldwin,	,,	,,
,,	6411.	,, R. Cresswell,	,,	,,
,,	4141.	,, W. Dakin, -	,,	,,
,,	6500.	,, T. Goldby, -	Dangerous,	,,
,,	1886.	Cr.-Sgt. J. Herrod, -	Severe,	,,
,,	3251.	Lce.-Cpl. R. Dixon, -	,,	,,
,,	3978.	Private J. Caveney,	Slight,	,,
,,	3405.	,, C. Chambers,	,,	,,
,,	5762.	,, A. Stevens, -	,,	,,
,,	943.	Arm.-Sgt. C. Avenell, (A.O.C. attached),	Severe,	,,
,,	5097.	Private F. Bancroft,	Slight,	,,
,,	3972.	Sergt. A. Young, -	,,	,,
,,	5639.	Corporal T. Worthington	,,	,,
,,	5641.	Private R. Shipman,	,,	,,
,,	4793.	,, T. Caroline,-	,,	,,
,,	3560.	,, R. Handley,	,,	Bank
,,	5702.	,, J. Barnes, -	,,	Moedwil
,,	5773.	,, C. Ball, -	,,	,,
,,	4215.	,, J. Knowles,	,,	,,
,,	—	Sergt. H. Beet, -	,,	Edenburg

SUMMARY OF CASUALTIES.

Rank.	Killed, Died of Wounds, etc.	Died of Disease.	Wounded.	Total.
Captains, - -	—	1	4	5
Subalterns, - -	1	—	5	6
Colour-Sergeants, -	—	—	2	2
Sergeants, - -	1	3	9	13
Corporals, - -	1	3	7	11
Lance-Corporals, -	3	3	5	11
Drummers, - -	1	2	1	4
Privates, - -	58	41	117	216
Total, - -	65	53	150	268

APPENDIX B

Officers who embarked with the Battalion for South Africa.

Lieut.-Colonel and Brevet - Colonel H. L. Smith-Dorrien, D.S.O. (Commanding)
Major E. A. G. Gosset (Second in Command)
Major F. C. Godley
Major F. C. Shaw
Captain A. T. England
Captain F. H. Weldon
Captain P. G. Rigby
Captain P. Leveson-Gower
Captain F. J. Radford
Lieutenant R. P. Sadler (Machine Gun)
Lieutenant R. H. Keller (Transport Officer)
Lieutenant L. St. H. Morley

Lieutenant P. F. R. Anley (Signalling Officer)
Lieutenant B. F. Burnett-Hitchcock
Lieutenant A. S. Murray
Lieutenant H. F. Watson
2nd Lieutenant G. F. de Pledge
2nd Lieutenant H. F. P. Percival
2nd Lieutenant J. H. Wybergh
2nd Lieutenant W. R. Frend
2nd Lieutenant H. V. Rhodes
2nd Lieutenant C. J. L. Gilson
2nd Lieutenant W. H. Wilkin
2nd Lieutenant G. L. H. Manby
2nd Lieutenant R. S. Popham
2nd Lieutenant M. B. Webb
Staff Medical Officer, Major S. E. Duncan, R.A.M.C.
Adjutant, Lieutenant F. Casswell
Quarter-Master, Lieutenant F. Tyler

Joined during the Campaign.

Lieut.-Colonel H. C. Wylly, - - -	On promotion to Command
Major C. N. Watts, - - - -	On appointment to Second in Command
Major and Bt.-Col. G. G. Cunningham, D.S.O.,	At Sterkstroom
Major L. S. Gordon Cumming,- - -	On being posted from Adjutant, Volunteers
Captain T. H. M. Green, - - -	On posting from 2nd Battalion
Captain M. P. Phelps, - - - -	With draft from England
Captain J. F. Ritchie, - - - -	On promotion
Lieutenant R. J. F. Taylor, - - -	With 1st party section "D" Army Reserve
2nd Lieutenant P. C. Shepard, - -	On appointment
,, G. D. I. Armstrong, - -	,,
,, G. Mayall, - - -	,,
,, H. L. Napier, - - -	,,
,, H. S. Butler, - - -	,,
,, M. K. Hodgson, - -	,,
,, M. B. Rimington, - -	,,
,, H. M. Milward, - -	,,
,, C. D. Harvey, - - -	,,
,, G. E. Mills, - - -	,,

2nd Lieutenant J. H. W. Becke,   -   -   On appointment
    ,,   L. O. Mott,   -   -   -   ,,
    ,,   A. F. M. Slater,   -   -   ,,
    ,,   E. N. T. Collin,   -   -   ,,

Volunteer Officers.

Captain T. Lee,   -   -
Lieutenant R. K. Ellis,   -   } With 1st Volunteer Co.
Lieutenant F. C. Wright, -
Lieutenant T. C. Newbold,   -   Volunteer Draft
Captain G. D. Goodman,   -
Lieutenant R. W. Webb, -   } With 2nd Volunteer Co.
Lieutenant J. H. F. Marsden,
Lieutenant J. Blackwall, -   -   With 3rd Volunteer Co.

Attached for Duty.

Lieutenant W. Leahy,   -   -   5th Battalion, Royal Munster Fusiliers
Lieutenant F. S. Popham,   -   3rd Battalion, Royal Munster Fusiliers
Civil Surgeon Worth,   -
    ,,   Caldwell,   -   } At various times and for varying periods
    ,,   Tennent,   -   in Medical Charge
    ,,   Allen, -   -
    ,,   Linton,   -

APPENDIX C

Roll of Warrant Officers, Staff-Sergeants, Colour-Sergeants, Sergeants, Corporals, and Drummers who embarked with the Battalion for Active Service in South Africa.

Sergeant-Major C. Gurney
Quartermaster-Sergeant T. Griffin
Quartermaster-Sergeant, Orderly Room Sergeant W. Bolton
Sergeant, Orderly Room Clerk S. Fielding
Pioneer Sergeant A. Read
Sergeant Drummer W. Roberts
Band Sergeant C. Evans
Signalling Sergeant S. Jones.
Machine Gun Sergeant W. Andrews

Transport Sergeant W. Margereson
Sergeant Master Tailor J. Brophy
Sergeant Master Cook F. Hoare

Colour-Sergeant T. Murphy,	- - - - -	" A " Company
,, C. Randall,	- - - - -	" B " ,,
,, W. Roberts,	- - - - -	" C " ,,
,, H. Girling,	- - - - -	" D " ,,
,, A. Tobbell,	- - - - -	" E " ,,
,, M. Corrigan,	- - - - -	" F " ,,
,, A. Ewin, -	- - - - -	" G " ,,
,, J. Herrod,	- - - - -	" H " ,,

No. 3561.	Sergeant M. M'Pherson
,, 3954.	,, F. Simpson
,, 4566.	,, T. Thorpe
,, 4236.	,, A. Jackson
,, 4007.	,, T. Joyce
,, 4340.	,, H. Foulds
,, 3126.	,, H. Warren
,, 2261.	,, J. Caudwell
,, 2485.	,, E. Pollard
,, 2878.	,, J. Binks
,, 2951.	,, W. Cooper
,, 2300.	,, W. Storer
,, 2894.	,, R. Dodd
,, 85.	,, W. Heapy
,, 1774.	,, J. Beecroft
,, 2225.	,, J. Musson
,, 2510.	,, E. Lovatt
,, 2889.	,, E. Rowell
,, 3639.	,, F. Parker
,, 3942.	,, E. Spencer
,, 4202.	,, J. Roberts
,, 4308.	,, C. Willmott
,, 4312.	,, E. Robinson
,, 4440.	,, W. Seaton
,, 4446.	,, G. Crapper
,, 4553.	,, A. Grant
,, 4591.	,, G. Wilson
,, 4687.	,, O. Geissler
,, 4715.	,, S. Good
,, 4789.	,, J. Gilham
,, 5112.	,, J. England
,, 5115.	,, A. Arnett

No. 5146.	Sergeant C. Turton	
,, 5157.	,,	W. Wells
,, 5276.	,,	H. Brompton
.. 5083.	Lce.-Sergt. G. Carrington	
,, 3431.	,,	W. Sims
., 2251.	,,	G. Cooper
., 2181.	.,	A. Draper
., 3167.	.,	J. Evans
,, 3010.	·,,	G. Cursley
,, 2630.	.,	H. Ellis
,, 2184.	,,	G. Briggs
,, 2195.	,,	H. Winn
,, 4275.	,,	F. Stokes
,, 5272.	,,	J. Mallett
,, 2380.	Corporal D. Coggins	
,, 2382.	,,	W. Witts
,, 2487.	,,	W. Carbury
,, 2542.	,,	J. Dexter
,, 2778.	,,	E. Walker
,, 3539.	,,	H. Beet
,, 4046.	,,	A. Smith
,, 4159.	,,	A. Payne
,, 4364.	,,	H. Stevenson
,, 4367.	,,	J. Bradshaw
,, 4468.	,,	W. Bedford
,, 4546.	,,	W. Simpson
,, 4606.	,,	C. Fasham
,, 4629.	,,	F. Ward
,, 4730.	,,	A. Francis
,, 4763.	,,	W. Tinsley
,, 4801.	,,	E. Gregson
,, 4831.	,,	B. Haskard
,, 4918.	,,	J. Henshaw
., 5013.	,,	J. Hind
,, 5053.	,,	W. Coxon
,, 5137.	,,	J. Davis
,, 5210.	,,	H. Tyers
,, 5411.	,,	C. Barton
,, 5422.	,,	C. Chambers
,, 5453.	,,	E. Cope
,, 5526.	,,	W. Wilson
,, 5531.	,,	G. Roper
,, 5633.	,,	R. Castor

,,	5664.	,, J. Bedford
,,	4259.	,, P. Morley
,,	4770.	,, F. Sargent
,,	4249.	,, E. Lindley
,,	4592.	,, T. Munro
,,	5117.	,, J. Tomlinson
,,	2522.	,, A. Edge
,,	2899.	,, J. Webb
,,	2867.	,, R. Pinnock
,,	2492.	,, T. Johnson
,,	3116.	,, S. Roberts
,,	3114.	,, F. Hickling
,,	2230.	,, C. Gates
,,	2825.	,, W. Dowson
,,	2518.	,, W. Robinson
,,	3157.	,, T. White
,,	2486.	,, C. Shardlow
,,	2902.	,, W. Bishop
,,	2833.	,, A. Smith
,,	2640.	,, A. Knight
,,	4447.	,, W. Louch
,,	2887.	,, D. Warner
,,	3041.	,, R. Yardley
,,	4376.	Drummer A. Riste
,,	3341.	,, I. Rowarth
,,	2226.	,, J. Smalley
,,	3593.	,, S. Elliott
,,	2200.	,, A. Shaw
,,	1175.	,, H. Smith
,,	2476.	,, A. Reid
,,	2923.	,, H. Smith
,,	3478.	,, J. Pottinger
,,	4019.	,, W. Coles
,,	4105.	,, T. Unwin
,,	4436.	,, F. Vickers
,,	4509.	,, T. Joy
,,	4551.	,, H. Chillenor
,,	4599.	,, T. Reece
,,	4658.	,, W. Kerr
,,	4790.	,, G. Leahy
,,	4875.	,, E. Goodman
,,	5489.	,, W. Frearson

APPENDIX D

*Extract from a speech made by General Viscount Kitchener of Khartoum,
G.C.B., O.M., G.C.M.G., on the 5th August, 1902, when present at the
Welbeck Tenants' Agricultural Society, at Welbeck Abbey, Notting-
hamshire.*

"You will be interested, I am sure, also to know that the Yeomanry
of this neighbourhood did excellent service, and that your Territorial
Regiment—the Sherwood Foresters—have always distinguished themselves in a most marked manner during this war.   They were one of
the Battalions that I *most trusted*, and on numerous occasions, which you
could perhaps remember, when they were under Colonel Kekewich and
Colonel Dixon, and were attacked by vastly superior numbers, they showed
what true British Soldiers are, and gave them a very good licking."

APPENDIX E

RANK AND NAME.	ACTION, ETC., FOR WHICH MENTIONED.	DATE OF GAZETTE.	AWARD GRANTED.
Local Major-General H. L. Smith-Dorrien, D.S.O.	(1) When in command of 19th Infantry Brigade rendered valuable and distinguished service on each occasion on which his Brigade was engaged.	31st March, 1900. (Lord Roberts.)	
	(2) Has done extremely well with 19th Brigade. He has shown exceptional aptitude for command in the field, being sound in judgment, quick to see and act, and full of resource. He is, moreover, a good organiser, and possesses in a marked degree the confidence of those in his command.	2nd April, 1901. (Lord Roberts.)	Promoted Major-General.
	(3) General good service.	23rd June, 1902. (Lord Kitchener.)	
Lieut.-Colonel H. C. Wylly.	... ...	8th April, 1902. (Lord Kitchener.)	Companion of the Order of the Bath.

RANK AND NAME.	RECOMMENDED BY COMMANDING OFFICER FOR.	MENTIONED IN DESPATCHES.	AWARD GRANTED.
Capt. T. H. M. Green.	(1) At Diamond Hill on 12th June, commanded the Company which advanced on the extreme right of the Brigade. He led his Company up to within 800 yards of the enemy, and when ordered by Brevet-Colonel G. G. Cunningham to withdraw to a less exposed position, did so most skilfully, although himself suffering from a very painful wound. Colonel Cunningham speaks most highly of Captain Green's conduct.	... ...	... ...
	(2) General service.	4th September, 1901. (Lord Roberts.)	D.S.O.
Capt. P. G. Rigby.	(1) At Diamond Hill led his Company to an advanced position in support of Captain Green's, and throughout the day was exposed to a hot fire. He showed much coolness and skill in the handling of his men.	... ...	... ...
	(2) Repeatedly volunteering for special and dangerous service.	4th September, 1901. (Lord Roberts.) and 23rd June, 1902. (Lord Kitchener.)	Brevet-Major.

O

RANK AND NAME.	RECOMMENDED BY COMMANDING OFFICER FOR.	MENTIONED IN DESPATCHES.	AWARD GRANTED.
Brevet-Colonel G. G. Cunningham.	(1) General service.	... ...	... ...
(Brought to notice while serving in the Battalion, and by Lord Roberts when commanding a Brigade.)	(2) Has been in command of a Brigade in the Rustenburg District for some months. He has acquitted himself well and to my satisfaction. I consider him a promising Commander.—(Lord Roberts.)	2nd April, 1901. (Lord Roberts.)	Companion of the Order of the Bath.
Capt. M. P. Phelps.	General service	4th September, 1901. (Lord Roberts.)	Brevet-Major.
Capt. F. J. Radford.	Do.	Do.	... ...
Capt. R. P. Sadler.	Do.	Do.	... ...
Capt. R. H. Keller.	Do.	Do.	D.S.O.
Capt. P. F. R. Anley.	(1) General service.	Do.	... ...
	(2) For good service in the Magaliesberg in September, i.e., keenness and energy displayed in capturing prisoners from 1st to 15th September, 1901.	and 8th October, 1901. (Lord Kitchener.)	... ...
Lieut. A. S. Murray.	(1) General service.	... ...	... ...
	(2) Keenness and energy displayed in capturing prisoners from 1st to 15th September, 1901.	... ...	... ...

RANK AND NAME.	RECOMMENDED BY COMMANDING OFFICER FOR.	MENTIONED IN DESPATCHES.	AWARD GRANTED.
Lieut. C. J. L. Gilson.	(1) General service.	4th September, 1901. (Lord Roberts.)	... ...
	(2) Good service and gallantry at Vlakfontein.		
Lieut. H. V. Rhodes.	(1) General service.	4th September, 1901. (Lord Roberts.) and	... ...
	(2) Do.	23rd June, 1902. (Lord Kitchener.)	... ...
Lieut. R. S. Popham.	(1) General service.	4th September, 1901. (Lord Roberts.) and	... ...
	(2) Specially recommended for gallant conduct at Bethulie, when he removed the dynamite charges from the Road Bridge, thus preventing its destruction.	23rd June, 1902. (Lord Kitchener.)	D.S.O.
Lieut. W. H. Wilkin.	General service.	4th September, 1901. (Lord Roberts.)	... ...
Lieut. F. A. C. Wright (1st Volunteer Coy.).	General service.	4th September, 1901. (Lord Roberts.)	... ...
Lieut. and Qr.-Mr. F. Tyler.	General service.	4th September, 1901. (Lord Roberts.)	... ...
Lieut. G. L. H. Manby.	Good leading in action at Vlakfontein, 29th May, 1901.	28th July, 1901. (Lord Kitchener.)	... ...
2nd Lieut. M. B. Rimmington.	Good service in action at Vlakfontein, 29th May, 1901.	... ...	... ...

RANK AND NAME.	RECOMMENDED BY COMMANDING OFFICER FOR.	MENTIONED IN DESPATCHES.	AWARD GRANTED.
2nd Lieut. H. M. Milward.	Good example and bravery in close fighting round the guns of 28th Battery at Vlakfontein, 29th May.	8th October, 1901. (Lord Kitchener.)	... ...
2nd Lieut. G. E. Mills. (Since dead.)	Gallantly encouraging his men at the attack on the camp at Moedwil, 30th September, 1901.	... ...	... ...
Major C. N. Watts. (1) Was not posted to Battalion at the time.	(1) Very useful service on Lines of Communication as Station Staff Officer, Mooi River and Volksrust, and latterly as Commandant, Volksrust.	30th March, 1900. (General Sir R. Buller.)	... ...
	(2) Good work throughout the campaign, especially at Moedwil, 30th Sept.	8th March, 1902. (Lord Kitchener.)	Brevet Lieutenant-Colonel.
Capt. L. St. H. Morley.	Good work throughout the campaign.	... ...	... ...
Lieut. M. B. Webb.	Do.	... ...	... ...
Lieut. G. Mayall.	Do.	... ...	... ...
2nd Lieut. M. K. Hodgson.	Do.	... ...	... ...
Major F. C. Shaw.	(1) General service whilst serving with General Bruce Hamilton as Brigade Major. (2) Do. as A.A.G.	2nd April, 1901. (Lord Roberts.) and 23rd June, 1902. (Lord Kitchener.)	Brevet Lieutenant-Colonel. ... ...

RANK AND NAME.	RECOMMENDED BY COMMANDING OFFICER FOR.	MENTIONED IN DESPATCHES.	AWARD GRANTED.
Captain F. H. Weldon.	General service whilst serving with Major-General Smith-Dorrien as Brigade Major.	23rd June, 1902. (Lord Kitchener.)	D.S.O., and qualified for employment on the Staff.
Capt. P. Leveson-Gower.	General service whilst serving with No. 2 M.I. Company of the Battalion.	Do.	... ...
Captain F. Casswell.	General service whilst serving with No. 1 M.I. Company of the Battalion.	Do.	... ...
Lieut. H. F. Watson.	Do.	Do.	D.S.O.
Lieut. J. H. Wybergh.	General service whilst serving with No. 2 M.I. Company of the Battalion.	Do.	... ...
Cr.-Sgt. C. D. Randall.	(1) At Diamond Hill was in charge of a half Company, which he led with much boldness, setting his men a splendid example by his coolness and intrepidity.	... ...	... ...
	(2) General service.	4th September, 1901. (Lord Roberts.)	D.C Medal.

RANK AND NAME.	RECOMMENDED BY COMMANDING OFFICER FOR.	MENTIONED IN DESPATCHES.	AWARD GRANTED.
Sergeant A. Jackson.	At Diamond Hill was in charge of the Right Section of Captain Green's Company, maintained his forward position when the remainder of the Company was withdrawn, and for several hours was under a very heavy fire. He controlled his men well, and set a good example.	... ...	... ...
Sergeant J. Gilham.	(1) Attending to his wounded Officer at Diamond Hill, a long sustained action of great coolness and devotion, lasting for considerably over an hour.	... ...	... ...
	(2) General service.	4th September, 1901. (Lord Roberts.)	D.C. Medal.
	(3) General service.	... ...	... ...
Private A. Alton.	(1) Is highly commended by Captain Rigby for his coolness and imperturbability when bringing up ammunition under extremely heavy fire.	... ...	... ...
	(2) General service.	4th September, 1901. (Lord Roberts.)	D.C. Medal.

RANK AND NAME.	RECOMMENDED BY COMMANDING OFFICER FOR.	MENTIONED IN DESPATCHES.	AWARD GRANTED.
Private A. Smith.	(1) Noticed by the Adjutant and Colonel Cunningham for his *sang-froid*, and the excellent example he set when distributing ammunition in the firing line.	... ...	... ...
	(2) General service.	4th September, 1901. (Lord Roberts.)	D.C. Medal.
Qr.-Mr.-Sgt. W. J. Roberts.	Do.	... ...	D.C. Medal.
Cr.-Sgt. A. Tobbell.	Do.		
Cr.-Sgt. H. Girling.	Do.	4th September, 1901. (Lord Roberts.)	... ...
Cr.-Sgt. D. Denihan (Volunteer Coy.).	Do.		
Sergeant S. Jones.	Do.	... ...	... ...
	(2) Good service throughoutt he war, and at Moedwil in signalling under fire.	... ...	... ...
Sergeant S. Fielding.	General service.	4th September, 1901.	... ...
Pr.-Sgt. A. Read.	Do.	Do.	... ...
Lance-Sgt. W. Dowson.	Do.	Do.	D.C. Medal.
Private A. Bullous.	Do.	Do.	D.C. Medal.

RANK AND NAME.	RECOMMENDED BY COMMANDING OFFICER FOR.		MENTIONED IN DESPATCHES.	AWARD GRANTED.
Private J. Cunningham. (Since dead.)	General service.		4th September, 1901.	D.C. Medal.
Private R. Isaacs. (Since dead.)	Do.		Do.	D.C. Medal.
Private T. Spencer	Do.		4th September, 1901.	... ...
Private C. Maddison.	Do.		Do.	... ...
Private C. O. Hickenbottom (Volunteer Coy.).	Do.		Do.	D.C. Medal.
Private W. Mason (Volunteer Coy.).	Do.		Do.	... ...
Private J. Flaherty.	Do.		... ...	... ...
Private J. Caroline.	Do.		... ...	... ...
Private C. Lymn.	(1)	Do.	... ...	... ...
	(2)	Do.	... ...	... ...
Qr.-Mr.-Sgt. W. Bolton.	(1)	Do.	... ...	... ...
	(2)	Has served throughout campaign with Battalion Head Quarters. Has latterly done excellent service in command of the few mounted men with the Battalion, who have been almost daily employed for the months of April to September, 1901, on rear and flank guards on the march.	28th July, 1901. (Lord Kitchener.)	... ...

RANK AND NAME.	RECOMMENDED BY COMMANDING OFFICER FOR.	MENTIONED IN DESPATCHES.	AWARD GRANTED.
Corporal W. Coxon.	(1) General service .	... ...	... ...
	(2) Chiefly instrumental (with Lance-Sergeant Bailey and two men) in 50 captures made by their Company in a week's work in the Magaliesberg.	23rd July, 1902. (Lord Kitchener.)	Promoted Sergeant.
Private M. Sullivan.	General service.	... ...	... ...
Private T. Topham.	Do.	... ...	... ...
Private A. Holmes.	Do.	... ...	... ...
Private W. Harris.	Do.	... ...	... ...
Private A. Terry.	Do.	... ...	... ...
Private H. Moss.	Do.	... ...	... ...
Private G. May.	Do.	... ...	... ...
Private A. Marriott.	Do.	... ...	... ...
Private A. Place.	Do.	... ...	... ...
Cr.-Sgt. J. Herrod.	(1) At Vlakfontein, in attack on Convoy after being taken prisoner, exhibited great courage and coolness in removing our wounded from bursting of our shells.	28th July, 1902. (Lord Kitchener.)	... ...
	(2) Good and reliable service throughout the campaign.	23rd July, 1902. (Lord Kitchener.)	... ...

RANK AND NAME.	RECOMMENDED BY COMMANDING OFFICER FOR.	MENTIONED IN DESPATCHES.	AWARD GRANTED.
Sergeant W. Howard.	(1) Helped to recapture guns at Vlakfontein, and general good service.	23rd June, 1902. (Lord Kitchener.)	... ...
	(2) Repeatedly volunteered for special and dangerous service.	... ...	... ...
Sergeant J. Evans.	Helped to recapture guns at Vlakfontein, and general good service.	... ...	... ...
Lance-Sgt. H. Bailey.	(1) Helped to recapture guns at Vlakfontein.	... ...	... ...
	(2) Keenness and energy in capturing 50 prisoners between 1st and 15th September.	8th October, 1901. (Lord Kitchener.)	Promoted Sergeant.
Private A. Holmes.			Promoted Corporal.
Private G. Marson.	At Vlakfontein, 29th May, in the attack on Boer position, were the first men up.	28th July, 1901.	Do.
Private Mc. Dermott.			Do.
Private T. Worthington.			Do
Private G. Whitehead.	At Vlakfontein, in attack on Convoy after being taken prisoner, exhibited great coolness and courage in removing our wounded from bursting of our shells.	... ...	... ...

RANK AND NAME.	RECOMMENDED BY COMMANDING OFFICER FOR.	MENTIONED IN DESPATCHES.	AWARD GRANTED.
Private J. Wiseman. Private W. Bacon.	Noticed by the Officer commanding Royal Artillery for good conduct at Vlakfontein.	... ...	... ...
(4778) Private C. Maddison. (Killed.)	Great gallantry and good example at Vlakfontein.	8th October, 1902. (Lord Kitchener.)	... ...
Corporal J. Simpson.	Repeatedly volunteering for special and dangerous service.	23rd June, 1902. (Lord Kitchener.)	... ...
Sergeant A. Francis. (4698) Private C. Maddison. Private R. Handley.	Repeatedly volunteering for special and dangerous service.	... ...	... ...
Private W. Boyle.	Keenness and energy in capturing 50 prisoners between 1st and 15th September, 1901.	8th October, 1901. (Lord Kitchener.)	Promoted Corporal.
Private G. Sanderson.	Sanderson held up 24 men practically single-handed.		Do.

RANK AND NAME.	RECOMMENDED BY COMMANDING OFFICER FOR.	MENTIONED IN DESPATCHES.	AWARD GRANTED.
Private W. Bees.	Gallant conduct while with Maxim Gun Detachment during attack at Moedwil, 30th September, 1901. (Gazette.) Was one of the Maxim Gun Detachment which at Moedwil, 30th September, had six men hit out of nine. Hearing his wounded comrades asking for water, he went forward, under a heavy fire, to a spruit held by Boers about 500 yards ahead of the Gun and brought back a kettle full of water. In going and returning, he had to pass within 100 yards of some rocks also held by Boers, and the kettle which he was carrying was hit by several bullets.	8th October, 1901. (Lord Kitchener.)	Victoria Cross.
Private F. Bancroft.	At Moedwil rushed out from cover in broad daylight and bayoneted a Boer who was firing at his section.	8th October, 1901. (Lord Kitchener.)	Promoted Corporal.
Private J. Brierly.	Gallantly bringing water for the Maxim Gun under very heavy fire from 60-yard range during attack on the camp, Moedwil.	8th October, 1901. (Lord Kitchener.)	D.C. Medal. Promoted Corporal.

RANK AND NAME.	RECOMMENDED BY COMMANDING OFFICER FOR.	MENTIONED IN DESPATCHES.	AWARD GRANTED.
Private F. Carr.	Attending his wounded Officer under heavy fire at Moedwil.	... ...	... ...
Sergeant C. Chambers.	Gallant conduct while in charge of a picquet at Moedwil. He refused to surrender when called upon, and shouted, "Fight on, fight on!" till wounded.	8th October, 1901. (Lord Kitchener.)	D. C. Medal.
Lce.-Corpl. R. Dixon.	All were members of Sergeant Chambers's picquet, and held on till five were killed and seven wounded, while only one was left unhit. They refused to surrender when called upon by the enemy.	8th October, 1901. (Lord Kitchener.)	Promoted Corporal.
Private J. Caveney.			Do.
Private P. Picard.		... ...	Do.
Private G. Newton. (Died of wounds.)	Do.	... ...	... ...
Cr.-Sergt. T. Murphy.	Recommended for keenness and energy in capturing prisoners, by wading with four men to cut off the retreat of 12 Boers, 15th September, 1901.	... ...	... ...

RANK AND NAME.	RECOMMENDED BY COMMANDING OFFICER FOR.	MENTIONED IN DESPATCHES.	AWARD GRANTED.
Private H. Marriott.	This man undoubtedly saved other men from being taken prisoners. He, being in the hands of the Boers, was threatened with being shot if he gave any signal to his own men who were approaching, but he stood up and warned his party till pulled down by the Boers.	23rd June, 1902. (Lord Kitchener.)	D.C. Medal.
Private W. Upton.	Always volunteered for any special duty, and did first-rate work scouting in the Gatsrand.	... ...	... ...
Corporal E. Cope.	Recommended as being a first-rate leader of patrols, and doing good work in the Gatsrand.	... ...	... ...
Private J. Birchenough.	Recommended as intelligent Scout and good, all-round M.I. man.	... ...	... ...
Private A. Wright.	Always volunteered for special work.	... ...	... ...
Private S. Rawson.	Good, intelligent Scout.	... ...	... ...
Private T. Peacock.	Recommended for good work about the Gatsrand.	... ...	... ...

RANK AND NAME.	RECOMMENDED BY COMMANDING OFFICER FOR.	MENTIONED IN DESPATCHES.	AWARD GRANTED.
Arm.-Sgt. G. Avenell.	Serving Maxim Gun to the last at Moedwil, 30th September, 1901.	23rd June, 1902. (Lord Kitchener.)	D.C. Medal.
Private E. Turner (2nd Volunteer Coy.).	Good service at Vlakfontein and Moedwil.	... ...	... ...
Private W. Seymour.	Mentioned by Colonel Kekewich, C.B., for good work at Moedwil.	... ...	... ...
Sergeant R. Hardy. Sergeant J. Mallett.			
Private T. Gould.			
Private T. Columbell.	For good and reliable service throughout the campaign.	... ...	... ...
Private G. Taylor.			
Private J. Yeomans.			
Private C. Ager.			
Private G. Wyvill.			

RANK AND NAME.	RECOMMENDED BY COMMANDING OFFICER FOR.	MENTIONED IN DESPATCHES.	AWARD GRANTED.
Corporal H. Beet.	(Gazette.) At Wakkerstroom, 22nd April, 1900, No. 2 Mounted Infantry Company, 1st Derbyshire Regiment, with two Squadrons Imperial Yeomanry, had to retire from near a farm under a ridge held by Boers. Corporal Burnett, I.Y., was left on the ground wounded, and Corporal Beet, on seeing him, remained behind and placed him under cover, bound up his wounds, and by firing prevented the Boers from coming down to the farm till dark, when Dr. Wilson, I.Y., came to the wounded man's assistance. The retirement was carried out under a very heavy fire, and Corporal Beet was exposed to fire during the whole afternoon.	12th February, 1901. (Lord Roberts.)	Promoted Sergeant. to Cross.
Sergeant A. W. Young.	In Boer attack on Bank Station, 12th February, carried a wounded man into the trenches, thereby saving his life, and afterwards returned to the fight.	28th July, 1901. (Lord Kitchener.)	... ...
Cr.-Sgt. A. Ewin.	General Service with No. 1 M.I. Company.	4th September, 1901. (Lord Roberts.)	D.C. Medal.

RANK AND NAME.	RECOMMENDED BY COMMANDING OFFICER FOR.	MENTIONED IN DESPATCHES.	AWARD GRANTED.
Cr.-Sgt. W. Seaton.	(1) General service with No. 1 M.I. Company.	4th September, 1901. (Lord Roberts.)	D.C. Medal.
	(2) At Wolverand, Transvaal, 28th October, returned under fire and picked up a wounded man within 200 yaras of the enemy. (Recommended for V.C.)	8th December, 1901. (Lord Kitchener.)	... ...
Sergeant W. Cooper.	General service with No. 2 M.I. Company.	4th September, 1901. (Lord Roberts.)	... ...
Private M. Bowen.	„ 1 Do. Do.	Do.	... ...
Private H. Bradbury.	„ 2 Do. Do.	Do.	... ...
Private H. Long.	„ 1 Do. Do.	Do.	... ...
Private J. Murphy.	„ 1 Do. Do.	Do.	... ...
Private J. Shaw.	„ 1 Do. Do.	Do.	... ...
Private J. Broome.	Whilst serving with No. 2 M.I. Company, recovering his Officer's horse, which had broken away on Grazing Guard owing to heavy fire of Boers, 11th April, 1902.	... ...	... ...
Private T. Chapman.	General service with No. 1 M.I. Company.	... ...	... ...
Private J. Harris.	General service with No. 1 M.I. Company.	... ...	... ...

RANK AND NAME.	RECOMMENDED BY COMMANDING OFFICER FOR.	MENTIONED IN DESPATCHES.	AWARD GRANTED.
Cr.-Sgt. E. Lovatt.	Good work generally, and good half Company leader with No. 2 M.I. Company.	... ...	... ...
Sergeant J. Yates.	Good work generally, and good Section leader with No. 2 M.I. Company.	... ...	... ...
Corporal J. James.	Good work generally with No. 2 M.I. Company.	... ...	... ...
Private H. Moult.	Good Scout with No. 2 M.I. Company.	... ...	... ...
Private F. Grosvenor.	Good Scout and reliable man, with No. 2 M.I. Company.	... ...	... ...

INDEX

Slipstein, affair at, 116
Smaldeel, 32, 169
Smith, Corporal, 191
Smith, Private, gains D.C.M., 77, 81
Smith-Dorrien, Colonel, 4, 5 ; commands a Brigade, 9, 24, 25, 30, 33, 34, 39, 41, 42 ; sends supplies, 50, 56, 64, 94 ; inspects M.I., 152
Smithfield, 21
Smuts, 113 ; Mrs., 136
Somerset Light Infantry, 93
Spaarwater, 85
Spens, Colonel, 31, 56
Springfontein, 21 ; Regiment at, 22, 156, 169
Springs, 85
Spytfontein, 29
Standard Diggers' and Miners' News, 60
Steinkamp, 125
Stephen's Nek, 35
Sterkfontein, 91
Sterkstroom, Regiment proceeds to, 5, 6, 7, 9
Stevenson, General, 31, 64
Steyn, President, 1, 44
Storer, Sergeant, 152
Stormberg, 5, 6, 15 ; Regiment leaves, 18, 154, 155
Suffolk Regiment, 26
Sullivan, Private, 19
Sussex Regiment, 27, 29, 42, 73, 100, 101, 103
Symons, Sir Penn, death of, 2

TABACKBERG, 169 ; action at, 171
Tafel Kop, 117, 175
Talana, 2
Tarkstad Valley, 6
Taylor, Lieutenant, 26, 28, 57, 73, 83, 94, 113
Tchrengula, 3

Thaba Mountain, 25 ; action at, 29
Thaba 'Nchu, 29 ; concocted, 162
Tigerpoort, 69, 73
Tobbell, Colour-Sergeant, 72
Topham, Private, 19
Towse, Captain, 29
Transvaal entered, 52
Tucker, General, 29, 39, 41, 64
Turner, Private, drowned, 167
Turner, Lee, Captain, 26, 28, 67
Twelfth Lancers, charge of, 67
Twenty-first Brigade, composition of, 27
Twismeit, 44
Tyers, Corporal, mortally wounded, 113
Tyler, Quartermaster, 28, 96

VAALKRAAL, 94
Vaalkrantz, 92
Valsch River Valley, 46
Van Heerden executed, 141
Van Tonder, 137
Van Wyk's Rust, 55
Van Zyl's Spruit, 25
Veekraal, 147
Vermaas, 174
Ventersberg, 43 ; occupied, 44
Ventersberg Road Siding, 41, 102
Ventersdorp, 115, 117
Venter's Drift, patrol drowned at, 167
Venterstad, 155
Viljoen, 98
Villiersdorp, 45
Vlakfontein (Orange Colony), 28
Vlakfontein, 117, 121 ; action at, 122 ; losses at, 128
Volunteer Company, 26, 28, 69 ; ordered home, 105; 2nd joins, 146
Von Donop, Colonel, captured, 177
Vrede, 137
Vredepoort, 94

Printed by Cowan & Co., Limited, Perth.